Handbook for Folklore and Ethnomusicology Fieldwork

HANDBOOK FOR FOLKLORE AND ETHNOMUSICOLOGY FIELDWORK

LISA GILMAN AND JOHN FENN

INDIANA UNIVERSITY PRESS

This book is a publication of

Indiana University Press
Office of Scholarly Publishing
Herman B Wells Library 350
1320 East 10th Street
Bloomington, Indiana 47405 USA

iupress.indiana.edu

Manufactured in the United States of America

Cataloging information is available
from the Library of Congress.

ISBN 978-0-253-04025-1 (paperback)
ISBN 978-0-253-04026-8 (ebook)

1 2 3 4 5   24 23 22 21 20 19

To Anika and Nora

For bringing us joy by joining in our adventures and helping us lug our gear!

CONTENTS

Accessing Supplemental Materials

Supplemental course materials are available for this volume and can be viewed online at https://www.iupress.indiana.edu/books/folkethno handbook

Acknowledgments

First and foremost, we are grateful to each person who has welcomed us into their lives, generously invited us to activities and events, and patiently listened to our not always well-articulated probing questions. Over the course of more than two decades of fieldwork we have done, it has been the participants in our projects who have been our teachers. By doing fieldwork we continue to learn how to do it. We also acknowledge all of our students over the years—teaching and guiding you through your many projects has expanded the breadth of our perspectives far beyond what any one fieldworker could experience in a lifetime.

Thank you to the anonymous reviewers whose detailed and concrete feedback has greatly strengthened the project. We appreciate Indiana University Press's director, Gary Dunham, for recognizing the need for this handbook, and are much indebted to editor Janice Frisch for her clear and careful guidance throughout the process.

Most important, we are thankful for our patient and adventurous daughters. They have joined us on so many fieldwork excursions—sometimes coerced, sometimes enthusiastically. Having two folklorist/ethnomusicologist parents must have benefits as well as challenges. Know that you have enhanced not only our lives but also our research.

Handbook for Folklore and Ethnomusicology Fieldwork

INTRODUCTION

THIS HANDBOOK PROVIDES AN OVERVIEW of fieldwork approaches relevant to folklorists, ethnomusicologists, and those in allied fields who explore artistic and communicative practices as they manifest in lived social environments. Recognizing that folklorists, ethnomusicologists, and others utilize multiple research strategies—including but not limited to archival and library research, literary analysis, and quantitative surveys—our focus is explicitly ethnographic fieldwork methods and not these other approaches. This handbook should be most useful for students and researchers whose methods involve engaging directly with the participants who produce and consume the cultural materials they are studying, and it is expected that many users will combine field methods with some of the others listed.

In as much as they are distinct, folklore and ethnomusicology share a great deal in their foci, theoretical frameworks, and methodological strategies. The authors consider themselves to be at the intersection of the two overlapping fields, and we have targeted this handbook accordingly. Folklorists and ethnomusicologists often study some type of creative culture as it occurs in contemporary life, attending to the processes and contexts of artistic engagement in interaction with the creators and their products. While there are many valuable textbooks about ethnographic methods produced by cultural anthropologists and those working in other disciplines, this volume adds to these resources with its explicit emphasis on how to do fieldwork about the arts and other forms of creative activity with attention to the contexts for and processes of their production, reception, distribution, and preservation.

Our objective is to provide guidance about methodological strategies and skills, which are important in the planning and execution of research projects, and in working with field data afterward. We also address theoretical and methodological issues integral to the ethnographic enterprise, such as positionality, ethics, representation, intellectual property, and reciprocity. Additionally, we provide guidance on preparing materials for archiving and preservation—steps that start during the planning and continue through the postfieldwork phase of research.

Our scope includes what typically has been the topic of folklore and ethnomusicology research methods guides—face-to-face research with individuals and communities who are involved in expressive culture. In as much as we value these methods as described in existing texts, most of which were published in the last decades of the twentieth century, we also recognize the need for a new text that addresses fieldwork in face-to-face as well as technologically mediated settings. Given the rapidity with which technology changes, any handbook about using technology in research will most likely be outdated by the time of publication. We therefore attempt to provide guidelines and ways of thinking that will be useful for the technologies current at the time of writing and applicable to new ones that emerge in the future.

Most existing guides on folklore and ethnomusicology fieldwork are intended to train future academics and provide research models based primarily on academic objectives and schedules. These generally assume that a researcher will spend extended amounts of time with a community in the field, often over multiple years, to gain deep intensive and extensive knowledge about the people and the cultural practices under study. These guides often also assume that the end products will be written descriptions and interpretations. Many professional folklorists and ethnomusicologists, however, do not work in academic settings. Rather, they work in the public sector or nonprofit environments where timelines tend to be shorter and research objectives more restricted and directed, thus necessitating a different approach to fieldwork. This handbook provides information valuable to those in academic and nonacademic settings and is adaptable to those doing research across professional and personal contexts and with diverse objectives.

This volume is relevant to those doing fieldwork in their home countries or in foreign countries, and in communities of which they are a part and those of which they are not. We provide information about research tools useful in different contexts and address some strategies and challenges of doing research in a variety of situations. We discuss how different types of relationships between researchers and the people that are the focus of a project can result in different types of research outcomes. Throughout, we have attempted to use gender neutral pronouns to the greatest extent possible.

The three parts represent three phases of fieldwork typical for many projects: "Preparing for the Field," "In the Field," and "After the Field." In part I, "Preparing for the Field," we cover the process of identifying a topic; creating a fieldwork plan; developing the intellectual, linguistic, cultural, and technological foundation necessary for successfully carrying out a project; potential ethical concerns; the practical details of preparing for research; and some of the bureaucratic details that often need attention prior to beginning field research.

Part II, "In the Field," outlines strategies and issues associated with entering the field for the first time, making contact, establishing relationships with people, and developing research questions. It then introduces different methods available to fieldworkers, including collection, observation, participant observation, and interviewing. It also provides approaches for using a variety of documentation strategies, with an emphasis on the importance of gathering appropriate information in anticipation of depositing materials into archives after the conclusion of a project. Throughout is a discussion of ethical and other difficult issues that can arise during fieldwork.

Part III, "After the Field," addresses what happens after one has completed the bulk of the fieldwork and is ready to work with research material to produce any number of research products. Some possibilities include an archival collection, class paper, thesis or dissertation, documentary, exhibit, podcast, radio program, or interactive website. We begin by exploring how to review and manage data, identify themes and code, and develop the process of analysis. We also address some of the ethical and legal issues that can arise in relationship to intellectual property, who gains from the research endeavor, and the politics of representation. We end by detailing ways to consider preservation of the data for long-term benefits, discussing practical steps involved as well as some of the social dimensions of where, how, and to whom to make materials accessible.

The arrangement of topics is not necessarily linear since much of what we describe occurs simultaneously or can take place in a variety of sequences during fieldwork. The book could be used as it is from beginning to end. Some readers will choose to read only select bits, and others may want to structure the chapters into a sequence that works for their needs. We have organized information into relatively short focused chapters to enable readers to easily access information about specific topics and to reorder as desired. Some readers will find this volume useful in and of itself. Others, especially those teaching courses, leading workshops, or running training sessions, could combine this handbook with other texts that provide more in-depth information about different phases of the research process, elaborate on the theoretical foundation of much of what we discuss, or address disciplinary-specific strategies or issues.

Throughout we include suggested exercises. They are framed for classroom use and assume that an instructor and students will be the participants. The exercises are equally useful for workshops, training sessions, or other nonclassroom settings. They can be adapted or used as inspiration for other types of skill-building opportunities. For those reading the book individually, we recommend reflecting on the exercises privately and doing some of the activities with friends or family members.

Fieldwork is based in social interaction, and fieldwork experiences are often as varied, unpredictable, and messy as life itself. Neither of the authors have ever been involved in what we felt was perfect fieldwork. We have enjoyed our successes while also appreciating the process of continuing to develop research skills—always learning from moments of discomfort or times when we wished we had done things differently. We intend this handbook to be a guide useful for planning, structuring, and reflecting on the research process. Ultimately, it is the people involved in all capacities that shape the research experience and determine its outcomes. The authors have each had the opportunity to conduct different types of projects (academic and applied) in many types of communities (in the United States and abroad, and face-to-face and mediated). We have taught courses in face-to-face and digital fieldwork methods and have mentored students doing a wide range of different types of projects. We will share examples and reflections from our experiences, as relevant, and look forward to continuing to learn and expand our skills in the process of writing this book and receiving feedback after.

Bruce Jackson cogently writes in the introduction to *Fieldwork*:

> Learning to do fieldwork is like learning to drive a car: you can be taught the techniques, but each utilization of the technique is a new creative moment, one absolutely specific to itself. You may know how to work the levers, buttons, and pedals of your car perfectly, but to get somewhere you must have your own plan of action and you must do the driving and deal with whatever impediments the world puts in your way as you go. You must bring to the task sensitivity and sensibility, factors very much beyond technique and technology. The same is true for fieldwork. (1987, 6)

This handbook provides plenty of detailed information about how to plan for and conduct ethnographic fieldwork, what to do with the materials amassed after, and how to think about and address a range of ethical and methodological issues. In the end, each fieldwork experience is unique, and we hope that this guide will be helpful as you create your plan of action and deal with "whatever impediments the world puts in your way."

PART I

PREPARING FOR THE FIELD

ETHNOGRAPHIC FIELDWORK IS AN EXTENSION of what each of us does in our day-to-day lives as we learn how to be social and creative people through observations and interactions within the worlds we occupy. Most of what one does in fieldwork resonates with what we already know how to do: learn about something by spending time with people, observe what is going on around us, and ask questions while listening carefully to responses. Yet, adapting everyday life activities into research methods requires developing a level of awareness and set of skills that enables one to systematically gather, document, interpret, and present information.

Part I begins with an overview of folklore and ethnomusicology fieldwork and then addresses many details associated with preparing to do fieldwork. Chapter 1 presents some terms and concepts that are important to fieldwork processes and outcomes. Chapter 2 discusses how to identify potential fieldwork topics and the importance of developing the necessary knowledge base prior to entering the field. Chapter 3 emphasizes the importance of creating a proposal that clearly outlines the objectives and plan for the project. Fieldworkers may be required to submit such proposals to instructors, funders, employers, or research compliance officers. And most significantly, proposals serve as important guides and tracking devices during the fieldwork process.

In the final three chapters of part I, we shift our focus to the logistical details that are often necessary prior to beginning fieldwork. Chapter 4 addresses some institutional requirements that are typical for fieldwork projects, such as a university's policies for conducting research with human subjects and some governments' requirement that foreigners obtain clearance prior to conducting research in a country. We then discuss some practical issues around doing research in domestic versus international settings and between face-to-face versus digital realms.

Documentation is an integral part of the fieldwork process often requiring a certain degree of skill and careful consideration about equipment and accessory needs, and this is the topic of chapter 5. The final chapter in part I is chapter 6, a detailed discussion about resource considerations that covers some sources for funding and the types of expenses that fieldworkers should expect.

1

DEFINING FIELDWORK

THIS CHAPTER INTRODUCES SOME BASIC terms and concepts for the beginning fieldworker. It begins by explaining what ethnographic fieldwork involves by describing what is meant by the "field," followed by a discussion of what kinds of people and cultural forms tend to be the focus of fieldwork projects. We consider the "work" by outlining the activities that are typical to this type of research. Folklorists and ethnomusicologists do fieldwork in a variety of settings and with varying relationships to organizations, establishments, and community groups. We present different types of institutional contexts for fieldwork and discuss the differences between individual and collaborative approaches. Human relationships are at the center of fieldwork, so we also consider various types of relationships between fieldworkers and the people they study.

What Is Ethnographic Fieldwork?

The method of fieldwork has been defined multiple ways by different scholars. For example, in *Folklife and Fieldwork: An Introduction to Cultural Documentation*, Stephen Winick and Peter Bartis explain that fieldwork is "the difficult but rewarding work of recording firsthand observations and interviews with community experts" (2016, 4). Similarly, in "Casting Shadows in the Field: An Introduction," Timothy J. Cooley writes that "fieldwork is the observational and experiential portion of the ethnographic process during which the ethnomusicologist engages living individuals in order to learn about music-culture" (1997, 4). And Bruce

Jackson explains in *Fieldwork* that he likes Everett C. Hughes's 1960 definition: "Field work refers . . . to observation of people *in situ*; finding them where they are, staying with them in some role which, while acceptable to them, will allow both intimate observation of certain parts of their behavior, and reporting it in ways useful to social science but not harmful to those observed" (1987, 7). Echoing these scholars, we conceive of ethnographic fieldwork as encompassing those research strategies based on direct involvement with the individuals and communities studied. The goal of fieldwork is to try to understand how people experience the world from their perspective—doing and experiencing similar activities in similar spaces with them will enable a fieldworker to develop a deep perspective on the lives and cultural practices of the people they study. Fieldwork takes many different shapes depending on the topic and objectives of the researcher and community members involved. Though the term "community" is a complex and contested term, we use it throughout this text for lack of a better term to refer generally to the networks of people involved in a specific folklore or musical form that is being studied. The ethnographic approach to fieldwork, often referred to as "participant observation," is founded on the idea that a great deal can be learned about a community's creative expressions by immersing oneself within the contexts in which the cultural practice being studied occurs. This usually involves developing relationships and spending significant time with the communities involved, while participating in and observing people's engagement with the cultural form in its so-called natural context.

At the core of ethnographic research is the idea of cultural relativism: an understanding of cultural practices from the perspectives of the practitioners rather than through the interpretive lens of the fieldworker. In addition to participating in and observing a community or the cultural forms in action, more targeted information-gathering strategies are often used that vary depending on the research topic and objectives. Some common strategies include attending occasions where the cultural practice takes place, such as social gatherings, concerts, festivals, practice or instructional sessions, craft markets, or participating on social media sites; pursuing interviews with individuals or groups of participants and community members; conducting surveys; and documenting using textual, audio, and visual media. Library, internet, and archival research often complement fieldwork, and engagement with digital communities can constitute all or part of one's fieldwork approach.

People do fieldwork with a number of objectives in mind, and they use the knowledge and materials they gather in a variety of ways. Some fieldwork is individually driven; the fieldworkers have the option of choosing a topic and can shape the project around their own interests and goals. Other fieldwork is done at the behest of an organization, company, instructor, or community, in which case the topic and objectives may be already determined. Some people enter the field with clearly delineated expectations about what they should learn and gather for a specific goal. Other projects are more open-ended. Depending on the goal, fieldwork can contribute to knowledge building, as in when someone does field-work because they are interested in learning about a community or cultural practice. Often, fieldwork supports some type of product: class assignment, documentation for an archive, master's thesis or doctoral dissertation, museum exhibit, documentary video, podcast, multimedia online exhibit, school curriculum, festival, or radio show. In addition to or alternately, the goal might be advocacy or to produce some type of social change through action research. The desired outcome will necessarily influence how fieldworkers approach the project, what questions they seek to answer, how and what they document, and what they will do with the information after.

What Is the "Field"? What Is the "Work"?

"Fieldwork" is a compound word, suggesting that some kind of work is being done in a field. Multiple academic and professional fields employ the term, but in the context of folklore and ethnomusicology, "field" refers to the sites where cultural expression occurs or where people involved live and do a variety of activities. The "work" refers to the researcher going into that field to learn something about the people and cultural practices, as well as everything a researcher does before and after related to the project.

What is considered the "field" can vary greatly and is dependent on the type of project. Ethnomusicologists Marcia Herndon and Norma McLeod explain that "a field may be a geographic area; a linguistic area; a particular village, town, city, suburb, or rural area" (1983, 3). The field can refer to spaces, such as a geographic location, a digital platform, an institution, or according to some, a state of mind (see Kisliuk 1997). It can refer to events, such as concerts, festivals, family gatherings, or art markets. And, it can entail a community of people who are participants in any number of capacities, which could comprise anything from a family, set of friends, ethnic group, musical ensemble, artist collective, social media network, political association, occupational group, digital community, the population of a town or country, or an international network.

If one is doing research about a family's holiday traditions, the field could involve spending time with individuals in a variety of activities in different locales relevant to the holiday as well as potentially interviewing participants in spaces unrelated to the practice. In this case, the field could include the home where a holiday is celebrated, the grocery store where

Figure 1.1. Gilman's students from Mzuzu University posing during a field trip during which they learned fieldwork methods. Malawi, 2013. Photo by Lisa Gilman.

special foods are purchased, the coffee shop where a family member is interviewed, the website where cooks find recipes, and the social media site where members share images of their holidays to a disparate audience. Some projects have a single focused field site, while others have multiple ones. Those doing research on a musical tradition might choose to focus their project on a single practitioner or physical site, whereas someone else might select to research in several communities where the music is practiced. Such choices emerge from, and produce, different perspectives.

Fieldworkers' relationship to the field varies. The field can be in their own backyard if they do research within a community of which they are already a part or that is nearby. It can be in other locations either within the region and country in which the fieldworker lives or a foreign one. Where the field is will necessarily shape the kind of preparation required and methods used, as will be elaborated on in chapters 4 to 6.

The "work" refers to what one does in the field, the methods used to research or gather information. It also extends beyond the field with regard to assessing materials gathered and preparing them for preservation or future use. The work can include spending time with people engaged in a practice or a location where it's happening, engaging in the practice, having informal conversations about a topic, conducting more formal directed interviews, attending events, and reading news or social media coverage of them. One of the most valuable components of the "work" or methods in folklore and ethnomusicology is the documentation of folklore and music practice that is part of the information gathering process. Folklorists and ethnomusicologists record multiple aspects of social life, often using combinations of textual, audio, and visual media. We will elaborate on cultural documentation in chapters 5 and 10.

The People

Fieldwork is ultimately research with people and can include those involved in folklore or ethnomusicological practice in a myriad of capacities. In her 1993 article, "Power and the Ritual Genres: American Rodeo," folklorist Beverly Stoeltje suggests that when doing fieldwork on rituals, folklorists should attend to (1) form, (2) production, "the organization of forces, energies, and materials that constitute the actual production," and (3) the discourse that surrounds them (1993, 141). Though each person will plan fieldwork based on what is most productive and appropriate for their topic of study, Stoeltje's framework is useful for thinking about whom might be worth spending time with when doing research. Below are some of the types of participants that may be useful to consider:

- The practitioners—for example the musicians, artists, joke tellers, or cooks
- Consumers or audience members
- The people involved in instruction or learning
- Those involved in or invested in organizing opportunities for the practice to occur
- Those knowledgeable about the history of the practice
- The people buying or selling or otherwise making money from the practice
- Individuals who have strong opinions about the practice: its legitimacy, value, and whether or how it should be practiced or continued
- Those producing the discourse about the practice, which could include those involved in informal conversations, journalists, bloggers, or scholars

Exercise

Can be done individually, in small groups of two to three, or with a single large group.

1. Identify a category of folklore or musical practice that would be interesting to research.
2. Brainstorm what "fields" could be appropriate for doing fieldwork on this topic.
3. What kinds of methods or "work" could be productive?
4. Which types of participants could be relevant?

Fieldwork Situations

Fieldwork can provide effective methods for people researching in a variety of contexts with a wide range of goals. Here, we discuss a variety of settings and briefly consider how these impact planning and design.

The Individual Researcher in an Academic Setting

Individuals who do research for academic goals often have a great deal of autonomy in selecting a topic and field setting. They often enjoy the flexibility of changing topics, settings, or timelines in relationship to their personal goals and to what is happening on the ground. Despite this autonomy, they usually operate within certain restrictions as dictated by their personal situations, their field or discipline of study, or institutional demands or policies. The model of the individual in the field is the one most commonly assumed in most ethnographic field methods guides.

Collaboration

All fieldwork, whether academic or applied, is inherently collaborative because it involves the participation of multiple people who together make the project possible. Even in the individual model, the success of the research is dependent on the participation and collaboration of those in the fieldwork setting. A fieldworker doing research on an Irish music scene by attending events, spending time with participants, and interviewing performers relies on access to the events and on participants welcoming the researcher and being willing to be interviewed. And, they might rely on participants collaborating by providing their own perspectives and assessment, which contribute to the researcher's analysis.

Some contemporary fieldworkers feel that collaboration should be the basis for all fieldwork and that the topic and goals of a project should always be conceived collaboratively by a community and the fieldworkers. Rina Benmayor, for example, promotes "the philosophy that investigation should be structured in ways that privilege reciprocity and mutual 'returns' among community members and researchers" (1991, 160). Rather than an individual selecting a project on their own that they introduce to participants, the community itself should conceive of the research topic, and objectives should be developed collaboratively. And most importantly, participants should benefit from the process and outcomes of a project. This approach is common among academic and applied researchers and is often a central tenet of projects done in the public interest. The mission of many public folklore organizations, for example, is to work directly with communities in ways that support cultural sustainability. Community objectives often shape approaches to sustainability, and fieldwork can assist by providing rich documentation used to support grant applications or contribute to interpretive exhibitions.

Collaboration also can mean two or more fieldworkers working together on a project. Because social interaction and artistic practice is inherently subjective, integrating the perspectives of multiple people in the research design can produce a more nuanced outcome. As will be elaborated throughout the handbook, a fieldworker's own identity and their relationship to the cultural community will have an impact on their access to research opportunities and their understanding of what happened. Research teams that integrate people with a variety of relationships to the group and topic—in other words, people who are insiders and outsiders and people who have a range of different identities across such factors as age, gender, knowledge of the practice, and so on—can be especially exciting and can produce deep and detailed outcomes. Collaboration is especially useful for projects drawing on a range of skills. For example, a project intending to produce an exhibit might require people with expertise in conducting participant observation fieldwork, producing high-quality recordings of performances or interview data, taking dynamic photographs, and designing the physical or virtual exhibit. A team that includes a photographer, sound recorder, and skilled interviewer would be ideal for the successful completion of the project (see Lassiter 2005).

Exercise

1. Divide into small groups of three to four people.
2. Identity a possible fieldwork topic.
3. Discuss the pros and cons of an individual versus team approach:
   - What would be the benefits of pursuing this project as an individual?
   - What would be the benefits of pursuing this project as a team?
   - What roles could different members of the team play?
4. What types of collaboration would be valuable for the success of this project, regardless of whether it was conducted by an individual or by a team?

Working within the Parameters of an Institution

A fieldworker's relationship to organizations (e.g., universities, nonprofits, government organizations, international nongovernment organizations [NGOs]) greatly influences a research topic and outcome. On the one hand, institutions can provide the rationale and excuse to do research. It can be difficult for an unaffiliated individual working on personal goals to

Figure 1.2. Fieldwork team interviews painter, Su Xinping, in his Beijing studio. Fieldworkers take notes, shoot video, record audio, and take a photograph. All materials eventually supported the ChinaVine project website. Beijing, China, 2009. Photo by John Fenn.

gain the same kind of access to research settings as those whose goals are aligned with an institution. Being associated with a university, museum, or nonprofit can provide legitimacy and ultimately increase the chance of gaining permission to conduct the fieldwork.

Institutions also can restrict and shape fieldwork in multiple ways. The objectives of the institution may determine the topic, product, and timeline of a project. Working for a museum that is researching its local immigrant communities to produce an exhibit about the cultural diversity in the locale may require the fieldworker to pursue interviews with specific categories of individuals using predetermined questions. The researcher conducting a survey of traditional artists for a state folklife agency will likely be given parameters for what is considered to be "traditional" that might differ from the researcher's own definitions. Similarly, a graduate student in ethnomusicology might be restricted from doing research on storytelling even if that seems to be the most salient expressive form in a community, as it could be seen by an advisor as falling outside the intellectual scope of a department. Note also that some institutions may evoke suspicion or distrust among certain communities, such that being allied with certain organizations may create challenges. Institutions often determine timelines, whether it is the deadline for a term paper, doctoral dissertation, tenure review, survey, exhibit, or music festival. Each situation is different, so it is important to keep in mind how institutional constraints and parameters will impact how, what, with whom, and when fieldwork takes place.

Positionality

Fieldworkers' positionality—their identities combined with their relationship with practitioners or the people they research—can vary widely. Fieldworkers can be members of the communities they study or they can be outsiders, but their positions vis-à-vis the community always have implications for the research process. A fieldworker's positionality can relate to one's gender, sexuality, race, ethnicity, nationality, religion, politics, and other identity dimensions associated with a cultural practice or community. Fieldworkers need to be aware of their own identities as social beings and how their identities relate to those of the people they are studying—a theme discussed throughout this handbook. For now, use the following exercise to explore some illustrative examples.

Exercise

1. Divide into small groups.
2. Each group selects one of the relationship scenarios below, or alternately comes up with its own. Ideally, groups will discuss different scenarios from one another:
   - A man trying to research narratives about women's first menses in his own culture.
   - A woman researching a predominantly male music scene.
   - An African American doing research on his community's singing traditions.
   - A Euro-American researching Navajo rug weaving in the United States.
   - A lesbian from the United States doing research on Malawian political dancing.
   - A Korean woman doing research on US male fraternity rituals.
   - A Euro-American male college student who is not in a fraternity doing research on Euro-American male fraternity rituals.
   - A Euro-American male college student doing research on his own fraternity's rituals.

3. Discuss how the positionality of the fieldworker in relationship to those of the people studied might impact fieldwork. Consider the following questions:
   - What successes might the fieldworker encounter?
   - What difficulties might the fieldworker encounter?
   - Should this project be carried out given these potential difficulties?
   - If yes, what strategies could be used to address possible issues?

Insider and Outsider Perspectives

Sometimes a person does fieldwork with a group or network of people with which they consider themselves to belong. Sharon Sherman (1998), for example, made a film *Passover, A Celebration* about her own family's religious feast. Others do fieldwork outside any of the multiple groups to which they belong, such as Fenn's research with young hip-hop artists in Malawi or boutique guitar pedal builders in the United States (2004, 2010). The distinction between insider and outsider is often not very clear because we each have varied and complicated relationships to different groups and individuals, and our relationships are not always clearly defined. If a woman in her twenties did fieldwork with her own extended family, her perspective would seem to be clearly that of an insider. Yet, within her family, there may be divisions based on age, gender, or education level that are associated with different access to knowledge and artistic practice. For example, only the women quilt, only the men play instruments, or only the elders tell stories about family history. She may find that though she is a member of the family, she would have more of an outsider perspective if she chose to study instrument playing or storytelling within the family. Yet, though she was not a participant in making music or telling stories, she might nevertheless bring a certain insider perspective, having grown up listening to the music and stories. In this hypothetical example, the student's perspective could be considered a complex combination of insider and outsider. Similarly, Fenn had very different relationships to the people and topics in each of the two projects mentioned above. In his research on Malawian hip-hop, Fenn identified as more of an outsider than he did with the pedal builders. In Malawi, he did not share the nationality, age, or lifestyle of the youth he studied, nor was he himself a hip-hop musician. However, he could connect over shared gender, an appreciation of the music, and respect for what the musicians were doing. With the boutique guitar pedal builders, he was also an outsider. However, he shared a nationality and broad musical-generational orientation with the participants in his project. Additionally, that he was an avid collector and user of pedals gave him some insider status despite not being a builder himself.

To complicate things even further, Deborah Wong emphasizes how the same person represents different insider/outside relationships—not only in varying contexts, but even as a result of the media through which they communicate and the acts of communication in which they engage. Wong is both a Taiko player and an ethnomusicologist. In her essay "Moving: From Performance to Performative Ethnography and Back Again," she explains that she shifts back and forth between the roles of performer and interpreter when she is writing about Taiko, at times writing "like a Taiko player" and at other times "writing like an ethnomusicologist" (2008, 77). Though she is an insider in that she is a performer, she is simultaneously an outsider when she analyzes a performance from the perspective of her scholarly training. As she puts it, "The ethnographer is always an outsider." She elaborates that even creating an ethnography of a close family member "would presumably entail crafting a new relationship beyond that of daughter or sister" (82).

Though there is neither clear nor consistent distinction between being an insider or outsider, one's relationship vis-à-vis the people studied has an impact on the fieldwork experience and outcomes, and thus is worthy of consideration. For the sake of discussion, we will refer to insider and outsider status, knowing that these perspectives do not exist in any clear-cut way. There are advantages and disadvantages to either being a member of a group studied or not. Each research situation will have its own social dynamics. The advantages or disadvantages of the researcher's relationship to the community will be dependent on such things as identity dynamics within the specific context, the personalities of the individuals involved, the nature of the project, the duration, who determines the goals, and the anticipated and actual outcomes. Understanding the impossibility of generalizing to all situations, we offer a discussion of some possible advantages and disadvantages to inspire fieldworkers to think about how their relationships could impact their projects.

Insider Perspective: Some Possible Advantages

Being a member of a group can be advantageous if the fieldworker already has linguistic and cultural competency and contacts with members of the community. They may also already understand the cultural form from the group's perspective. Insiders often already have positive relationships and do not need to spend extended time developing trust and acceptance. It may be easier for insiders to gain access to events relevant to the project. Moreover, their presence may attract minimal attention, allowing them to focus their energies on observation and documentation rather than gaining access or relationship building.

Insider Perspective: Some Possible Disadvantages

Insiders may not notice important information because they are so familiar with the group and its practices that they perceive cultural activity to be "normal" or even unimportant. It may not occur to the fieldworker to explore the significance of certain dynamics or assumed meanings. Insiders may be aligned with certain members of a cultural group, making it difficult for them to access other members. Their relationships and previous interactions may impact how participants treat them. Sometimes fieldworkers' own experiences with the people or topics may make it difficult for them to understand or accept perspectives that conflict with their own. And, insiders sometimes assume that they know how people feel about things when in fact they do not and are projecting their own thoughts on others. Furthermore, by engaging in documentation, the fieldworkers remove themselves from the group, which may strain familiar relationships or interfere with their obligations as members of the group.

> In his first folklore class at the University of Oregon in fall 2017, Bryan Rodriguez interviewed his father about stories that had fascinated Bryan as a child. At the time of the interview, his father was in poor health. Bryan's project was a success in that he received an excellent grade. More importantly, it was meaningful to him, his father, and other members of his family: "I remember waking up early, one Saturday morning for a walk with my father. The air was crisp, the leaves' colors were as warm as the rising sun. As a kid, I didn't like walking, or hiking, or anything that required me to walk more than a hundred meters. My father dragged me out of the house to go to the trails; I was tired and hoped it was worth waking up early. I recall tying my laces on my blue Vans, making sure I didn't step over them in the five-mile trek that was ahead. As we started to walk, I asked my father to tell me any scary stories he knew. Being interested in Halloween and the paranormal, I was excited to hear what my father had to offer. 'Oh, I know so many of them!' he replied with a smile. He started telling countless stories about when he was a young boy and how he came across several witches or brujas in his small village of Jomulquillo, Mexico. My eyes grew bigger with excitement and fright about how my father described these shapeshifting creatures called *Lechuzas*: an old woman who preys on young children, having the power to shape-shift into a birdlike animal, ultimately flying off with the hopeless victims into the mountains. The fieldwork project allowed me to share the folklore of the Rodriguez family, the small village of Jomulquillo, and of many Mexican-Americans."

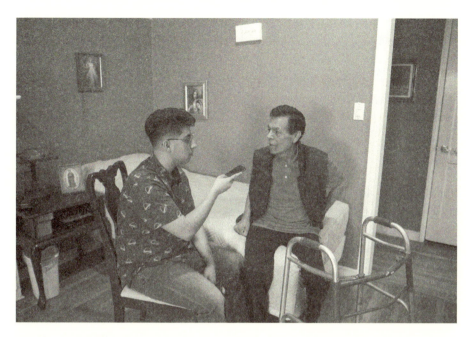

Figure 1.3. Gilman's student Bryan Rodriguez interviews his father Jesse Rodriguez about La Lechuza stories for his fieldwork project for the class "Introduction to Folklore." Los Angeles, California, 2017. Photo by Estefania Salgado.

Outsider Perspective: Some Possible Advantages

When one is not a member of a group, everything can be new and unfamiliar. An outsider can be unusually attuned to details and pay attention to and pursue information that an insider might take for granted. Outsiders may be less likely to assume that they understand something, so they may ask questions about things that an insider would take for granted. Because participants may not assume that the outsider will understand very much, they may be more likely to indulge their questions and thus answer what might seem to be simple or obvious questions. Furthermore, an outsider can sometimes be received more enthusiastically than an insider. An outsider's interest can sometimes feel exciting and legitimating, inspiring people to want to participate. Members may perceive some benefit for their group or cultural practice gaining recognition from a larger audience. And, everyone involved may enjoy the process of developing new relationships, which can energize a project.

Outsider Perspective: Some Possible Disadvantages

Outsiders may lack linguistic competency, which refers to both the language of the research context being foreign to the fieldworker and to situations where the fieldworker may be fluent in the language but where there may be distinctive speech patterns, accent differences, or idiomatic expressions with which they are unfamiliar. Cultural competency can also be an issue because it can take a long time for the fieldworker to learn how to behave appropriately in the research context. It could even be that the fieldworker never gains access or acceptability to a community. Outsiders can make assumptions about people, information, or cultural practices based on their own frame of reference. When a fieldworker is identified to be in a more socially powerful or privileged position, members of a community may select to protect their cultural materials and privacy and not divulge information or grant the fieldworker access to important events. Even when granted access, the outsider's presence may be disruptive. Furthermore, outsiders may not be aware of social relationships and how their connections to certain individuals or positions of status are impacting their research. Not knowing much about the people, fieldworkers may not recognize misinformation or biases. Furthermore, people may be suspicious of the fieldworker's motivations and be distrustful of what will be done with the information gathered.

Exercise

1. Divide into pairs.
2. Identify a fieldwork topic for which one member of the dyad would have an insider perspective.
3. Consider the following questions:
    - Would the individual have access to this topic? Why or why not?
    - In what ways would their perspective be insider? Is there anything that would complicate this perspective?
    - In what ways might their relationship to the group or topic be an advantage for completing the project?
    - In what ways might the relationship to the group or topic produce challenges?
4. Identify a fieldwork topic for which one member of the dyad would have an outsider perspective. Based on the above discussion, consider the following questions:
    - Would the individual have access to this topic? Why or why not?
    - In what ways would their perspective be that of an outsider? Is there anything about this topic that would provide an insider perspective?
    - In what ways might their relationship to the group or topic be an advantage for completing this project?
    - In what ways might the relationship to the group or topic produce challenges?

No scenario is perfect. Awareness of the issues that might arise should help fieldworkers develop research plans that take these issues into account, mitigate problems that arise, and be honest about their limitations and biases in their presentation of the material. In academic settings in the fields of folklore, ethnomusicology, and other allied disciplines, research by individuals is often privileged. Students are often expected to do research on their own for class assignments, theses, or dissertations, while scholars often get the most credit for individual projects that produce single-authored works. However, a team approach that gathers fieldworkers who have a range of relationships to people and topics can be the most productive approach because the project benefits from the strengths and weaknesses of each perspective. And most importantly, the project can benefit from the interactions between the fieldworkers who can discuss differences in their interpretations, which can yield important insights.

What to Call the People Involved?

What to call the people who are the focus of fieldwork has long been a controversial and contested question. Some terms that have been featured in fieldwork include "informant," "research subject," "citizen," "participant," "consultant," "collaborator," and "interlocutor." Yet, each of these terms has been critiqued at one point. Referring to someone who provides information about a cultural practice as an "informant" could be problematic because of the term's common use in police or intelligence realms. "Research subject" depersonalizes people and treats them as objects of study. "Subject" also can have pejorative implications and be associated with "political inferiors and, in the context of medical research, with cadavers" (Finnegan 1992, 221). "Collaborator" has a similar connotation to "informant" in the intelligence world; it also often suggests a much greater degree of collaboration in such things as research design, writing, and benefit than what actually transpires. "Interlocutor," meaning someone engaged in a dialogue, can seem impersonal and could imply much less engagement than is typical for many participants.

So, what to call people? There is no easy answer. The authors usually refer to people by their social position or by their research role. In his work with the ChinaVine project, Fenn referred to participants as "artists," and in his fieldwork with guitar pedal makers, he referred to them as "builders," using the term they used to refer to themselves in relationship to their artistic practice. In her project on political dance in Malawi, Gilman referred to people as "women dancers," "politicians," or "journalists." In her project on the musical listening of US troops, she used names or referred to those she interviewed generally as "participants in this project" or the "people whom I interviewed." This approach is clunky, but it avoids labeling participants with a term that implies a static relationship between the fieldworkers and those who are involved, and it uses terms more appropriate to how people identify themselves or their positions vis-à-vis the project. As there is no correct way to refer to participants, we encourage fieldworkers to reflect on the options and make a decision that feels appropriate to the context of the project. For the purposes of this handbook, we use the vague term "participant."

Bruce Jackson

"I use the word 'informant' a great deal in this book. I'm not happy with it, but I don't have another word that serves all its functions quite so well. Denotatively, the word means simply 'someone who provides information,' but connotatively it can be more troublesome. The historian or folklorist or anthropologist or sociologist speaking of his or her 'informants' better not do that around individuals who have been or who fear being the subjects of investigations by one government agency or another" (1987, 7).

Conclusion

There are many reasons why people do fieldwork and many different contexts in which they do it. Regardless, the emphasis is always on the lived experience and social interactions that occur through immersion in a social setting. Human relationships are at the center of all fieldwork projects. Being aware and constantly reflective about one's identities and one's relationship to a project, relevant institutions, and the people involved is critical for success and can go a long way toward mitigating some of the problems that could occur.

2

DEVELOPING A PROJECT

IN THIS CHAPTER WE SHIFT our focus from important concepts and terms to the practical steps of conceptualizing and developing a fieldwork project. We consider the following questions: (1) *what* to research and what methods would be most productive for that topic, (2) *who* might be involved in a number of different capacities, (3) *when* to begin and end, and (4) *why* is the project significant.

Knowing that readers will be conducting fieldwork on a wide range of topics with a variety of goals and in various contexts, we do not provide detailed guidelines about more formal aspects of research design. Instead, we provide guidance for identifying a project and making a research plan. As you read through the sections, bear in mind that each project is idiosyncratic and will unfold in relationship to the individuals involved and the nature of its context and goals. We provide an overview of steps, though the specifics for individual projects or the sequencing of steps will vary from project to project.

Finding a Topic

An obvious jumping off point for any project is identifying a topic. Some fieldworkers are drawn to ethnographic methods because they already have a topic that interests them, or they have been told to research something specific by an instructor or supervisor. Others may know that they want to do research on some type of folklore or musical form or they may have been assigned to do so, yet they may have little idea of where to start.

For the purposes of this chapter, we will assume that the fieldworker has not already identified a topic. We briefly address how to come up with a topic and how to narrow it to something that is doable given the time and resources available to you.

Folklore and music happen all around us in formal and informal settings. If you are seeking a topic, we recommend that you pay attention to the things you encounter in your life. Look through newspapers, archives, and the internet for interesting activities. Discuss possibilities with friends, family members, classmates, or people in communities with which you are familiar or that interest you. Read posters and announcements in physical and virtual spaces or visit local community centers. As you peruse what is happening around you, consider what you find most interesting and engaging, what fits within the parameters of what you are expected or hoping to accomplish, and whether you think you would have access. You might do a project associated with some type of activity done by you or those you know, or you may decide to branch out into a topic that is less familiar. Depending on your time, ability to travel, and funding, you may decide to do a project in a local setting, or you may choose to do one in another location nearby, in another part of your country, or in a foreign one.

If you have the freedom to select a topic of your choosing, we recommend identifying something that interests you already. Fieldwork requires self-motivation, so finding something that energizes you is important. Below are some questions for reflection as you consider your options.

- *What is the projected outcome?* What do you hope or what are you expected to produce from the fieldwork? Some typical outcomes include archival materials, class papers, theses and dissertations, physical or virtual exhibits, festivals or other events, videos, podcasts, or policy papers. Some projects are not oriented toward producing tangible outcomes but rather are intended to be educational, contribute to community building, or to effect social change
- *Whose goals?* Will you be collaborating with the community to produce something that is desired and beneficial for its members? Or are the project's goals primarily your own or that of an organization for which you are working?
- *What will you do with the materials gathered?* Will you archive the materials you document for the community's record keeping? Will you archive the materials for your future use or that of others?
- *What is your timeline?* How much time do you have to do the project? Is there a deadline? How much time do you have in your schedule to devote to your project?
- *What resources do you have to put toward the project?* What financial resources do you have for equipment, travel, and accommodation? Do you have contacts or the necessary expertise?

Figure 2.1. Art show at Lincoln Gallery, taken during fieldwork by Fenn's students that supported the creation of a strategic plan for the Oregon Supported Living Program's Arts and Culture Program. Eugene, Oregon, 2015. Photo by Sarah Wyer.

- *What limitations might impact what would be feasible to you?* Are there family or other social obligations, physical or mental health issues, personal challenges, or anything else that might make a particular topic or project difficult or even impossible?

It is important to realize that not all topics would be appropriate for all individuals or for all desired outcomes. Certain folklore practices or musical forms are better suited for certain types of projects. As an example, if you want to make a documentary video, it is important that the topic be visually engaging, that you would have access to the individuals and settings that you hope to capture, and that you have the linguistic and cultural competency to work with the people involved. Some possible topics would not work well because the visual components are limited or because participants would refuse to be visually identifiable. Some subjects or communities are not accessible to filmmaking, and there may be culturally sensitive information that people feel should not be shared with others. Though a topic may not be appropriate for a documentary, the same topic might be feasible and appropriate for another outcome. Something that is not visually engaging for a video might be interesting to write about. Participants who do not want their faces shown in a video may be willing to participate and share information for a written format. Similarly, some topics are better suited for exhibits than others.

An exhibit about storytelling can be limiting if the curator is restricted to providing texts of stories and images of storytellers. An exhibit about baskets and basket-making might be more visually stimulating. There are no hard and fast rules about what kind of format is best for any given topic, but we recommend reflecting on these issues before launching a project.

Access

One of the most important things that you need to evaluate is whether you will have access. As you explore possible topics, consider whether there are aspects of your identity that could make it possible for you to do this research or ones that might make it challenging. Is membership in a community necessary to be present or participate? Are you old enough to attend the events where something happens? Would your gender, sexuality, ethnicity, race, or religious identity give you access or could aspects of your identity be a limitation? In considering these questions, think about the extent of the limitation. For example, if you are a man wanting to do research on a topic that is associated with a group of women, it may be that you could gain access but that you would have to work a little harder to develop relationships and gain trust. On the other hand, there may be topics or groups to which you could not have access regardless of your efforts. A 19-year-old in the United States wanting to do research on a blues music scene that happens in a bar that does not allow minors would not have access to those events. Access might, however, be granted to practice sessions and interviews that occur in other settings.

Some types of activities and knowledge are intended for insiders of a group, and members may be committed to keeping the information private. Whether or not you were a member of the group would determine whether you would have access to the material. It would also impact whether people would be willing to allow you to do the research and make it publicly available. Other things to consider that could affect access include whether the activity will occur during the time you have available to do the fieldwork. Would the people involved be available? If the research requires travel, would you have the time? Do you have the resources to pay for the travel or to take care of your needs at home while you are away?

An aspect rarely discussed in fieldwork guides is the importance of knowing your own personal strengths and limitations. If you are gregarious and comfortable in most social situations, a topic that requires you to interact with people you do not know may be a good one. If you experience anxiety in social situations or find them paralyzing, you may decide to select a topic that is more feasible for your personality. That said, many fieldworkers have found that pushing themselves beyond their comfort zone has resulted in some truly interesting and insightful experiences.

While some issues of access can be assessed prior to entering the field, bear in mind that others will emerge only after a fieldworker begins to engage with the people or site. It is important that you continue to actively reflect on the issues raised above throughout the fieldwork process.

Knowledge and Skills

An important part of preparing for fieldwork is learning as much as possible about the topic to gain the necessary background, learn what has already been done by other researchers, and help develop a focus. Some might dedicate a great deal of time to library, archival, or internet research prior to finding a topic. Others might identify a topic and make initial forays first and then begin to explore the library, archives, and internet for pertinent information. There is no correct order to these activities. The logic of the sequencing for any given topic will often emerge from fieldworkers' prior engagement with the topic or community, their access to the topic, and the timeframe involved.

Library Research

Though there may be more emphasis on scouring relevant scholarship in academic research, reading what has already been written about a topic is valuable regardless of the setting for or goals of the project. In deciding what books, journal articles, or materials to review, think broadly. You may find scholarship that is specifically about your topic. But broadening your reading to what has been written on other dimensions related to it will enrich your understanding. We recommend looking for writing on the artistic practice under consideration, the cultural group or community in which it occurs, relevant theoretical perspectives that might shape your research questions and analysis, and scholarship on unrelated topics that draws on similar methodological or theoretical frameworks to your own.

Suggested Resource

Jennifer Post's *Ethnomusicology: A Research and Information Guide* (2011) is an excellent text for identifying bibliographies, discographies, filmographies, indices, journals, encyclopedias, dictionaries, and other relevant sources. While the focus is on ethnomusicology, she includes many sources relevant to folklore or ethnographic research more generally.

As an example, if someone were to do a project on the performance of gender in contemporary burlesque in the United States, useful topics for library research might be:

- The history of burlesque
- Gender and contemporary burlesque in the United States
- Contemporary burlesque (not specifically about gender) in the United States and other countries
- Theoretical approaches to gender as performance
- Other types of performance genres that involve gender play
- Bar culture in the United States
- Music and gender
- Costuming and gender
- The demographics of the people who perform burlesque compared to the setting in which the research might take place

You may also want to read about issues associated with the format you have selected. Those making documentaries may want to research scholarship on issues of representation in audiovisual media. Those writing books may want to explore issues of authorial control in interpretation of ethnographic material. Those creating exhibits may want to read about how to contextualize material culture in an exhibit.

When you search for relevant materials, do not be surprised if you cannot find publications that are specific to the topic you have chosen. One of the most exciting dimensions of ethnographic fieldwork is that fieldworkers sometimes select topics that have received very little previous attention from scholars or others, making a project especially valuable. Though you may not find much directly about your topic, you should have no problem identifying relevant scholarship if you think broadly. You may also be surprised by the topics that have already been researched. In our experience teaching, it is not unusual for students to declare that they cannot do the library portion of an assignment because nothing has ever been written about their topic. A quick search in our library database sometimes produces extensive materials, a great surprise to the student who assumed that the topic would not have garnered scholarly attention.

On the other hand, in scouring the library database for existing scholarship, you may find that somebody has already done almost identical research to what you are planning. This may or may not be an issue. For those doing fieldwork for class papers, it may not be a problem given that the specifics of your project will necessarily be distinct from what has already been written. For those doing master's or PhD projects, original research is often a requirement, in which case some effort to distinguish one's project from what has already been done will be necessary. Bear in mind that even if your topic or research focus is similar to what has already been done, your perspective may be different enough that you feel confident your fieldwork would make a contribution. Remember that all fieldwork is original research. Somebody else may have done a similar project in the same community, but your research would be unique if only because of your questions and perspectives. You would most likely attend different events. You might interview different people, or you might interview the same people and ask different questions. Or the same people might feel differently than they did previously or respond differently to you. Furthermore, your personality, positionality, interests, academic training, and foci would impact the research situation and the outcomes in ways different from your predecessors.

Take advantage of librarians! They can help you find sources and appropriate search strategies. In addition to the library's main search engine, search databases that index publications on specific topics. For folklore and ethnomusicology, the following databases are useful: JSTOR, MLA, Music Index, RILM Abstracts of music literature, Anthropology Plus, Project Muse, or Academic Search Premier. We recommend searching multiple databases. Though there is overlap between them, each index has different foci. Systematically searching several relevant databases often yields the best results.

Finding sources can be overwhelming, and, if you find a lot of material, even paralyzing. Establish a system for organizing materials. One option is to build a single bibliography of everything you find and then begin to work your work way through the readings. As you find sources and read, be sure to write down a full bibliographic citation in the style that is appropriate to your discipline. You may need to return to a source to review or cite it in a later phase of your project. Building a full and consistently formatted bibliography as you go might be time consuming and tedious; yet, it will save you the headache of having to find the details again when you require them in the future.

Reading everything in the bibliography organized alphabetically can feel like too much. An effective strategy to make the reading more manageable and facilitate better recall is to organize the readings from the master bibliography into smaller lists. In the example given above about burlesque, organizing readings into the search categories already listed would produce clusters of related readings. The fieldworker could then divide their time by reading publications on similar topics together, which could maximize memory and comprehension.

As you read, we recommend that you create an annotated bibliography by writing short summaries for each reading that include a brief description of the topic, a summary of the author's main arguments, and a brief discussion of what evidence they are using to make the arguments. The annotations should be just a few sentences to allow you to quickly review them in the future so that you remember what was in the reading and quickly determine whether it is worth revisiting as you work through various phases of your project. You may feel like skipping annotating when you are strapped for time and eager to begin fieldwork. However, in the end, it will save you a great deal of time. It is much easier to read through your annotations to determine a publication's relevance than it is to find the book or essay again and skim through it to determine what it was about or the authors' arguments that was relevant to the project.

Archives

Exploring archival collections—such things as video footage, interview recordings or transcripts, newspaper articles, photographs, and ephemera—to identify primary source materials related to your project can help you gain a historical perspective and can inspire you to think of topics or foci. Finding whether, and where, these materials exist can be complicated; the process of discovery will vary greatly from project to project. Should you find that someone has conducted research on the topic in the past, you will want to determine if they deposited their materials in an archive. If so, contact the archives to find out if it is possible to access the materials.

Many universities with folklore programs and state public folklore organizations have archives whose holdings include materials from professional and student folklorists, including documentation about music that might be relevant to ethnomusicologists. Universities with ethnomusicology programs—including University of Washington; Indiana University; and University of California, Los Angeles—have robust ethnomusicology archives. Many university libraries have manuscript or special collections that include materials relevant to folklore and ethnomusicologists. Additionally, museums and historical societies in the United States often have archival holdings associated with local culture and heritage, and countries frequently have national archives where fieldworkers might find valuable primary data. National institutions in the United States, including the American Folklife Center at the Library of Congress and the Smithsonian Institute's Center for Folklife and Cultural Heritage, have extensive holdings on many folklore and music topics that span global geographic areas, historical periods, and cultural groups.

Keep in mind that if you find that an archival institution holds collections relevant to your fieldwork topic, the materials may not be immediately available to you. And, in some cases, they may not be available at all if either the researcher who conducted the initial fieldwork or the community they worked with placed restrictions on access. It is best to contact the archives and communicate with a staff member about whether you can access a collection, either on-site or remotely. Be sure to ask about the timeframe for delivery of copies and be prepared to pay for duplication fees. If physical items are involved, you will also likely need to pay for shipping. More and more, archives are able to produce digital copies for researchers to use, and in some cases, collections are easily accessed through online portals. But be prepared to wait if materials are not already digitized or to travel if collections are restricted to on-site use only.

Internet

The internet can be an excellent resource for doing background research to establish a knowledge base and foundation for fieldwork. Internet sites may include important background information, written descriptions of communities or people, audio and visual recordings, spaces where participants in your topic interact or discuss the topic, news coverage, opportunities to buy and sell materials, reviews, and information helpful in preparing for logistics. As you peruse the internet, be sure to consider who is providing the information in order evaluate the quality or validity of the information provided.

In addition to obtaining background information, exploring internet sites to identify whether there are digital spaces where participants in your topics are active can be important, both for gathering information but also for identifying potential research strategies and sites. You may find that musicians from a community you are interested in have a blog in which they discuss their practice or that they post musical selections online. Or, people making a type of craft you are studying may be posting how-to guides or using a website to sell their crafts to people in other communities or countries. These types of discoveries can be important for shaping what kinds of questions you want to pursue, give you insights, or may influence you to shift your project altogether.

Existing Data Sets

For some projects, it could be useful to look for relevant quantitative data, such as census data or other data sets that will help you understand the topic as you develop research questions, compile data, or analyze. Data on census data or other demographics of a community—for example about gender, occupation, and economic levels—can be key for situating a study in a larger context or understanding social dynamics. This data is sometimes published in paper or online reports and can be accessed fairly easily. Other types of data may have restricted access, in which case you would need to determine whether and how to obtain the materials.

Linguistic Competency

Many of you will be doing fieldwork in situations where the majority speak the same language as you. Others will need to learn a foreign language in order to communicate with the people involved and successfully accomplish other fieldwork activities. Learning a foreign language is time consuming; allow for adequate time in your planning. Though you may become proficient in a language, your linguistic abilities may be inadequate for doing all that the fieldwork requires. Many fieldworkers benefit from hiring research assistants or otherwise getting help from local members of the community to better understand and translate materials.

Linguistic competency can also be important in relationship to access. Certain members of a community may use language differently than others. You therefore need to think about what specific language or linguistic modes you need in order to talk to the people or interact with the practice you are researching. For example, in many African countries the official language is the language of the former colonizer—generally French, English, or Portuguese. Knowledge of the official language can be enough to operate in the country and do some fieldwork. However, it is common in many African contexts that highly competent speakers of the official language are those with more formal schooling, who live in urban environments, or who have occupations that bring them into regular contact with foreigners. If a fieldworker only knows the official language, their ability to interact may be limited to only those who speak this language—thus greatly limiting their perspective and likely resulting in bias.

Developing linguistic competency is important even for those doing research in a language in which they are fluent. James Spradley explains that fieldworkers often neglect to develop linguistic competency when researching people who speak the same language as them "because informants *appear* to use a language identical to that spoken by the ethnographer. But such is not the case; *semantic* differences exist, and they have a profound influence on ethnographic research" (1979, 18). Different groups and individuals use language differently, often in ways associated with cultural difference or power differentials (see Briggs 1986; Etter-Lewis 1991). An important step in preparing oneself for fieldwork is identifying one's linguistic relationship to the people who will participate in your project. Developing linguistic competency is necessary and can include learning idiomatic expressions and codes, understanding which words are value-laden, becoming familiar with kinds of language used between people of different status, identifying how metacommunicative devices operate, and gaining appreciation for the kinds of communications appropriate among various social categories.

Cultural Competency

In this early phase of your project, you should try to learn as much about the community and practice as possible to help you formulate a doable research plan. Developing your own cultural knowledge and competency will enable you to effectively participate within the research setting (see Briggs 1986). Strategies for accessing information will vary from project to project. Forays into a community; attending public events; exploring relevant internet activity; reading books, newspapers, and magazine articles; or following blogs can be helpful. In some cases, there may be formal archives—collections of photographs, audiovisual recordings, documents, or ephemera associated with communities—that you can review. Reading novels by authors who are writing about the cultural area, listening to musical recordings, watching relevant documentaries or other footage, and watching local TV shows and feature movies can be instructive.

Ask these questions as you engage in initial research about your topic: Is there a particular cultural form that interests you? If so, how do practitioners refer to it? How is it learned and taught? When and where does it most likely occur? What value does the practice carry: positive, negative, or neutral? Is there broad agreement about the value? What can you glean initially about its aesthetics or social function? What seem to be the most important or significant dimensions of the practice for the people who are involved?

Find out what you can about who participates. Consider the following questions: Is this an individual or group cultural form? If it is associated with a group, is it associated with some type of cohesive group or broadly defined individuals? Are there categories of people who are more likely to participate? Are there different types of participation? Are there people who are excluded? Are there people who choose not to participate? Are there people who are likely to be organizers? Are there benefits? If so, who seems to benefit? What is your relationship to the practitioners? Alternately, your project might revolve around a desire to learn something about a social group, engage with a set of social issues, or participate in advocacy, which would require a different set of questions.

Exploring these types of questions in the initial phase of research will help you develop a foundation for a research plan, while you gain adequate knowledge to effectively engage with participants. This initial phase of planning will help you figure out whom to approach, how best to approach them, what kinds of events you might be able to attend, and the appropriate ways to interact within the relevant spaces and with the participants

Many of you, especially those doing research in cultural contexts that are less familiar to you, whether they are on- or offline, will need to learn about culturally appropriate behavior in the setting. How do people greet one another? Who interacts with whom? What social hierarchies are operating? How do people in different strata behave with one another? How do you fit into the social hierarchies? How should you interact with people at different levels? Developing cultural competency at this phase is the goal but bear in mind that this process will continue throughout the fieldwork. As a researcher, you will likely need to acclimate to an unfamiliar cultural space and work to navigate acceptance in the field environment. Prepare yourself to be continually aware and ready to adapt as needed. Note that even if you are already a participant in the event, this type of questioning should help open your analytical lens.

Preliminary Fieldwork

Once you have a general idea for a topic, we recommend that you spend time doing preliminary research, investigating such things as when the activity occurs, what locale or locations are associated with it, who is involved with it in a variety of capacities, and determining whether you will have access. The goal in this phase is to familiarize yourself with the topic and to start to develop initial contacts. Spending time "on-the-ground" (whether online or offline) figuring out what is most interesting and salient to the group or about the topic can be valuable as you identify research questions and a focus for the project.

It is useful to make initial forays into the field, if at all possible. For those doing research on a type of music or folklore practice that happens in public places, you may want to spend some time at the event or locale where it takes place. As an example, if you are studying Irish music circles, you should attend one as an audience member. If you are

Figure 2.2. Gilman recording video of a Malawian dance performance during preliminary fieldwork for her dissertation project. Malawi, 1996. Photo by Lisa Gilman.

studying foodways at a festival, attend the event, taste the food, sit with others who are enjoying a meal, and engage in conversation. For those who are interested in a topic that is predominately online, begin to follow relevant activity or become a participating member of a group. If there are no events or activities for your topic or none that you can easily attend anonymously, it could be useful to introduce yourself to a practitioner or to one or more members of the community. Engaging in preliminary conversations with these individuals and possibly obtaining opportunities to attend some of the activities associated with the topic could be valuable. If you plan to do fieldwork with a group of which you are already a member, you may want to participate in some activities with your developing research questions in mind. This will help you determine if they seem appropriate. You can also begin talking to some members to find out whether they would be agreeable to contributing to your project.

If the activities or practices you are interested in are located far from you, it may be difficult to engage in this type of initial foray. Ideally you would plan a short visit to help define the project and determine its feasibility. There also may be other ways to obtain preliminary information. There may be people associated with the place or topic living nearby whom you could contact to have some initial conversations, or there may be internet sites or social media networks that you could use to start to learn more about the topic and make initial contacts.

Conclusion

We outlined the process of identifying a topic, doing preliminary field-work, developing linguistic and cultural competency, making initial forays into the field, and developing a knowledge base. Developing this foundation is crucial for the next steps, which include formalizing what you plan to produce, what questions you are pursuing, and what research methods you plan to use to gather information.

3

CREATING A RESEARCH PLAN

AFTER YOU HAVE FORMULATED AN idea for a topic that is accessible, and you have developed a knowledge base, it is time to establish a focus for the project. In this chapter we outline how to develop an overarching line of inquiry and a set of associated questions that will be the basis for your fieldwork. We then suggest a strategy for establishing a plan that will be effective for answering your questions and obtaining the information needed for the desired outcome. Some ethnographers emphasize that research questions should come after the researcher has spent a great deal of time with a community learning about the people and the practice. The idea is that a project's focus should emerge from what is most relevant to practitioners or makes the most sense within the context of its production and consumption. While we agree with this approach, we are also aware that many students and beginning fieldworkers have limited time to spend doing preliminary research before having to focus their efforts. This chapter assumes that fieldworkers are developing a new project on a topic of their choosing, though we realize that some readers may be working in situations where they are contributing to existing projects or developing foci collaboratively with communities rather than controlling a project themselves. We intend for the material discussed in this chapter to be informative and adaptable to those doing fieldwork in a variety of settings. Much of what we cover is relevant to those working in both public and academic settings, though the sections on establishing analytical foci likely will be most relevant to academics.

Developing a Research Plan

Some of you will have to produce a proposal to submit to an instructor, institution, research compliance board, or potential funder. Proposal guidelines usually provide specific instructions about required sections and length. Though each differs, most expect information about the following:

- Description of project that explains the topic and questions to be explored
- Research locations
- Expected outcomes
- Significance
- Methods and work plan
- Timeline

Whether or not you are required to submit a proposal, we recommend that all fieldworkers take the time to write down information about all the items on this list to ensure they are prepared and focused. The process of considering each of these questions could also reveal problems, weaknesses, or areas in need of improvement.

Research Focus/Lines of Inquiry

Working from the preliminary information on the topic you have gathered, you are ready to begin refining your project and creating a focus. One strategy is to identify a primary line of inquiry around which to structure the project—what is it that you are trying to learn about this topic or group of people? Many folklore and ethnomusicology fieldworkers use a grounded approach to develop their research questions. Rather than choosing in advance to apply a particular theoretical approach or deciding what is important to the fieldworker, they elicit what is important to the practitioners and then they develop the project around that. Other fieldworkers identify questions based on their own interests. And some fieldworkers draw on issues or theoretical approaches that interest them, choosing their fieldwork topic because it provides the opportunity to explore these.

Your main line of inquiry will be contingent on the desired outcome of the project. Someone writing a thesis or dissertation might have more theoretically driven questions than someone doing fieldwork to design an exhibit or effect some type of social change. Regardless, a fieldworker needs a focus that guides the research; otherwise they might gather a lot of information but end up with not enough of it in the right format to meet their goals. Once you have decided on a main line of inquiry, we recommend coming up with subquestions that will help support your primary focus. Below is an example adapted from a proposal Gilman wrote to do fieldwork with US troops.

The main line of inquiry for the project tracked the leisure dance activities of US soldiers as an entry point for learning how soldiers at lower ranks experience and negotiate the embodied experiences of preparing for and participating in their country's war efforts. There were several subquestions that contributed information addressing the main line of inquiry:

1. What kinds of embodied experiences are common during wartime?
2. Do soldiers dance during deployments or when on leave or postdeployment? If so, where, when, with whom do they dance, and what kind of dance do they enjoy?
3. How does the embodied experience at war compare to that of dancing?
4. What role (if any) does dancing play in soldiers' reflection, interpretation, or response to their war experience?

Note that each of the subquestions is designed to produce information that will shed light on the main line of inquiry—using dance to learn "about how soldiers experience and negotiate their embodied experiences of preparing for and participating in their country's war efforts."

The second hypothetical example is someone doing fieldwork in a public rather than academic setting. The topic is basketry in a particular community, and the goal is a physical exhibit:

Main line of inquiry: How do basket makers interact with the natural environment in the production of baskets?

The main line is divided into four subquestions or interrelated lines of inquiry:

1. What materials from the local environment do basket makers use?
2. Who gathers the materials? When, where, and how?
3. What is the process through which the materials are prepared and woven into baskets?
4. How are natural materials valued compared to synthetic ones?

Notice that each of these questions comprises many other subquestions. By developing your observation and interview tools, you will also develop questions from the broader guiding ones.

When asked to identify a main line of inquiry, we have noticed that students frequently come up with broad and ambitious goals. For example, students interested in the telling of contemporary legends might indicate that they are interested in learning why people tell legends about sex and how these legends impact how girls in the United States think about their own sexuality. Although these are excellent questions, they are too broad in scope. One student doing fieldwork can determine neither why people tell these legends nor the impact that legends have on all girls in the United States. With this interest in legends, sex, and the socialization of girls in mind, the student could come up with a much narrower topic about what kinds of legends are told by a particular group of friends, what those legends express about sexuality, and how the members of that group think about their own sexuality in relation to their interpretations of the stories. Correspondingly for the project on dance, war, and embodiment, the project could be focused on soldiers at a specific base, those who enjoy a particular kind of music and dancing, or those who share the same job.

Going through the process of creating questions and doing the steps described above is an effective first phase in developing a proposal. You can build your project description around your questions and then develop your methods and timeline around what would be required to answer each of the questions. You can then build your bibliography and theoretical framework (if applicable) by identifying library, online, and archival resources that would be most relevant to each of your main questions.

Exercise

1. Divide into groups of two to four.
2. Consider a project about music at a local festival.
3. Brainstorm three possible main lines of inquiry that could be the focus for this project.
4. For each, what are three subquestions that would contribute to answering the main question?
5. Reflect on each set of questions by considering the following:
   - Do the questions make sense?
   - Are they answerable?
   - Are they important?
   - If so, to whom would they be important?

Research Locations

Where to do your fieldwork will depend on your topic and research questions. It may make sense to focus your project on a physical location (e.g., club, city, neighborhood, social media network, or village) or a specific group of people (members of an arts collective or band, family, participants on an internet fan site, members of a cultural community, or children in a neighborhood). Pick a location based on whether you would have access. Somebody interested in small town festivals should pick a town not only based on physical access but also on whether it is feasible to attend the festival when it is scheduled.

Consider whether you have narrowed your topic enough to be able to effectively do the research. Someone interested in African American quilting, for example, will not be able to do fieldwork with all African American quilters across the United States. They would need to narrow their focus to a specific region, group of quilters, age group, quilting style, family, or time period. For some, determining the location for the project will be facilitated by the topic itself. Someone with a very specific topic—for example, Irish music jams in Eugene, Oregon—will be able to establish a place and community for the research based on the topic itself. There is a small community of people who gather in the same bar each Sunday in Eugene to play music together. Someone interested in Irish music jams in New York City will have a much larger selection of groups and locations to navigate. And, someone interested in Irish music-making in the United States more broadly would probably need to identify a specific geographic location or community of people to focus the project.

If interested in phenomena that occur online, question whether you should plan to do fieldwork exclusively online or whether you should plan some combination of online and offline fieldwork. In the essay "Ethnographic Approaches to the Internet and Computer-Mediated Communication," Angela Cora Garcia et al. recognize that some fieldworkers hope to do only online research because it can be easier and faster than doing face-to-face fieldwork (2009, 56). It is important, however, that you devise methods that are most productive and appropriate for your project rather than ones that are the easiest. Garcia et al. suggest that "rather than deciding in advance to conduct an ethnography of an online site or community, the ethnographer should first choose their topic of interest, and then define the field in terms of whether and how that topic involves different modes of communication or technological locations" (56). They make the important point that "virtually all ethnographies of contemporary society should include technologically mediated communication, behavior, or artifacts (e.g., websites) in their definition of the field or setting for the research" (57). Anthropologists Samuel Collins and Matthew Durington offer a nuanced discussion of field sites and fieldwork in the digital age, pushing ethnographers to consider "networked anthropology"— the inclusion of diverse media platforms and social media into research— as a methodological approach to bridging online and offline spaces (2015, 16–17). We would argue that many projects about digital topics would also benefit from some face-to-face fieldwork. As with those doing "in real life" fieldwork, digital fieldworkers need to identify the best sites for answering their questions or producing the desired outcome.

Figure 3.1. Deviation, an installation created by Fenn for the exhibit "Designing Sound," an outcome of his fieldwork with boutique guitar effects pedal builder, Devi Ever. Eugene, Oregon, 2011. Photo by John Fenn.

Expected Outcome

What is it that you hope to end up with at the conclusion of the project? The objectives for your project will necessarily determine how you go about doing the fieldwork and, for many of you, will shape the questions you pursue. Some readers will already know what they want to produce, but others will have to decide among several options. Bear in mind that

Figure 3.2. Traditional Tibetan knife maker, Tse Ring Dolga, discusses his craft with ChinaVine fieldwork team. The material from the fieldwork at his workshop resides on the ChinaVine website. Gato Monestary Village, Sichuan Province, China, 2015. Photo by John Fenn.

as with everything in fieldwork, plans may change in the middle, or you may end up with enough materials to produce something different or in addition to what you had initially planned. When considering the desired outcome, reflect on why you have selected one format over the other. Is there a reason to produce a book rather than a film or an online exhibit rather than a concert?

Significance

Why is this fieldwork important or significant? This is often one of the hardest questions for fieldworkers to answer. Fieldworkers will find a topic that interests them but may find it difficult to articulate its significance beyond their own individual curiosity. Bear in mind that a funding agency, your instructor, a thesis committee, or the people with whom you hope to do fieldwork will often expect you to articulate a reason for why this project is worthwhile. Spend some time answering the question, "So what?" Why should someone invest in or care about this project? If you cannot come up with an answer, you may need to refine your project or redirect your questions or goals to increase the topic's significance. Note that the value could be across many different dimensions. Folklore and ethnomusicology studies can contribute to academic knowledge, understanding of difficult social issues, entertainment, showcasing talented individuals, documenting valued history or cultural practices, intercultural exchange, revenue production, or any number of other things. When reflecting on significance, be sure to explore to whom it is significant. The project may have different value for different constituents. If you have difficulty thinking about why your idea is significant, do not give up too quickly. It can be helpful to talk to a friend, colleague, or mentor who may have enough distance from the topic to help you identify its value.

Research Methods

What will you need to do to answer the main and subquestions you have outlined for your project? And, what will you need to do to produce the desired outcome? These two questions are related but distinct. In thinking about the hypothetical basketry project described above, two methods useful for answering the first subquestion could be to ask a basket maker what materials they use and to go with them on a gathering expedition. These methods would help answer the research questions, but they may not be the best strategy for producing the desired outcome. A physical exhibit would require the fieldworker to identify materials to display in addition to gaining knowledge. Methods might include joining the basket maker on expeditions to gather materials, taking photographs or video recording of various steps in the process to obtain compelling audiovisual materials, and collecting objects, such as pieces of fibers or finished baskets.

In part II, we provide guidelines on methods typically used in folklore and ethnomusicology projects. For those new to fieldwork, we recommend reviewing those chapters prior to creating a plan. Then, ask yourself, "What would I need to do to answer each of my questions?" Depending on the question, your answers may include a review of relevant scholarship on the topic; visits to archives to explore relevant documentation; online research for information or online participation in the activity; attending events where it happens; observing the activity happening; communicating with people involved in a variety of capacities through conversations, emails, interviews; participating in the activity; and maybe learning how to do it.

In creating a methods plan, be as specific as possible. For example, rather than stating "interview participants," stipulate an ideal number of each type of participant that you hope to interview and why you have selected certain types of participants. If you plan to attend a group's rehearsals, estimate the number of rehearsals you think you would need to attend. You can always change it as you go, but having a firm plan will enable your mentors, instructors, and supervisors to give you feedback and help ensure that you end up with the information necessary for achieving your goals.

An important part of your planning should be about documentation. How will you gather your data? Will you rely on fieldnotes or do you plan to use other recording strategies, such as audio or video? Explain the reasons for your choices and consider whether they will be appropriate to the fieldwork setting. Your planning should extend beyond your immediate goals. Will you be gathering information that would be valuable to deposit in an archive so that it could be available to the communities of origin or future scholars? If so, we recommend contacting potential archives in the planning phase to determine what information about data they require, what formats they accept, what criteria they have for accepting materials, and what release forms are necessary. Once you have this information, you can align your data-gathering system with their requirements.

Exercise

Creating a research plan. Recommended for groups of two to four.
The project: Basket making in a community.
Goal: A physical exhibit.
Main line of inquiry: How do basket makers interact with the natural environment in their production of baskets?
Subquestions:

1. What materials from the local environment do basket makers use?
2. Who gathers the materials? When, where, and how?
3. What is the process through which the materials are prepared and woven into baskets?
4. How are natural materials valued compared to synthetic ones?

Using the example above, consider the following as a group:

- In what locations could you do this project?
- Who would be the participants?
- What methods would be productive for answering *each* of these questions?
- What forms of documentation would be useful for pursuing these lines of inquiry and producing the desired outcome?

Timeline

Fieldwork requires a great deal of flexibility, and your plan will most likely change as your research progresses. Having a clear timeline is useful for making sure that you take advantage of important research opportunities, make progress, and ultimately do what you need to do to achieve your goals in the time available to you.

An important first step before creating your timeline is gathering information about relevant activities that are already scheduled. Are there performances, events, rehearsals, instructional activities, planning sessions, meetings, or gatherings that you should attend? Are there times when key individuals will be available? What deadlines or time restrictions will impact your own availability? You may want to schedule for multiple research activities during the time you have available. For example, if you know that there will be a major performance happening, this may also be a great opportunity for you to make initial contacts and schedule some interviews. Or, if there is a festival scheduled, you may want to plan for a series of fieldwork activities prior to the festival, such as meeting organizers, attending planning meetings, volunteering, and interviewing participants, in addition to documenting the festival itself and interviewing participants after.

Be sure to account for the time it takes to do preliminary research, make initial forays, make contacts, schedule events, travel to and from locations, think, eat, write fieldnotes, process fieldwork materials, rest, and produce the final products. Be specific. Create a schedule with date ranges in which you detail what you hope to accomplish during each phase. Some dates will be specific and can be included on your calendar, such as a concert or special meal that is scheduled for a specific time and day. Other activities might be more vague, such as attending rehearsals that happen regularly, reviewing a social media site, or interviewing people. Although these activities may not occur at a certain time, it is a good idea to schedule these within a general time frame to ensure progress and completion.

Conclusion

There are many benefits to developing a clear plan with lines of inquiry and a structured research proposal. Such planning can help you obtain access to a community, funding, and approval from an instructor or supervisor. And, most important, a project plan will serve as a guide and framework during the fieldwork in addition to helping you track your progress.

However, this plan should only serve as a guide. Fieldwork is about people and social interactions, and these can rarely be fully anticipated or controlled. Things often do not happen as planned. People often do not think or behave as we anticipate or foresee. Sometimes activities are cancelled, organizations dissolve, people who are central to our projects leave, or resources run out. Sometimes we realize that the questions we planned are not relevant, or no one is willing or interested in answering them. These are only a fraction of what can happen to disrupt well-meaning goals. Fieldworkers should always be prepared for things to not go as they hoped and be prepared to feel discouraged and disappointed. Sometimes fieldworkers must adapt or even terminate a project, and that should be accepted as part of the experience. If researchers approach fieldwork with an open and flexible attitude, knowing they often will not have control or things might deviate from the expected, they will have more fun, develop stronger relationships, and ultimately do better fieldwork and produce the best products possible.

4

ORGANIZING AND LOGISTICS

AS YOU DEVELOP A PROJECT plan, you will need to move from the conceptual to the practical when launching your fieldwork efforts. In this chapter we highlight important considerations that figure into organizing yourself and your project prior to starting fieldwork. As with all other considerations discussed thus far, the specifics of your project will determine the particular decisions you need to make or resources you need to gather. For example, if your fieldwork project does not involve international travel, you will not need to think about visas and passports. However, you still may need to source funding for travel—whether this travel is short-distance commuting by car or airplane flights across the country. Although we do not cover every contingency, the orienting framework we provide will help you plan: making arrangements for any clearance or permissions you might need, organizing travel and/or communications, and gathering the appropriate gear or technology for your documentation needs.

Tips
- Talk to people who have been to or worked in the area (international or domestic).
- Read travel guides about the place.
- Look at other academic work about the place or community, even if from other disciplines.
- Find contacts through a local university or students.

Clearance, Consent, and Permission

Getting consent and permission to do fieldwork is a multifaceted process. At the level of working with individuals and small groups of people, you will need to have their consent to record or photograph—or to even be there at all! Remember that doing fieldwork often involves asking to be invited into people's lives in order to inquire about things they create, believe, or practice. It seems obvious, but if they do not want you there, you should not be there. Folklorists and ethnomusicologists do not "follow a story" in a journalistic sense so much as they seek understanding and interpretation in collaboration with individuals and communities. Consent and permission flow together in the people-centered practice of fieldwork, and ultimately folklorists and ethnomusicologists need to be responsive to the needs, desires, and well-being of the people they work with during research. Both the American Folklore Society and the Society for Ethnomusicology have ethics statements posted on their websites, and we recommend that all fieldworkers review these statements to understand a fieldworker's accountability to the people they work with in their research.

The American Folklore Society (AFS) and the Society for Ethnomusicology (SEM) have statements on ethics in field research. See AFS's 1988 "Statement on Ethics: Principles of Professional Responsibility" online at http://www.afsnet.org/?page=Ethics, and SEM's 1998 "Position Statement Ethical Considerations" online at http://www.ethnomusicology.org/?page=EthicsStatement.

Obtaining consent and permission to document happens in the field when you are working directly with people. There are other kinds of permission that fieldworkers need to navigate, though. For the most part, this navigation happens prior to beginning a project on site—whether the site is physical or virtual. This category of permission is more institutional than individual, and there are several facets of it to examine.

If you are planning to conduct fieldwork as a member of a US-based university—whether you are a student, staff, or a faculty member—you will likely encounter the acronym IRB. This is certainly true if your university accepts federal funding from the US government, whether or not that funding has a direct bearing on your project or your position in the university. IRB stands for "Institutional Review Board," an institutionally specific body of individuals designated to review research projects involving "human subjects"—the formal term for what folklorists and ethnomusicologists call "people." The presence of an IRB on university campuses stems from legislation by the US Congress that emerged out of ethical and legal controversies surrounding research in the biomedical fields. The 1991 legislation is formally called the Federal Policy for the Protection of Human Subjects, but it is popularly known as the "Common Rule" because the first subpart (A) applies "commonly" to all human participants in research (there are other subparts that seek protections for specific or vulnerable populations, such as pregnant women and fetuses, prisoners, and children).

Although seemingly distant from the fieldwork concerns and interests of folklore and ethnomusicology, the goal of protecting people from exploitative misguided research practices that the legislation established is relevant to many folklore and ethnomusicology projects. There is often a training component alongside the process for submitting an IRB protocol at your university, through which you will learn about the history and parameters guiding research on human subjects. It is useful to note that most universities exclude class projects from IRB oversight, but it is important to become familiar with your home institution's priorities given that the federal legislation offers institutions latitude with regard to implementation.

While the IRB process can be cumbersome, it is not without value for folklorists and ethnomusicologists. In part this has to do with some of the colonial assumptions and structures embedded in the disciplines, but more directly, the value of the process relates to the ethical framework it foregrounds. The American Folklore Society's ethics statement emphasizes the concepts of welfare, dignity, and privacy with regard to participants in any research, and these should be guiding principles in all fieldwork projects (1988). In that fieldwork should be a collaborative endeavor supported by both permission and consent, it is important to recognize that interacting with individuals and communities in order to observe, inquire about, and document cultural practices will have some sort of impact on them. Acknowledging and negotiating ethical concerns in a formal way is one step toward mitigating any negative impact and (ideally) advancing positive outcomes. However, both the American Folklore Society and the Society for Ethnomusicology have formal position statements on human subjects research that call for modification to the Common Rule with regard to ethnographic fieldwork. These statements, in coordination with other fields and disciplines that work directly with living people during research, make the argument that the Common Rule erroneously categorizes ethnographic fieldwork as entailing the same potential danger or exploitation as clinical or bioinvasive research. The Common Rule is under continual consideration by federal officials, so be sure to seek the most updated guidance as you develop your project.

Human subjects and IRB represent only one facet of the place permissions and clearance hold in fieldwork. In effect, IRB approval provides you with permission from your institution to proceed with your project. The IRB process also provides tools that might be required and are often useful in the field, such as consent forms, which are intended to give information and protection to the participants in your project while generating an official record of what they have agreed to and what special stipulations they may have made.

The official process aside, you still cannot just show up at your fieldwork site and start observing or conducting interviews. There are other considerations regarding permission and clearance, and these are situationally specific. One of the first domains of consideration is international research. For the purposes of this section we will assume US citizens conducting fieldwork on cultural practices outside the political boundaries of the United States, and we hope those of other nationalities using this text will consider the specifics of their home countries and of those where they are conducting fieldwork. The other domain of consideration is domestic research—again, we'll assume students who are US citizens and conducting fieldwork within the United States.

International Contexts

International ethnographic fieldwork can be exciting and formative. It can also involve much bureaucracy, may require a lot of patience, and can be quite expensive. In this section, we will address the bureaucracy/patience element by calling attention to key factors involved in the logistical organization of fieldwork, especially with regard to permission and clearance; we address financial matters in chapter 5. There is not one way to navigate the logistical concerns discussed here, as each country will have its own legal and cultural structures regarding research. Furthermore, if you are affiliated with a university, you may not need to navigate these structures on your own, as most universities have a division focused on international affairs. Faculty advisers or fellow students who have worked in the country where you are hoping to do research also can be great sources of information or guidance.

One of the first considerations with international fieldwork will likely be getting official research clearance at the state or national level. Such clearance could come from a ministry or governmental office or may flow through a university or research center that functions as an agent of the government. The process may be highly formal, or it may simply require showing up and getting a signature. Ultimately, though, the process of receiving official research clearance will result in paperwork or documentation that indicates you have governmental approval to conduct research in the country. If you have no information about how to find out what is required in a particular country, we recommend as a first step contacting a professor or other researcher in the country who should be able to either answer your questions or put you in touch with the appropriate institution or a knowledgeable individual.

This official research clearance at the national level is likely only one piece of the puzzle. You should also find out if you need further clearance at the sites for your fieldwork, or for other partner organizations with which you intend to work. For example, if your project involves a local or international nongovernmental organization (NGO), their home office may want to know the extent of your research activity. If you are working with a local university or research center, they may provide some oversight for your research, which might necessitate that they give approval as well. And, should your fieldwork take you to a city, town, or rural population center that has a local government structure (district commissioner, traditional authority, chief, or mayor), there could be other levels of authorization you should seek.

There is also the consent you will need to seek from project participants. Completing the IRB procedures will familiarize you with the informed consent process. Bear in mind that the IRB consent procedure does not always account for the process that might be most suitable to a particular fieldwork situation. For example, standard IRB procedures emphasizes the importance of individuals signing forms. In some contexts, approaching individuals to seek consent would not be appropriate. Rather the first step could be to approach a community leader or the head of family and seek that person's permission. Part of your job in developing cultural competency is determining what would be the most appropriate, respectful, and ethical process for the situation in which your particular project takes place.

Beyond, but intertwined with, the structures of clearance and permission are legal questions around photography, video, and audio recording in public. At the international level, laws can be quite different from country to country—and can change quickly in certain political contexts. You will want to familiarize yourself with the laws governing the place in which you'll be conducting fieldwork, as it would be disruptive to find out about these laws through unanticipated interaction with authorities.

Domestic Contexts

The considerations around clearance, permission, and consent do not change too much with domestic fieldwork, although the type of bureaucracy is a bit more uniform or predictable since it occurs within one nation-state. Navigating research clearance and permissions will not necessarily be any easier within a domestic context, however. Depending on the nature of your fieldwork project you may need to negotiate site-specific permissions with private or corporate entities who will have internal policies and concerns. Or you may work with public institutions, such as school districts or park agencies that will be bound by legal or governmental policy structures. The point is that you should be thorough in identifying the entities with which you must seek permission or clearance, even in a domestic project.

Most often in the United States, if you are conducting fieldwork with people as private citizens, your responsibility as an ethnographer is to seek their consent as individuals to participate in the project. However, if you are seeking to work with them in their capacity as employees of an organization, as members of a civic group, or as participants in a public event (whether privately or publicly run), you could encounter concentric or overlapping rings of permissions. Make sure you are aware of any site-specific needs for additional research clearance or permission your project might necessitate. And, under no circumstances, whether in private or public settings, should you record or otherwise document in a clandestine manner (true for international settings, too).

Unless you are working in sites affiliated with a federal agency, you should not need any official research clearance from the federal government for doing fieldwork in the United States. But, it will be important to become familiar with government regulations or policy that may impact your research design. For example, if you plan on gathering field documentation at public celebrations, you may need to educate yourself about federal or state regulations related to fieldwork activities such as photographing or video recording in public places. While you will be gathering consent from people you directly interview or photograph, people in the background who do not actively give you consent may be protected by privacy laws—and these vary from state to state. Photojournalists often encounter similar situations, and many professional associations or organizations provide up-to-date guidelines. A bit of searching online will be fruitful in this regard.

If you plan to conduct any of your planning research in archives, or plan on integrating archival materials into your fieldwork project, be prepared to navigate consent or permissions as well. Folklorists and ethnomusicologists who donate their field collections to archives may do so with restrictions about what materials researchers can access. Research participants may also have placed restrictions on materials, which constitute part of the conditions under which they gave consent to the initial fieldworker. Ultimately, you will be bound by these restrictions in exploring archival field collections, such that even if you can locate an interview through an online finding aid, you may not be able to listen to it or read it right away. Contacting staff at any given repository is the best means for gaining a full understanding of access to specific collections.

Travel

Some sort of travel is associated with most folklore and ethnomusicology fieldwork. Whether your travel will be across town or across the world, you will want to account for the logistics and economics involved. Increasingly, travel in the twenty-first century intersects with digital domains, and it could be that your fieldwork sites exist in a virtual environment. In this section we will offer suggestions and approaches for planning travel activities connected to fieldwork across physical and nonphysical spaces. Travel activities comprise transportation, as well as lodging, luggage, food, documents, and communications. All these activities usually come with a cost. In this chapter we help plan, while in chapter 5 we address budgeting.

A primary consideration in planning travel revolves around how you will get to your fieldwork sites. This consideration is highly contextual and will relate directly to how far you must travel from where you currently live—a distance that could be four miles, or four thousand. You might have several transportation options to choose from, such as bus, train, airplane, or personal vehicle. Think of this stage of travel as the round trip or initial travel and explore the range of options you might have for this step. A secondary consideration with fieldwork travel is the internal or local travel you will navigate once you have arrived. Again, you may have many options—walking, bicycle, taxi, bus, informal ride sharing, or rented/borrowed car—and you should start to plot how a combination of options could work to support your fieldwork plan. Some factors to account for are financial (see budgeting section), but others are tactical and logistical: What sources of local travel are reliable? What options might enable you to engage more directly with regional cultural norms or expectations? What modes of transport will be efficient, but not too ostentatious? What forms of transport are available or work for you given your physical condition, timeline, budget, and safety concerns?

For a fieldwork project exploring the emerging community of boutique guitar effects, Fenn began his "travel" on discussion boards and websites. Once he determined that a significant number of established builders were located in Portland, Oregon, he was able to plan short field trips to their shops for interviews. This physical travel was relatively simple and inexpensive since it was close to his home, and it comprised a narrow geographic focus for his project. However, he also "traveled" via email and video call technology to builders who lived across the country to conduct interviews that established a broader context for the culture and community of hand-built music technology in the United States.

Figure 4.1. Gilman and the authors' two daughters, Anika and Nora Fenn Gilman, walking down the road lugging recording gear. The field trip involved much driving and walking on dusty roads. Kawaza Village, Embagweni, Malawi, 2013. Photo by John Fenn.

Figure 4.2. A lorry (truck) filled with Malawian Ngoni passengers heading to Nc'wala, a harvest ceremony hosted by Ngoni in Zambia. This type of public transport is common in the region. Mchinji, Malawi, 2013. Photo by Lisa Gilman.

Exercise

Recommended for small or large groups.

A fieldworker plans to do international fieldwork in a region that is 2500 miles away from their current home. They need to purchase airplane tickets that will get them into the capital city of a country in the region. However, the area in which they want to do fieldwork is 150 miles from the capital and consists of numerous small villages and towns that are anywhere from 3 to 30 miles apart from each other. With regard to transportation alone, what are the elements or factors for which they would need to account?

Beyond transportation, there are other elements of travel planning. If you are going to do fieldwork internationally, you will need to have a passport (make sure it does not expire while you are traveling!), as well as visas required by countries you might be visiting. Contact regional consulates or embassies to determine if you need to get a visa beforehand or whether you get it upon arrival. You will also need to determine the appropriate type of visa, taking into considerations factors such as the length of your stay and the kind of work you plan to do. Other questions about travel visas will include: How much time will it take to obtain it? How much does it cost? Should you need to procure the visa before you travel, investigate whether it is best to do it yourself through an embassy or pay a visa processing company to take care of this for you (often expensive, but efficient). You may also require certain vaccinations or medicine, such as malaria prophylaxis, so it is important to consult with a travel doctor well in advance.

You should gather information about how and where you can access money. Having cash on hand is a good idea, and in some international contexts, this might be the only option for purchasing food or paying for housing. It is often the case that you can have reliable ATM access to your bank account while traveling internationally, but sometimes that access is only in major urban areas. Credit cards may be an option, though not necessarily as your main source of payment. You should always let your bank and/or credit card company know that you are traveling internationally so that they will not block access to your accounts in response to a fraud alert. For domestic fieldwork (i.e., within the United States), you should not have to worry about electronic access to money, though you may end up paying ATM access fees if your bank does not have machines where you are. Contact your bank beforehand so as not to be surprised by these charges later.

Whether you are traveling internationally or domestically you will likely need to organize accommodations. Accommodations may be for a few nights or long term and can take a variety of forms: hotels, hostels, homes (with friends, family, or formal hosts), or rentals. In planning accommodations for your fieldwork project, give thought to how housing might impact your research. There could be socioeconomic or cultural considerations (is the place you are staying too fancy?) or logistical ones (is it hard to get public transportation or are you far away from key sites?). There might also be localized political considerations: if you stay at a certain house owned by the family of someone you are doing research with, does that align you with them in ways that might alienate others in the community? Some of these considerations or concerns emerge during fieldwork itself, such that you have no way of planning around them prior to arriving on site. If you have explored several options for housing, however, you might have alternatives at the ready should you encounter tension or discomfort. Of course, in some communities there may only be one place to stay—whether you are there for two nights or two months—and you will have to navigate tricky situations by being an astute and empathetic fieldworker.

Safety can be a concern for anyone, but concerns might be heightened for women and LGBTQ+ (lesbian, gay, bisexual, trans, queer/questioning, and others) fieldworkers in some settings (see chap. 11). Consider whether you will be secure where you plan to stay, and whether you can move to and from the location safely. If your research involves moving around at night, or if you are relying on public transportation, think about how close transit stops are to your accommodation, lighting, whether there are people out and about, or whether someone can escort you. Are taxis readily available? Many fieldworkers travel with expensive gear—computers, cameras, and smart phones. You may also need to consider whether your accommodations will be relatively safe from theft.

Considerations around safety and comfort while traveling for fieldwork come together around clothing. You should familiarize yourself with climate as well as cultural expectations when planning for the clothing you will need to have on hand. Take into consideration temperatures and weather, but also investigate biting insects, potential for sun exposure, or the types of terrain and surfaces you will likely need to navigate (i.e., shoes are important!). You might plan for a balance of casual and more professional attire (depending entirely on the kinds of fieldwork settings you imagine), while staying attuned to the cultural norms around clothing. While conducting fieldwork in Malawi, for example, Fenn needed to be aware that in many places, people identified shorts with young boys, not men. So, while it would be acceptable for him to wear shorts while at home or working outside, it would not be fitting for him to wear shorts in public—regardless of the heat and humidity! Meanwhile, Gilman learned that it was considered inappropriate for adult women in Malawi to wear short skirts or dresses that did not fall below the knees, and that trousers were considered unacceptable for girls and women in many rural settings. Women who wore clothing that revealed their thighs were deemed in many settings to be prostitutes. She adjusted her dress accordingly. Think about what kinds of clothing are appropriate to the occasions you might attend. If you are studying a certain type of music, you may find yourself at an informal rehearsal, at a bar on a Friday evening, at a formal concert, or at a wedding. Think broadly about your dress needs so that you are clothed appropriately and prepared for unexpected opportunities.

Finally, travel requires luggage. You should have some way of carrying your stuff during the initial travel, as well as a means for toting fieldwork gear during local travel. There are several factors to account for: Are you traveling domestically for a few days at a time, or internationally for a year? Will you be hauling your luggage from site to site or walking long distances with heavy gear? Will your luggage and gear fit into luggage compartments of public transportation or small vehicles? Do you need secure and locking bags, or will a soft-sided duffle work? Will you be in a setting where a specialized camera bag signals "tourist" or "expensive gear inside," or will you be somewhere that such a bag does not call attention to you? Both authors spend a great deal of time thinking about bags. We always think about what might be the best and most appropriate way to carry the various cameras, tripods, audio recorders, notebooks, phones, pens, logs, sunscreen, hats, or business cards we might need for a particular field experience. When Gilman was doing fieldwork on dance practices in bars in Colorado Springs, for example, she carried a small camera in a bag just big enough to also carry a notebook and miniature pen that would pass as a purse in a bar. When she did fieldwork on dance in rural settings in Malawi, she had an old backpack that fit a still camera, video camera, notebook, pen, extra video, and extra batteries. She used the old backpack to avoid drawing attention to the gear that she carried in poor regions where most people did not have access to expensive equipment. While filming dance events, she strapped a fanny pack around her waist with extra batteries, film, a pencil, and logging notebook so that she could easily switch her gear and jot down information without disrupting the video recording.

You should think thoroughly about where you are going, how long you will be staying, how you will be traveling, and what you will be bringing. You will want to weave into these categories any relevant sociocultural elements that something as innocent as luggage might reflect: relative status of fieldworker, value of equipment/gear, or other characteristics that could very well impact how people in the communities you are working with understand you.

Digital Spaces and Fieldwork

The preceding discussion of logistics around travel for fieldwork pertains to the traditional conception of "site" as a physical place. Digital or virtual spaces have become rich sites for folkloristic and ethnomusicological fieldwork (Cooley, Meizel, and Syed 2008; Howard 2011; Underberg 2006; Underberg and Zorn 2013). There are still logistical considerations in terms of travel, which might be better thought of as a form of access. Whether your emerging project takes place solely in the digital realm or manifests as a hybrid of physical and virtual sites, a primary means of "travel" will be information and communications technology (ICT). ICT refers to the massive and emergent infrastructure that enables people all over the world to exchange information, whether that is through cellular data networks, satellite, or terrestrial cable-based networks (fiber optic or otherwise). ICT has become a ubiquitous feature of social and cultural life around the world, albeit to varying degrees (Coyne 2010).

In organizing digital, electronic, or virtual aspects of fieldwork travel and access, factors such as reliability, security, and cost take on different meanings than in normal, everyday travel. The reliability of a public bus can have a significant impact on fieldwork travel, meaning you may not get somewhere when you planned to, or may not even arrive at all. Such absolute disruption presents a different modality of reliability than one might encounter, for example, with data networks and connectivity. If you are relying on such pathways to communicate with fieldwork subjects or access sites, then reliability might encompass intermittent interruptions or restricted bandwidth. Access to virtual fieldwork sites can become impeded, slow, glitchy, and frustrating—factors that may be amplified when you conduct transnational digital fieldwork and must work across communication infrastructure systems that might have differential quality.

Given the complexity of data networks and web-based "transportation," it can be daunting and even unrealistic to find other options. With a broken-down bus, you can catch another one or find a different source for a ride—the sudden and absolute disruption in travel can, in other words, be resolved. Problems with digital travel might not have such obvious solutions and can be more persistent; this trouble can require creative and more extensive solutions. Paying attention to the specifics related to your fieldwork project—including access or reliability on all sides of the "field"—is our recommendation.

Security is another important factor in planning virtual travel. One aspect of security with digital fieldwork is ensuring you remain attentive to the confidentiality and privacy of the people with whom you engage. With virtual travel in or to digital sites, security entails making sure that interaction with fieldwork subjects—and the information they share—stays within reasonable expectations for privacy. "Reasonable expectations" can vary from context to context, and could manifest through community standards, end-user license agreements, or several other phenomena that have emerged at the intersection of virtual communities and technological development since the late 1980s. Because of the variability around privacy from community to community or space to space in digital environments, it is imperative that you become familiar with expectations and practices related to your topic. Keep in mind the standards of ethics outlined by professional societies such as the American Folklore Society or the Society for Ethnomusicology and operate under these standards while working in digital environments just as you would in physical ones.

Other facets of security to think about in relation to virtual settings include protecting your own identity and information, maintaining the integrity of your digital footprint, and ensuring that you maintain control over or otherwise monitor access to the spaces and mechanisms/technology you might use. Such spaces or technologies could include communications portals, documentation tools, and remote cloud storage. The concept of "digital citizenship" has gained currency in recent years, and organizations promoting the principles of privacy, security, and access underpinning digital citizenship offer guidelines and recommendations useful for fieldworkers.

Finally, there is cost to consider when organizing travel or access to digital fieldwork sites. Everything from registering for sites or services to purchasing computer or communications technology can bring costs to a virtual or digital fieldwork project. Ensuring reliability or security might also entail costs, monetary or otherwise, and you will want to be able to account for these in your funding planning.

Given both the ubiquity and speed associated with digital communications and culture in the twenty-first century, a social-psychological cost attached to fieldwork in virtual settings might be time. Travel/access related to digital fieldwork can manifest in synchronous or asynchronous modes—but these modes carry different values, meanings, or expectations when compared with more traditional face-to-face contexts. Synchronous engagement—being in the same "time" with someone you are interviewing, for example—occurs both in face-to-face and in virtual settings. Whether you use video call technology, live chat in a virtual community, or sit down at a table with someone in a café, you participate in synchronous conversation. But, the mediation of screens, data networks, and other technology alters the meanings and expectations around being in the same "time" with an interviewee. When in a café, you are there together—both physically and experientially. While interviewing someone at a distance via a video chat, you could be separated by time zones, political and geographic boundaries, and a host of other elements that shift how you or your fieldwork participant might think about time. Whether this cost has an impact on the quality of your fieldwork (and the experience of the people you work with) depends on so many factors that it is nearly impossible to make a decisive statement on best practices or things to avoid. However, having an awareness of these issues as components of digital fieldwork can help you think about them beforehand and plan accordingly.

Similarly, asynchronous modes of communication exist in both real world and virtual settings. Mailing a letter to someone using the postal service is an example of asynchronous communication. There is a time delay between the initial act of communicating—the letter—and the response. Email is a common instance of asynchronous communication, though the difference might be more about expectations around time than experiential realities. Within some technocultural environments, even a slight delay in response through email might result in a cost—irritation, a decrease in trust, miscommunication, or a missed opportunity. Discussion boards and community forums are other examples of asynchronous channels for access/travel in digital fieldwork, and these spaces will likely carry norms around timelines. Such norms will likely vary widely from community to community in that they are culturally structured, so understanding the expectations and practices in the spaces you intend to explore ethnographically will be crucial to your own travel planning.

There is an element of travel for fieldwork—whether physical or virtual—that involves both planning and constant attention: safety. It overlaps with many of the issues discussed above but is also so heavily contextual that discussion of it remains necessarily generalized. Fieldwork is often an individual endeavor, and folklorists or ethnomusicologists frequently find themselves solo in the field. Gendered dynamics and frameworks can figure into the experience of a solo fieldworker, sometimes with regard to safety and sometimes not. Securing money, gear, and other possessions are aspects of safety as well—though anchored more in physical settings than virtual. Fieldwork in digital environments can bring on safety concerns related to identify theft, hacking, and trolling (Phillips 2016). You need to know how and when you are safe, no matter where you are conducting fieldwork. And you need to consistently and constantly revisit your safety status throughout your fieldwork by checking in with yourself, friends in the field, colleagues, officials, family members, and any other resources you have access to as you immerse yourself in the cultural and social environments of those with whom you work—a topic we return to in chapter 11. Remember that your physical and emotional safety in addition to that of all those involved should always be the priority in fieldwork.

Conclusion

Developing a folklore or ethnomusicology fieldwork project involves numerous steps before you even enter your field sites, from crafting a research question to establishing a fieldwork plan. This chapter explored the organizational details related to permission and clearance processes, travel logistics, and issues of safety. We accounted for international and domestic contexts, as well as physical and virtual/digital ones, but remember that each fieldwork project will entail considerations of the communities, places, and cultural frames specific to it. We offered general strategies and questions to ask, but there are no singular approaches to organizing for fieldwork. In chapter 5, we explore the topic of cultural documentation and technologies.

5

DOCUMENTING AND TECHNOLOGY

A KEY ELEMENT OF SUPPORT for your research project is the gear that you will use for documentation, communication, and organization over the course of your project. Folklore and ethnomusicology fieldwork can be done with a range of equipment, from a little to quite a lot. You should align equipment needs with the main goals, questions, and methods driving your fieldwork to meet your budget, produce rich cultural documentation, and support a manageable and efficient experience. Too much gear, or the wrong kind of gear, can lead to a complicated time in the field as well as less money for other aspects of the project. In this chapter, we explore technology and the considerations that go into planning your fieldwork: familiarizing yourself with options and capabilities, understanding the accessories or auxiliary equipment you might need, and developing skills in using your gear. We provide you with a framework for identifying the kinds of equipment or technology that supports your research plan, rather than a list of the specific models or items to get. The chapter discusses budgeting and purchasing gear, and in chapter 10 we move through strategies for using equipment while in the field. All these steps work together, and we have separated them in this handbook to demonstrate a systematic approach to planning and completing a fieldwork-based project.

Deciding What You Need

In preparing to acquire fieldwork equipment, you should orient yourself to four general categories of technology or gear that are prevalent in the

Figure 5.1. Notebooks are common objects throughout the world, and invaluable field-work technology. Karonga, Malawi, 2013. Photo by Lisa Gilman.

digital era. That is not to say all technology you should consider is digital, as pen and notebook remain core tools in a fieldworker's toolkit. A significant shift with digital technology is that one device can do many things, and the categories we suggest here will help you prioritize the functions of a specific piece of equipment to ensure you consider how any given item supports your plan.

The three categories of equipment or technology we discuss are capture, storage, and communication. *Capture* refers to the area of documentation, those moments of collecting, recording, or gathering fieldwork data. As we will discuss further in chapter 10, the activity of cultural documentation can occur in at least three domains: textual, audio, and visual. The focus of this chapter will be on capture gear, specifically with regard to the words, sounds, and images we encounter in fieldwork.

Storage refers to the technology or equipment you use to house, protect, and backup your fieldwork materials or data. In this handbook, we assume "born-digital" materials for audio and visual capture, which refers to those recordings or documents that are digital from the moment you create them. For born-digital materials, storage means hard drives for transferring and backing up files created by capture devices. You should also think of storage in conjunction with fieldnotes, ephemera, and other analog materials that you might gather or create during your project. How will you keep such things safe and secure while in the field?

Communication has become an increasingly prevalent category for technology and equipment in fieldwork, especially since the rise of cellular networks and devices as prominent means for communication across the world. Through the late twentieth century, "communication" during fieldwork meant largely written (notes, letters), landline telephone calls, or face-to-face interactions. Email, social media, and SMS are currently significant means for communication before, during, and after fieldwork—and your planning around equipment to support your project should account for any (or all) of those modes.

Gathering Gear

Addressing a few questions during the prefield organizing phase will help you prioritize, especially around budgeting and finances, travel, and security. You should also consider documentation logistics and alignment with methods. If you plan to visually document a tradition of material culture, still photography might be more important to you than audio recording— but not necessarily. Interviews may figure into your research plan, so having audio recording capabilities would be important. In the end, planning accurately and cohesively for your capture equipment needs is a key step.

What are the questions you should ask yourself when planning for equipment? First, what do you need to do your fieldwork, and why? Second, is there a "mission critical" piece of equipment, something that you could not do without? Follow-up questions to the mission critical one include, what if the equipment fails, breaks, or is stolen? What kind of backup plan might you put in place? What do you need to know about the technology involved to make an effective decision about the equipment you need, and where do you find this information?

These questions point toward balances you will want to strike in assembling a fieldwork tool kit: between necessary and sufficient, between affordability and quality, and between ease of use and efficacy. A specific piece of gear, such as a camera, might be necessary to your fieldwork. But it might not be sufficient if you plan on doing more than taking photos, in which case you would need to augment it with another piece of equipment. When assembling your tool kit, think carefully about the relationship between your answers to the questions above and your ability to buy, borrow, or rent a piece of equipment. Pulling together your gear is more about strategic and thoughtful acquisition than gathering anything and everything you might want.

A good rule of thumb when contemplating the quality level of gear you acquire is to consider the uses you imagine for your documentation in relation to the value your documentation may hold in the future, for you, other researchers, communities of origin, or the public good. You may not need, or be able, to buy the "best" camera. A midlevel model could be capable of high-quality images or video that fulfill your immediate goals while also providing robust visual material for future, unimagined uses. The metrics or measurements for "quality" constantly change for digital devices, but all refer to a type of resolution or capacity for a device to turn the experiential world of sound and visuals into digital data: megapixel counts for still cameras, lines of resolution for video, and sample rates for audio recorders. Higher resolution or more capacity often equates to higher price, and you will want to determine where the quality requirements of your project intersect with your financial resources or the gear you are able to borrow. Quality will also have something to do with the ruggedness of a piece of equipment, determined by a wide range of factors from the material composing the housing for a piece of gear to the durability of particular components that see extensive use (buttons, knobs, connection ports). High-end gear that is oriented to fieldwork specifically will have weatherized features, such as sealed or insulated battery compartments or gaskets to prevent moisture, sand, or other problematic elements from getting inside the equipment. Paying attention to the ruggedness of a piece of equipment will enable you to prepare for its care and storage in the field.

Finally, you should keep in mind that fieldwork happens in complex cultural and social environments, wherein a lot of activity happens at once. Having gear that you can easily manage while capturing the quality and type of data you require is central to your success as a fieldworker. Identify equipment that will help you conduct quality fieldwork because your documentation efforts will be part of the flow, rather than getting in the way. Talking to instructors and peers about their recommendations or reading reviews of gear—by professionals as well as end-users like yourself—is a good way to become familiar with features and limitations of various models. Focused searching online can help you find websites that host reviews or discussion forums. In addition to reading about equipment, we recommend getting your hands on specific pieces of gear you have interest in using. This is not easy in all locations, so do pay attention to return policies if purchasing online is the only option for trying something out.

Since the earliest fieldwork manuals for folklorists and ethnomusicologists emerged, much has been written about capture equipment in terms of both using it and understanding the role of such technology in fieldwork (Brady 1999; Ives [1974] 1995; Jackson 1987; Society for Ethnomusicology 2001). Although the shift from analog to digital requires new terminology and technical understandings, many of the core concepts around tactics and strategies for use remain in place. For example, the basics of using an analog tape recorder to document an interview apply to using a digital audio recorder (see Ives [1974] 1995; Jackson 1987). The essential premise is to create durable audio documentation of an "event" in the field that you can return to for analysis or utilize in some form of presentation. A primary difference between analog and digital equipment, though, is that with digital there is a wide range of options and capabilities across devices. With a 35-mm film-based camera, a better lens noticeably improved image quality. With a digital still camera, however, the factors impacting quality of images are more numerous and can include lenses, larger internal sensors, software-controlled options, and even updates to the firmware that runs the camera's internal functions.

Given the dynamic landscape of digital devices, there are key aspects you should pay attention to when conceptualizing how equipment fits into your research plan. Start by thinking carefully through all the kinds of data or information that you will want to capture to best support your project. Primary elements of your fieldwork topic such as material objects, performances, or interviews will be at the top of your list. But, you should also consider important kinds of information or metadata: the information about your fieldwork materials that may not be contained within the materials themselves, such as the full names of people, places, dates, technical information about equipment, or contact information—a topic we elaborate on in chapter 7. In many cases, a notebook and pen work well to jot such things down. Even if you do not use notebooks during interviews to take notes (though we recommend you do so), they are a key piece of fieldwork technology.

An aspect of equipment or technology to consider is multifunctionality. Notebooks allow you to write many kinds of information down, but, in the end, you can only write (or draw) in them. For the most part, digital cameras currently available can capture still images as well as video, making it possible to carry one piece of equipment that documents in multiple modes. However, you may want to take still photos while also capturing video. In the era of smartphones and tablets it is possible to have a single piece of technology that functions across the domains of capture, communication, and storage (to a limited extent). Does your research plan enable you to rely on one piece of equipment? Does the smartphone or tablet produce cultural documentation of sufficient quality for your project and for potential future uses? Maintaining a focus on capture equipment, we will briefly outline aspects of assembling the visual and/or audio components of your fieldwork toolkit.

The Society of American Archivists offers a technical definition of "metadata": "A characterization or description documenting the identification, management, nature, use, or location of information resources (data)" (https://www2.archivists .org/glossary/terms/m/metadata, accessed January 26, 2018).

The American Folklife Center provides a more illustrative description: "Our digital files consist of data: bits and bytes of binary information, which computers can decipher into audio, video, pictures, and words. But there's also information ABOUT that information, telling us when and where it was created, how it has been changed, and who has changed it. That data about our data is called 'metadata.'" (Winick and Bartis 2016, 31)

Visual Capture

Whether seeking to do still photography, video, or a combination of both during your fieldwork, you will probably end up needing a camera of some sort. Choices can appear to be endless: point-and-shoot, digital single lens reflex (DSLR), camcorder, or smartphone? Consumer-level, professional, or prosumer? "Consumer" grade equipment is often readily available, and at a lower price point than "professional" video and still cameras. "Prosumer" equipment represents a blend of features and affordability that can appeal to fieldworkers on a budget. For example, consumer-level DSLR cameras offer interchangeable lenses and a range of resolution options, but professional cameras offer "better" components (including construction of lenses), high-resolution video capability, and even external microphone inputs. Prosumer gear in this category can provide video and high-quality still image, external microphone inputs, and even greater lens options—but might have a "less powerful" sensor. The quotation marks are key, as the comparison of quality across professional and prosumer is relative and context-specific. Spending $7000 on a professional set up might get you the "best" images or video but spending $700 on a prosumer set up might get you "great" images and video quality, while preserving money for other equipment or fieldwork costs (see Society for Ethnomusicology 2001, 25–26).

Audio Capture

Recording audio during fieldwork introduces choices parallel to those described above: stand-alone recorder or computer/tablet based? Stereo or multichannel? And, within these categories you will encounter the consumer, professional, and prosumer labels. "Stand-alone" refers to a dedicated audio recorder, a device that has the sole function of recording audio. To use a computer, tablet, or smartphone for audio recording in the field you will need appropriate peripherals or accessories. These items range from microphones that plug into the audio jack of a smartphone or

Figure 5.2. An outdoor recording opportunity, presented to the authors unexpectedly during a fieldwork trip in Malawi. Small tripods perform as microphone stands, and long cables enable the fieldworkers to keep gear out of the way. Headphones, notebook (for metadata!), and a hat are key accessories. Kawaza Village, Embagweni, Malawi, 2013. Photo by John Fenn.

tablet to USB devices that operate as microphones or as inputs for external microphones. Given the constant change in computing technologies, mobile or otherwise, it is difficult to offer advice that will not be undone or compromised by the next round of hardware updates, software changes, or market-driven "improvements." Smart shopping for these peripherals entails reading reviews, comparing features, and asking questions of friends, colleagues, and mentors.

There are risks or challenges to using computer or mobile devices for field-based audio recording, but as technology continues to shift, some of these risks decrease. One of the core differences between stand-alone audio recorders and computer or tablet-based options resides in the analog-digital conversion chip. And, to a large extent, there are differences in these chips across stand-alone recorders as well. While beyond the scope of this handbook to fully explain analog-digital conversion, a basic description may help. When you press "record" on your digital device, the microphone "hears" the audio waves and sends them through a circuit called a preamplifier or "(mic) pre" for short. The audio is still analog at this point, and it travels to another stage of circuitry that is the analog-digital conversion chip. In reviews or descriptions of recording devices, this is generally called the A/D chip or converter. The chip processes the analog audio signal by drawing on complex mathematical calculations that result in a digital audio stream. User-controlled settings mainly determine the quality or resolution of the stream, often discussed in terms of "sample rate" and "bit depth." There are many sources for learning more about these terms, and a search online will lead you to websites, tutorials, or books that can provide basic knowledge to inform your choices.

Laptop computers have long been components of a fieldwork toolkit beyond functioning as capture devices and can range from essential to convenient items depending on the kinds of uses you have for one in your own research project. A laptop facilitates transferring files from digital capture devices to external storage drives and will also enable you to organize metadata in the field—the information about who, what, where, and when that should accompany photographs, videos, and audio recordings. Laptops also afford in-field editing of audio and visual documentation, depending on the software and processing power of the machine, and allow you to write while on location: fieldnotes, working drafts of longer pieces, emails, or other types of documents.

Should you have a reliable internet connection, a laptop will enable you to use video chat for interviews or other synchronous communication with participants in your project. Laptops can also be useful for mapping or getting directions in some field settings. And, of course, you can use a laptop to conduct contextual research while in the field by accessing journal articles, news sites, or other digital spaces.

Tablet computers continue to emerge as viable options for much of the work that laptops enable and may very well be a replacement for a laptop for some fieldworkers. We strongly recommend creating a thorough list of all the possible uses you envision for a computer during your fieldwork to best evaluate whether a tablet will suffice.

Accessories and Other Considerations

In addition to the devices you borrow, rent, or purchase for your fieldwork, you will want to gather accessories and miscellaneous items. These include extra batteries and storage media, such as memory cards and hard drives, as well as cables for connecting your recording gear to speakers and monitors for playback purposes. We also suggest a set of headphones that are durable and of good quality. Not only will these be important for monitoring both audio and video field recording, but headphones can also be valuable in reviewing, transcribing, or logging your recordings. Headphones that fully cover your ears may be preferable and more effective in many situations but do consider your own budget, comfort level, and needs.

For audio capture you should seriously consider acquiring an external microphone. While many stand-alone audio recorders have built-in or onboard microphones, in most scenarios you will have more flexibility and control using an external microphone. Using an external mic allows you to separate the sound source and the recorder, use the polar (or pick up) pattern of an external microphone to create a focused sound field, and, most important, decrease handling noise often heard when you stop or start a recording while using onboard microphones. An online search for "microphone polar pattern" or "microphone pick up pattern" will provide current information that will assist you in your planning.

Using external microphones during video recording can be crucial, especially given the relationship between image and sound that video entails. Any video camera or still camera capable of shooting video will have built-in microphones, but there are benefits to using external microphones when it comes to having more control and better sound quality. Remember that a built-in microphone on a video capture device will be situated near the lens, so sounds will be "heard" from that perspective. Should you zoom in, the image will be decoupled from the sound since the microphone does not zoom like a lens. Similarly, in a wide-angle shot with video, an on-camera mic may not accurately capture the sound field as the visual field will be more expansive than the audio image. Using

Figure 5.3. Over-ear headphones allow the monitoring of recording in isolation from ambient sound. Authors' daughter, Nora Fenn Gilman, demonstrates how to work in style while helping record the Kawaza Western Crooners. Kawaza Village, Embagweni, Malawi, 2013. Photo by John Fenn.

well-placed microphones with polar patterns that map to the kinds of sounds you want will enrich video recordings.

It is important to align your gear with your research plan and expected outcomes. A documentary video requires high-quality audio, whereas video you shoot to analyze movement or spatial aspects of cultural performance will not depend as much on the audio elements. External microphones will require microphone cables, stands, and other accessories such as windscreens or boom poles (for holding the microphone over or near sound sources without getting into the video frame). For video or photography work in the field, a tripod can be important. With the correct adapters, a tripod can also serve as a microphone stand, which might be useful if you are hoping to travel lightly.

Other miscellaneous items to gather for fieldwork include a flashlight and a small tool kit. A versatile piece of gear for fieldwork is a multitool, such as a Leatherman or Swiss Army knife. While not directly associated with the cultural documentation aspects of fieldwork, a pocket tool will come in handy for a wide range of activities in the field, both expected and unexpected. Accessories should include a power strip with a surge protector, especially if you plan on conducting fieldwork in sites that have unreliable electricity. The voltage of the current where you will be working is important, keeping in mind that the United States operates at 110v, while other places in the world use 220v. Most electronics, including laptops, video cameras, and many audio recorders, have power adapters that can switch between these two voltages. However, it is imperative that you familiarize yourself with the requirements of your devices. Should you plug a 110-volt-only power adapter into a 220-volt wall outlet, it will be destroyed. The same is true of power strips, so keep this in mind when shopping.

We discussed general luggage in the previous chapter, but other considerations for gear are a bag to carry everything you need while in the field, as well as weatherproof and lockable cases for storing gear (and associated media) when you are not using it. We will address this issue more in the next chapter on budgeting, but it is useful to think through the appropriate cases and bags for moving around in the field while you are sourcing gear. In some settings, you will want these to be inconspicuous (such as a backpack), and in other settings you will want the maximum protection for your gear (such as a molded hard case). Seek to strike a balance that allows you to fit everything you intend to carry while giving you easy access to the most important items.

Documenting Virtual or Digital Culture

Whether your project spans physical and virtual spaces or is solely focused on cultural documentation in a digital environment, you will need to account for technology that can help you capture fieldwork occurring online. Much of this capture may happen through software, so it may be best to start there. If you are making video calls for interviews, explore whether there is recording capability built into the software platform you plan to use for the calls. If you do not have this capability, are there programs included in the operating system, or other pieces of software available for purchase or for free?

If you plan on utilizing websites as a component of your fieldwork data, being able to make high-quality screen captures will be important. A consideration here would be static or dynamic screen captures. Static captures entail discrete images of your screen (or a window in a browser), whereas dynamic capture would consist of a video or screencast. If navigating a series of pages within a site or scrolling through more than a screen's worth of content is important to your fieldwork, then having access to a piece of software that allows you to record your time on a website will be important. Again, some of this capacity might be integrated into an operating system or come as a suite of applications with your computer, but in other cases you may need to source separate programs.

As approaches to fieldwork in digital environments continue to emerge, both methodologically and theoretically, there is a good chance that technologies for documenting cultural interaction, experience, and expression will develop as well. The best advice we can offer is to pay attention and be receptive to opportunities at hand when it comes to gathering fieldwork data involving virtual environments. Look to how participants in the cultural communities your project involves document their own participation, as their techniques may be able to inform your data gathering.

Learning Your Equipment

The most effective way to become familiar with your fieldwork equipment is to use it often prior to conducting fieldwork. What follows are a few suggested exercises to do with your equipment, and these can form the basis for your own activities in practicing cultural documentation with specific gear.

Exercise 1

Run through set-up and tear down of equipment. Often you will be chatting with people or paying attention to activity around you while in the field, such that it is quite useful to become extremely comfortable with connecting everything, getting it all in place, and powering your gear up. The same is true of putting everything away, so we suggest running through this process multiple times before your first fieldwork session.

Exercise 2

Read the manual! Familiarize yourself with buttons and features on your device. While some field recording equipment will have only a few buttons for operating it, other gear will have many. And some features—such as sampling rate or ISO—might only be accessible via menus activated on a device's LCD or LED screen. Knowing how to set up your gear for recording in the way that you want or need will ensure that your fieldwork documentation is both adequate and complete.

Exercise 3

Work on microphone placement. Whether you use an external microphone or on-board in either video or audio recording, the position of the microphone in relation to the sound source will impact the quality of your documentation. Practice recording with the microphone or device in different locations. Sit or stand in one place and record yourself speaking. Move slightly to one side or the other, stating clearly which direction you moved. Try moving closer and farther from the microphone, also indicating the approximate distance. Listen back to the recording, making note of how the sound quality changes. You can also do this exercise with live music by playing an instrument in different locations relative to the microphone.

Exercise 4

Combine microphone placement and setup. Conduct a short practice interview with someone you know. Once you have everything ready, practice monitoring the audio using headphones before you record. This is important for both audio and video recordings. Then conduct a short interview, being sure to focus your attention on the interviewee while also periodically checking the recording device and taking some notes on levels. This can be much more difficult than it sounds, but once you do a few practice runs, you will likely be much more comfortable and confident in the field.

Exercise 5

Become familiar with lighting considerations. Video or still photography depends on light, and you will need to be able to navigate a range of lighting situations in fieldwork. Rarely do you have complete control over the light in a space in which you are conducting an interview, recording a video of a performance or cultural practice, or shooting still photographs. Practice using your visual documentation equipment in a range of light settings, paying attention to how the device handles low light and back lit situations.

Exercise 6

Set up a video chat with a friend or relative to conduct a mock interview. Record the interview using built-in capabilities of your software or computer. Pay attention to the interpersonal dynamics involved in conducting an interview over the web. What is important about the space or room? How does this space help or hinder the process? Review the recording and think about how the interview may have been different or similar if you were in the same room with the interviewee.

Tips

Over the many years that we have been conducting folklore and ethnomusicology fieldwork, we have developed practices or picked up tips from colleagues and mentors when it comes to cultural documentation. Below are a few suggestions, in no particular order. We encourage you to seek other tips and tricks from both seasoned fieldworkers and your peers.

- *Always note all relevant metadata prior to recording anything.* Writing down full names, dates, locations, and technology used will ensure that you have accurate information for all fieldwork activities; these details are often difficult or impossible to locate after the fact.
- *Test your equipment!* There is nothing more disappointing than realizing that recordings failed after a beautiful performance or insightful interview!
- *Set the time and date on your cameras and audio recorders.* This may seem obvious, but it is easy to forget when you travel across time zones. Having accurate metadata is key!
- *Put your keys in the freezer.* If you are interviewing someone in their home or workspace, there may be ambient noises from freezers or refrigerators, air conditioners, or other household appliances. In many cases, it is reasonable to ask if you can unplug or turn these off, explaining that the noise might interfere with the sound of your recording. But you do not want to leave at the end of the interview without plugging everything back in, so put your keys in the freezer. That way, you can't leave without remembering what you've unplugged.
- *Disable cellular network connections.* Should you use a mobile phone or tablet for field recording, it is a good idea to turn off the cellular capability. If you leave this feature on, it is possible that the device will try to connect to the network every so often while you are recording, likely ruining the recording with interference noise.
- *Transfer files from memory cards or device storage.* It is important to copy your audio, photo, or video files to external hard drives as soon as possible after you conduct fieldwork. Relying on SD card or other internal storage on the devices themselves puts you at risk of losing valuable cultural documentation.
- *Have extra batteries and storage media.* Running out of power or storage in the middle of a fieldwork session is both disruptive and disheartening. Make sure to have at least one extra charged battery and empty memory card for each of your fieldwork devices.
- *Monitor audio through headphones as well as meters on your device.* When setting up a video or audio recording, listen through your headphones to make sure you are hearing what you want to–the sound of your participants rather than noise from nearby appliances, for example. During the recording, remember to glance at any audio meters periodically, but also try to hold the headphones up to your ear occasionally to ensure that you continue to capture the sounds you intend to.

Conclusion

A primary feature of fieldwork in folklore and ethnomusicology is producing cultural documentation of the words, sights, and sounds we encounter through research. Equipment is a necessary component of documentation, and this chapter outlined strategies for choosing the gear that supports your research plan. All equipment is technology, from the pen and notebook to the latest digital device. Understanding the value of any piece of technology for your research project is central to making choices around what to include in your fieldwork tool kit. Draw on the suggestions we have made in planning for your specific project, keeping in mind that most fieldwork can be done with the minimum amount of gear. In chapter 6, we move from planning your project into budgeting and identifying sources of financial support.

6

FUNDING AND RESOURCES

ALL FIELDWORK ENTAILS SOME EXPENSES, whether you end up working in international or domestic environments, physical or virtual spaces. Most fieldworkers at some point travel, eat food, purchase equipment or supplies, and pay for accommodations, all to differing degrees depending on how close or far away the field sites are from where they are living. If you do fieldwork in the town where you live or within a reasonable distance, you can return home after a day's fieldwork, cook your own food, and sleep in your own bed. As such, project costs might be low. But if your research takes you to an international location, the scenario changes. In addition to geographic location, you will also have to consider time duration. If the project takes one month, you budget differently than if it takes a year. In this section, we address the kinds of expenses you should plan for, as well as the types of sources you might look to for funding.

Banking and Access to Money

At this point in the early twenty-first century, banking systems are connected through global networks of ATMs. We have encountered few problems in various parts of the world accessing our US bank accounts from overseas ATMs, but it is important to check with your bank prior to traveling internationally for fieldwork. You should ask about transaction fees, as some banks will reimburse you for these. You should also make sure your bank knows when and where you are traveling, so that they do not accidently block your account due to a fraud alert.

Whether you are applying for external research funding, grants or awards from your educational institution, or paying out of pocket for everything, you should start by creating a budget. This step will help you estimate and track your expenses across the full project. This section breaks possible expenses into broad categories to assist you in structuring a budget for your project; some categories and suggested subcategories may work as is for your project, while others may require adjustment. It is best to approach our suggestions as guidelines rather than absolute rules, and to draw on them when detailing the more specific costs your fieldwork might entail.

Travel

No matter what shape your project takes, you will likely need to travel. The exception might be a purely digital fieldwork project that takes place via electronic communications (virtual space or otherwise), but even such a project might require physical travel to a trade show or other gathering related to your topic. An initial consideration for travel is getting to a field-work site (and, eventually, home), whether via airplane, bus, train, or personal automobile. If your fieldwork is international, your transportation expenses will be quite a bit higher than with a local or domestic project. You might also have to factor in visas, excess luggage fees, or shipping costs. For all overseas travel, you will likely want to see a doctor to discuss recommended and required vaccinations or other travel medication. The visit—plus any shots or prescriptions—are part of your travel expenses. Most doctors will ask for your itinerary so that they can consult the most recent Centers for Disease Control travel recommendations. Although you could do this yourself, it is best to discuss the options with a doctor in order to be fully informed about your choices and related expenses.

A second consideration when budgeting travel will be the costs of moving around within your fieldwork site. That is, if you are traveling internationally, you will probably take a series of flights to your destination. How will you get around once you are in the area? Such travel includes everything from that first day of transport from an airport, to the means of getting to your destination (5 or 500 miles from the airport?), and then your daily or regular needs for moving around. You might consider purchasing a vehicle (expensive in most places, but sometimes necessary), using taxis or other public transportation, getting a bike, or drawing on local modes of transportation that you may have never encountered before. A preliminary visit to a location is a great way to become familiar with the options and expenses, but you might also ask around and gather information from colleagues, faculty advisors, and family who have been in the area.

Accommodations and Food

The category of "accommodations" comprises several elements, but the main question is this: where will you live while doing fieldwork? If you are staying close to home, the answer could be quite simple and the cost low. If you are traveling some distance, whether overseas or just a few states away, you will have to arrange for somewhere to sleep, work, cook/eat, and do laundry. Such arrangements vary from staying with a friend or relative to renting something long-term. Depending on where you are going, "renting" may mean staying in a stand-alone house, an apartment, or a hostel. In almost all cases, you need to budget for the costs of housing and food.

Collecting and assessing the options available to you at your chosen fieldwork site will take some time but is worth the effort. As with many other elements of fieldwork, you may not know some of the options prior to showing up! Budgeting beforehand still has benefits in such cases, as you should have a concrete idea of the amount of money you have available for monthly or weekly accommodations. In planning a preliminary budget that accounts for the options you know about beforehand, you might consider such elements as furnishings. Is there a bed, a desk? How will you care for your personal hygiene, such as bathing and laundry? How will you eat? Are there facilities in which to cook? Will hosts provide food as part of rent?

The question of food is an important one. You need to eat, food costs money, and therefore you need to budget for steady and reasonable food. This may mean buying it at restaurants, convenience stores, local markets, or from a host family. Depending on your fieldwork site and topic, acquiring food may mean growing it yourself or contributing to collective sustenance efforts at the local level. In thinking about food, the distinction between procuring it and preparing it can be a key factor. Elements may include your own dietary needs, the availability of ingredients or components in certain locations, or your own comfort with preparing food—or having it prepared for you. There may also be sociocultural expectations in your fieldwork site that push you to engage or disengage from the culinary process.

There are ethical considerations at this stage of budgeting, especially if food and accommodations will draw on interpersonal relationships. Whether these are people you already know or those you will come to know once fieldwork is under way, be aware that beyond the commercial realm of hotels and restaurants there may not be fixed prices for food and lodging in the areas where you plan to do fieldwork. Should you opt to enter a home-stay situation in which you live with a family who is part of the community you are working with, it is likely there will be negotiation. Depending on cultural norms and a range of other factors, the hosts may suggest a rate—or may expect you to do so. The same could very well be true if you are planning on crashing in a friend's apartment while doing fieldwork. In all instances where you are paying for food or accommodations outside of a commercial setting, make every effort to be informed about the cultural, social, and economic factors at play and navigate the situation with attention to ethics and the avoidance of unintentional exploitation of potential hosts. Budgeting for these types of arrangements is never easy but planning up front will be beneficial.

An additional consideration when budgeting for accommodation and food at this stage of planning should be the extent to which a community will be hosting you. Individuals or families may house you or help with food, and you will likely compensate them in some way, but what opportunities might arise in which you can acknowledge a broader community that is engaged in your fieldwork? Regularly occurring communal meals or celebrations to which you can contribute financially (or otherwise) might be one scenario, or it may be that you initiate a gathering by way of saying thanks to a community. Budgeting for such opportunities is not straightforward, and usually requires some knowledge of local expectations and costs. We recommend building room into your overall accommodations budget if you do not have means for getting information that is specific enough to help you craft a line item.

> The costs of international versus domestic travel can be surprising. Gilman was surprised to find that the cost of doing research in Malawi was equivalent to or even a little less than doing research in Colorado. While the cost of air travel to Malawi was four times as high as to Colorado, the cost of hotel accommodation, food, and hiring research assistants was far higher for her fieldwork in Colorado.

Although international travel for fieldwork carries significant costs and requires extensive planning, much (if not all) of the preceding discussion also applies to domestic fieldwork. Within the United States, fieldworkers should incorporate reimbursement mechanisms often utilized by federal and statement governments, as well as nonprofit organizations, to compensate individuals for travel expenses. The General Services Administration (GSA) of the US government maintains mileage and per diem charts that you can use to budget domestic travel costs. The mileage charts provide an estimated cost for using a personal vehicle. You can build this into your budget whether you are applying for a grant, bidding on a contract, or calculating expected out-of-pocket expenses for your fieldwork project. Equally useful are the per diem charts, which help account for both food and lodging costs in specific locations across the United States. The GSA organizes these charts by city and state and provides concrete figures for meals (breakfast, lunch, and dinner) as well as hotel accommodation. Note that the figures provided by the GSA in both mileage and per diem charts present the maximum allowable by federal law for reimbursement and are not necessarily the actual amounts you will spend. That is, you may spend less (or more) on food in a given area compared with that the GSA chart indicates—but the charts are nonetheless useful in budgeting. Additionally, these charts could be useful for tax purposes if you are able to itemize any fieldwork expenses. The GSA updates the charts annually and maintains them on a publicly accessible website.

Gear

Given the wide range of tools and technologies available for cultural documentation and the rate at which digital gear features and functionality changes, you may find that you need to purchase something to conduct your research. While it is not necessary for you to have the latest or best gear to conduct fieldwork, you do want to make sure that you have reliable, field-worthy, and functioning equipment. And, even if you are borrowing equipment for "free" from friends or family, there are still potential gear-related costs that you should budget for to ensure that you do not accidentally prevent yourself from gathering important field data (including replacement if something is stolen or broken).

This sample list of equipment useful in fieldwork comes from *Folklife and Fieldwork: An Introduction to Cultural Documentation* by Stephen Winick and Peter Bartis (2016, 11):

- Notepads, pens, and pencils.
- A camera with extra memory cards, batteries, charger, and accessories.
- A digital audio or video recorder with two microphones, microphone cables, extra memory cards, batteries, and a pair of headphones.
- A laptop, notebook, or tablet computer, with power source or charger, and if possible backup hard drive.
- A steel tape measure for recording the dimensions of material objects.
- A GPS or map.
- Appropriate dress, which is both comfortable and/or right for the occasion.

In addition to the items listed by Winick and Bartis, we suggest the following:

- An extension cord or power strip, with surge protection.
- A small multitool or tool kit.

As outlined in chapter 5, there are a few kinds of technologies to think about in the digital era: capture, storage, and communication. Capture technologies include cameras (video and/or still) or digital audio recorders, and these can be the higher priced items in a budget. Stand-alone digital audio recorders, for example, can range in price from under one hundred to over several thousand dollars. Budgeting should account for your fieldwork needs as well as the financial resources available to you. If you are drawing on institutional support (via a grant or research award from a university, for example) check on any policies related to ownership of equipment after the fieldwork is done; some institutional sources require transfer of equipment back to the institution if the cost exceeds a certain threshold.

Budgeting for certain gear does not stop with identifying the amount on the price tag. You need to price accessories, such as cases or bags, and other equipment you may need: microphones, stands, cables, batteries, removable media (e.g., SD cards), headphones, and tripods. In addition to budgeting for these more obvious accessories, you should also account for smaller and less obvious items, such as audio cable adapters, surge protectors or outlet expanders, a flashlight, and a small tool kit or multitool. As discussed elsewhere in this handbook, your fieldwork methods and the kinds of research questions you are asking will help determine the type of cultural documentation you will want to pursue, so in the budgeting phase you should make sure to identify gear for purchase that you absolutely need—rather than all the equipment that would be nice to have. Gear costs can add up quickly, and the longer your list, the more you will need to spend up front.

With born-digital materials, storage is an important cost factor. Beyond the removable media commonly used by digital cameras and audio recorders, you should have some form of hard drive storage and backup for the all the files you create. Hard drive or storage technology consistently changes so be prepared to do research into the most rewarding ratio of cost to performance available at the time you are preparing for fieldwork. An important consideration with hard drives is compatibility of drive formatting and the operating system of the computers to which you will connect a drive. Ultimately you have control over a drive's formatting, but it is worth understanding using format structures that have cross-platform compatibility (e.g., between Apple and Windows operating systems).

In chapter 5 we discussed the role of laptop or tablet computers with regard to cultural documentation and fieldwork technology. Important factors for budgeting are the user's needs and the research plan. Dedicating some of your planning time to assessing how you imagine using a computer of any sort in the field will benefit your budgeting process. If you already own a laptop that is dependable and can accomplish all

Figure 6.1. A sturdy black canvas duffle bag holds fieldwork gear: digital audio recorder, cables, microphones, batteries, external speaker (plastic black case in foreground), and headphones. A notebook and water bottle complete the setup. Malawi, 2013. Photo by John Fenn.

computing tasks you expect to do, then there might not be a need to buy a new one or invest in a tablet. However, if your laptop is older, heavy, or even too valuable to take into the field, then you might want to explore other options. Tablets can double as capture devices with the appropriate accessories and in certain fieldwork scenarios can be efficient solutions both economically and practically.

A final category of gear that you should take into consideration when budgeting for your fieldwork project is communications. A laptop or tablet will cover the realm of email and social media, as well as any video calls you might need or want to make while out in the field. Around the world, internet access takes on various forms, so it is well worth your time to search for information on the options available in the places where you will be conducting fieldwork. Increasingly, one of the more important pieces of communication technology for fieldworkers is a cell phone. Around the world, cellular communications technologies are established and expanding. Robust and accessible cellular networks—especially in developing areas—have increased access to regular and immediate communications within and between communities and individuals, and a fieldworker will benefit greatly from being able to engage these networks (Goggin 2006, 2008; Ling and Donner 2009). While this may appear as an obvious statement given the ubiquity of smartphones and the constant communication they afford in the United States and other western settings, fieldworkers should determine what kind of mobile phone makes the most sense in the context of the research they are setting out to do and within the limits of their budget.

One of the first steps in the budgeting process will be to determine if the phone you already own can be used where you are planning to do fieldwork. Of course, this is primarily a consideration with international research projects. Many models of mobile phones can easily be integrated into cellular networks and service providers around the world by swapping in a local SIM card. There are many factors determining whether a given handset can be used in a specific country or region, so your research should start with your current carrier. There are also numerous web-based resources you can consult to determine what, if anything, you need to budget for in this regard.

Once you have determined if you need to purchase a different handset or not, you will want to understand the options for local service providers in your fieldwork locations. While monthly plans may be the norm in the United States, many places in the world operate on a "pay as you go" model that revolves around smaller and more frequent expenses. For the most part, you can determine which option works well in your destination based on feedback found on websites used by travelers, but bear in mind that almost anywhere in the world that has cellular service will also have local offices and shops for the major carriers in that region—and staff will be able to help answer questions and set up your phone. Furthermore, unless you are planning to purchase an expensive smartphone, local prices on "feature phones" (a common term for handsets that can make calls, send/receive SMS, and run limited web apps) are usually competitive. There can be advantages to buying local phones when onsite, such as aligning yourself materially with the groups and individuals you will be working with in your research—so keep this option in mind when budgeting. A final consideration is paying for the service itself; this might amount to a few dollars per day, but you will want to make sure you have the money available once you get into the field!

Research Assistants

Depending on the kind of fieldwork project you have devised, you may end up needing to work with research assistants. These may be students from a university in or near your field site, culture-bearers from a community you plan to explore, or someone that travels with you from your own point of origin, such as a family member, partner, or friend. Across each of these scenarios, budgeting for research assistants might account for travel, accommodation, food, wages, or some combination of these categories. There may be formal arrangements, or agreements might be more informal—but in no case should you expect someone to help you for free. There are ethical and strategic aspects to this realm of budget consideration; planning up front will help you avoid unexpected or uncomfortable situations during your research. A good rule of thumb is to ensure that helping you with fieldwork does not bring financial or other burdens to your assistant. Whether you meet a potential assistant in the field, or you make arrangements with them far in advance of beginning your project, be sure to set guidelines and establish expectations for both yourself and an assistant.

Incidentals

There are often unexpected opportunities or emergencies that can have a financial impact on your project. A thorough list of these incidental expenses is impossible to generate, and certainly would include both predictable and unpredictable items. On the predictable side, you might prepare to buy small gifts for people involved in your research, purchase food and drink for individuals or small groups, offer taxi or bus fare, or donate to organizations that you encounter during your fieldwork. Should you conduct fieldwork with artists who make a living from their art, you should be prepared to purchase a recording, painting, sculpture, or other manifestation of their work. While doing so has economic impact on your fieldwork, it is also an aspect of establishing trust or rapport.

More unpredictable expenses range from emergency medical issues (travel health insurance is crucial) to paying for unexpected automobile repair in the field. In some international contexts you may be asked to assist with school fees, hospital costs, or some other type of financial burden

Figure 6.2. Emergency auto repair expenses can take many forms. Here, a tractor belonging to the company in charge of a rubber tree farm pulls the authors' car from a deceptively unstable sandy road. Nkhata Bay District, Malawi, 2013. Photo by John Fenn.

faced by families and individuals whom you encounter during fieldwork. Managing such requests in socially and culturally appropriate ways is complex and can be one of the more demanding aspects of fieldwork. If you plan for such contingencies in either preparatory or on-site budgeting, though, you can more readily navigate such unpredictable expenses.

Reciprocation

A final category for budgeting accounts for the "giving back" that folklorists and ethnomusicologists have come to embrace as an important component of their work (Lomax Hawes [1992] 2007, 1992). As discussed in chapter 14, "reciprocity" can entail fieldworkers sending copies of a dissertation, book, or article to those who participated; providing copies of audiovisual field recordings to communities of origin; or sharing documentation of exhibitions, performances, and other research-related products. Expenses related to reciprocation vary, and can include duplication costs, international shipping, travel costs for participants to come to an event or exhibit, or purchasing extra copies of a product that came out of your fieldwork. Such expenses can be shared with home institutions, such as universities and archives, or publishers, but planning ahead of time will help you avoid being surprised by such costs after your fieldwork is done.

Sourcing Financial Support and Resources

Once you have created a budget for your fieldwork project—even a preliminary and skeletal outline of basic costs—you will need to figure out your sources of money to fund the project. There are two broad contexts within which you might find yourself conducting folklore or ethnomusicology fieldwork: individual and institutional. These are not mutually exclusive categories—for example, an individual student conducts fieldwork for a dissertation within a large institution—but within each category there are different streams or options for funding. As with many other sections in this handbook, the following suggestions do not represent the only options for funding fieldwork. Instead, draw on the discussion to refine your thinking about your project and the sources of financial support that make the most sense for the work you want to do.

As an individual, whether you are a student or a contract fieldworker, you will probably encounter out-of-pocket expenses wherein you pay directly for aspects of your fieldwork using personal financial resources. Credit card debt, student loan money, or income from a job before or during fieldwork are all immediate out-of-pocket sources of money. This may not be the most preferred, or bountiful, source, but it is often the most accessible. Loans or gifts from family members and friends ("Hey, I'd really like this digital field recorder for my birthday!") fall into this category, and you should not overlook these options in your planning. Keep in mind that out-of-pocket expenses can be reimbursable at a later date should you get a research award or grant—so be sure to save receipts. It may also be useful to consult with a tax professional prior to making any out-of-pocket expenses, as these may qualify as itemized deductions on your income tax return.

The institutional context for sourcing financial support for your project can encompass research you do as a student at a university or college, as well as fieldwork you complete as an employee for a public or nonprofit agency. Institutional support might come through grants from internal or external sources (that you write, or are written into), research awards, budget allocations, or contributions from community organizations partnering on a project.

Opportunities for folklore and ethnomusicology fieldwork-based research in academic institutions include course-based projects, degree requirements (e.g., master's thesis and PhD dissertation), and collaborations with faculty (e.g., as a research assistant or member of a team). Outside of an invitation to participate in a funded project as a fieldworker, the expectation is generally that you will figure out how to finance your field research activities. Sources for funds that support academic research can be internal and provided through channels within the institution, or external funds that come from entities outside of the university.

Internal sources may include unit or department awards, dean's awards, and schoolwide competitive fellowships. There may also be humanities centers or area studies centers to which students can apply for research support. Start your search for money by asking your adviser or faculty members with whom you have worked about opportunities. In addition, contact the dean's office or a unit such as the graduate school. Offices at levels above your home department—such as an office of research that serves the entire campus—should have a list of financial support opportunities that are not discipline-specific, and you should pursue any funding for which your project is eligible.

External sources that fund fieldwork in folklore and ethnomusicology generally take the form of grants or programs supported by large foundations such as the Andrew W. Mellon Foundation or the Rockefeller Foundation. While the grant you are eligible for may not be managed by one of the foundations, it is useful to examine their websites early to familiarize yourself with any of their funding priorities. The Fulbright US Student Program provides support for a range of academic research, and you should review the program's current priorities and grants when mapping out your funding opportunities. Additional organizations to explore are the Social Science Research Council and the Wenner-Gren Foundation, both of which offer grant programs for which folklore or ethnomusicology fieldwork projects could be competitive. Yet another source for finding funding is a professional association, such as the American Folklore Society or the Society for Ethnomusicology. These organizations may offer direct support through research awards or fellowships, but they also can serve as clearinghouses for information about other research funding opportunities.

Institutional settings for folklore and ethnomusicology fieldwork beyond academia may include nonprofit organizations or public sector / government agencies, such as arts commissions, state folklife offices, or federal units. Within any of these settings, you may be conducting fieldwork as a staff member or as a contractor, and funding for fieldwork projects will flow from internal and external sources. Internal sources would be allocations from project or operating budgets, per diem allowances, or other instances when the money supporting fieldwork comes from the organization itself. External sources would include grants from private foundations, state arts agencies, or federal sources such as the National Endowment for the Arts. Financial support for fieldwork projects in public sector or nonprofit settings might also come in the form of partnerships with other organizations, fee-for-service situations (in which someone contracts your organization to do fieldwork), or private gifts and donations. Finally, you may be able to seek funding from community organizations either local to your fieldwork site or with interest in supporting efforts elsewhere. Organizations such as the Rotary Club are worth contacting, as even a small amount of funding may help propel your project.

Conclusion

Crafting a realistic and thorough budget takes time and patience, and the categories we have suggested in this chapter will certainly help you get started. These are common expenses, so keep in mind that fieldwork will entail costs specific to the locations, type of equipment needed, or idiosyncratic activities associated with the project. The most basic of budgeting will ensure that you account for expected and routine costs and will also help you be prepared for unexpected costs during your research.

PART II

IN THE FIELD

NOW THAT YOU HAVE PICKED a topic, established a research plan, and worked out some of the logistics, it is time to delve into the fieldwork phase. Review your plan regularly throughout fieldwork as it will help keep you focused and ensure that you complete all the steps necessary for achieving your goals. It is easy to stray into tangents and wild goose chases, losing touch with what you set out to accomplish. Flexibility and adaptability will be key to your success, so fieldworkers should frequently return to plans to assess whether they are still appropriate. Enthusiastically taking advantage of unexpected opportunities and embracing what we call the "just say yes" approach can lead to the most productive, exciting, and innovative research. Frequently, a fieldworker might find out about or be invited to do something, attend an event, or meet someone who was not originally in the plan. Knowing your initial plan well allows you to evaluate how a serendipitous opportunity might affect your project.

Part II is divided into five chapters that provide guidelines for strategies for gathering and documenting information while in the field. As we discussed in chapter 1, the term "fieldwork" is often used interchangeably with "participant observation" and refers to methods that involve immersion and participation in social situations. Common strategies associated with participant observation include observation, participating while actively observing, and talking to people both informally and in more formal interview frames. Also integral to this type of research is documentation through writing and audiovisual formats. The documentation that constitutes the metadata and data can be reviewed and used after fieldwork to produce the research products.

We have separated our discussion into the following components: observation, participant observation, interviews, and documentation. This division is inherently problematic because these are not always distinct activities. In a situation where fieldworkers are primarily focused on observing an event, they are having an experience and thus are also participating. And, when they are conducting an interview, they are observing details throughout the interaction. Documentation is not separate from any of these activities since fieldworkers continually record all fieldwork activities in one manner or another. Even though all these activities merge in the field, we have divided them into separate sections because each requires its own set of skills and deserves focused attention.

Chapter 7 describes different settings for doing fieldwork. It then discusses the collection of folklore and musical texts as either a final goal of a project or something that is done in conjunction with other methods. It ends with a lengthy discussion of the process of observation in which we emphasize the need for explicit and concrete attention to details, interactions, and social positioning. Chapter 8 adds participation into the mix, describing participant observation as the core method for much folklore and ethnomusicology fieldwork. It covers strategies for establishing relationships or developing rapport with people who are involved in your research project; how to decide how, when, and where to participate; and what one should do when participating. Chapter 9 addresses interview techniques, including the logistical considerations about where and when to hold interviews, how to develop questions, and the importance of flexibility. Throughout the chapter, we emphasize listening as the most important dimension of successful interviews. Chapter 10 is about technical dimensions of fieldwork, primarily exploring ways to produce cultural documentation using a variety of technologies and methods. Part II concludes with chapter 11, "Issues in the Field." Most fieldworkers have very positive and productive experiences; yet, some also encounter challenges around such issues as illness, money, power differentials, identity politics, prejudice, sexual dynamics, and sometimes violence. We discuss some ways that these issues can arise in the field and reflect on how fieldworkers might address them. The important message in this chapter is that the basic needs and safety of fieldworkers *and* research participants should always be the priority.

7

RESEARCH SETTINGS AND OBSERVATION

FOLKLORE AND ETHNOMUSICOLOGICAL FIELDWORK REPLICATES much of what we do in everyday life. These activities become research when we pay attention to details, focus on finding answers to our research questions, and importantly, document the information we gather. Because documentation is so important, we begin this chapter by providing a system for organizing and managing data and explaining the importance of fieldnotes. After explaining some different settings in which fieldwork typically takes place, we begin our discussion of methods by discussing collecting, and we end with a lengthy discussion of the importance of detailed observation skills, whether one is conducting fieldwork "in real life" or in virtual spaces.

Managing Data

The range and volume of data a fieldworker develops will vary by project and can include some combination of fieldnotes, descriptions of events and observations, interview recordings and transcripts, drawings, screen shots, audio recordings, video recordings, notes about or reproductions of archival materials, newspaper articles, event programs and other ephemera, and scholarly writing related to the topic. Gathering data in the field through fieldnotes, photographs, and recordings is one aspect of cultural documentation, but you should also plan for another aspect: creating metadata.

It is imperative to consistently use a system for organizing and managing all your data across formats. Creating this system *prior to beginning fieldwork* will enable you to fold metadata into your daily workflow. Doing so will ensure that all your materials are clearly marked and organized when you are done with fieldwork and will make it much easier to prepare your collections for long-term preservation (see chap. 15). A spreadsheet is a useful means for organizing metadata and will come in handy at the end of fieldwork as you analyze your data or prepare it for some other use. If using and maintaining a digital spreadsheet in your fieldwork sites is not feasible, a notebook will do the trick.

We recommend creating a simple document or spreadsheet with a list of all fieldwork activities you intend to carry out. The American Folklife Center provides guidelines in *Folklife and Fieldwork: An Introduction to Cultural Documentation* (Winick and Bartis 2016, 32–33), and recommends that a spreadsheet contain minimum description (also referred to as "essential descriptors") of a collection and the individual items that compose it. Columns for metadata should include: identifier or file name, title or caption (consisting of factual content about who, when, what, where), names of participants (including subject and creator—be sure to use full names and check for correct spelling), geographic location and place names, dates, brief description or summary, language, format (e.g., file type), rights or restrictions on use, and keywords.

A column for project code will be useful, as well. This is a unique identifier for the whole project and might include the year and geographic location or other umbrella feature of your research. The project code should be affiliated with each item in your spreadsheet as a means for connecting everything together as a whole collection. Examples include: 2018_Maryland, 1983_urban-legend-project, or 1999_LosAngeles_ethnic-music-communities. The project code should be general enough to label all materials but have enough specificity to tell you (or an archivist) what is contained within the collection.

In addition to the spreadsheet, we recommend that you create a template for recording metadata associated with each item of fieldwork material. This is often known as a log sheet. Whether you are writing about an event or organizing images or recordings, first record the necessary metadata that situates the activity and provides necessary information for you or someone else to contextualize it in the future. This includes such information as the full names of individuals involved, their social roles or status as is relevant to the project, people's ages, other relevant identity factors, the date, the occasion or other important information about the event, and the location. For location, be sure to provide as much detail as is useful; you may want to include the name of a specific site—such as the building, family's home, public ground, or website—in addition to information about the name of a neighborhood, town, region, city, and country. We return to a detailed discussion of using spreadsheets and logs in chapter 12, but below is an excerpt of a log from *Folklore and Fieldwork* (Winick and Bartis 2016, 26):

Identifier: afc2012034_00483
Title: Patrick interview, 2013-02-17
Names: Patrick Bovenzi (interviewee); Ellen E. McHale (interviewer)
Place: Tampa Bay Downs Racetrack kitchen.
Date: 2013-02-17
Description: Patrick Bovenzi talked about his work in the horse business, and especially his current work as a horse identifier.
Language: English
Formats: 1 audio file, digital, WAV (55 min.); 1 video file, digital, sound, color, mpeg4 (55 min.)
Rights: No restrictions, permissions completed.
Tagging: Horses, Racetracks

Even though this information may be on the spreadsheet, we have found that including it with each piece of data for which writing is appropriate saves us a great deal of time when we are in the analyzing and producing phase. When reviewing an interview you want to quote for an exhibit or thesis, for example, the information you need to properly cite the interview, such as full name, date, and location, is right there!

In general, metadata that helps identify or construct the context for a given piece of cultural documentation will be useful as you move into phases of analyzing, editing, or otherwise using materials. It is fairly typical for fieldworkers to forget information after leaving the field, making metadata especially critical. Metadata can also be useful to communities of origin, or to archivists should you decide to donate your materials. Detailed metadata will enable archivists to describe your collection, and accurate metadata will enable future researchers to discover your materials when using archival research tools, as will be discussed in chapter 15. A photograph or video is a rich piece of documentation, but a viewer unfamiliar with the cultural content or context would not easily be able to determine the name of a musical instrument, the identity of the person playing it, or the geographic location. Note that the date and time of fieldwork documentation is also an element of metadata, and increasingly can be captured automatically and embedded in digital files by cameras and audio recorders. *However, you should make sure to set the time and date stamp features of your recording devices accurately.* Bear in mind that digital cameras or audio devices do not automatically adjust when they move across time zones. In addition to date and time, most devices record other types of technical metadata into files, such as shutter speed and ISO for image files, or sample rate and bit depth for audio files. Many devices will also record the model of the device itself into the file (e.g., Canon EOS T3i).

Fieldnotes

In doing fieldwork, anything we hear, observe, smell, or even think can be considered data. However, in order to turn an experience into data, we must end up with some type of documentation to review, analyze, or otherwise use. There are multiple terms that we use to discuss the processes for documenting during fieldwork. "Documenting" is a general term for gathering data in the field. "Collecting" may refer to the gathering of particular "items" from a genre or type, as will be discussed in the section "Collection" below, or to the more general effort of documenting the cultural life of a community. Folklorists and ethnomusicologists also use the term "recording." While this word is typically used to reference documenting oral or musical culture through audio, it can also refer to textual documentation, such as fieldnotes or visual documentation.

The most important form of documentation for most projects is fieldnotes. Different recording media can be valuable for different types of fieldwork activities: video for a musical performance, audio for an interview, photography for architectural design, or screenshots for websites. However, *nothing replaces the value of fieldnotes*. In addition to the information recorded in audiovisual media, the fieldworker also needs written accounts that contextualize, explain, elaborate, and include any reflections associated with a fieldwork activity. As Gregory F. Barz puts it, "Fieldnotes are for many ethnomusicologists an essential aspect of knowing; they are not only critical in determining what we know, but also illustrative of the process of how we came to know what we know" (1997, 45). The same can be said for folklorists. Throughout this section, we will elaborate the type of information that can be valuable to note. Here, we provide some general guidelines about how to take fieldnotes.

Fieldnotes are used for recording all fieldwork activities, whether it is an informal interaction, an important event, or a scheduled interview. It is important to set up a system for maintaining your fieldnotes before your first foray—either a notebook, a single computer document, or a series of well-organized files. Make sure to create a numbering system to keep track of your notes, whether they are handwritten notes or electronic files. And, we recommend maintaining your fieldnotes in a private format. Some fieldworkers have experimented with public research blogs, which are typically inappropriate for fieldnotes because not all the information you document will be intended for a public audience. Furthermore, your fieldnotes will include such things as your feelings, emerging thoughts, and reactions to your experiences, much of which you will likely want

Figure 7.1. Fieldworkers from a UNESCO team doing an Intangible Cultural Heritage survey note metadata and document traditional culture via fieldnotes, hand written and electronic media. Karonga District, Malawi, 2013. Photo by Lisa Gilman.

to keep to yourself. You may decide at a later date to make some of this information public, but we recommend that you wait until you have a clear idea of what you are going to do with your data before making these decisions.

Writing Ethnographic Fieldnotes by Robert M. Emerson, Rachel I. Fretz, and Linda L. Shaw (1995) and *Fieldnotes: The Makings of Anthropology*, edited by Roger Sanjek (1990), are excellent sources about the intricacies of creating fieldnotes. Barz (1997) elaborates on multiple ways to think about and approach the actual writing of fieldnotes. We encourage you to pursue these and other sources. Here, we provide only a brief overview addressing two key steps. One step is what Emerson et al. (1995) call "jottings" and the other step is the more formal write-up into readable prose. Jottings refer to the notes we make in the field as reminders and to make sure that we have a record of important names and details, the "scratch notes, abbreviated words and phrases to use later to construct full fieldnotes" (18). The distinction between jottings and "full fieldnotes" is very important. In our experience, students sometimes rely on their jottings, which can be quite incomprehensible once the recent memory of an experience fades. We thus emphasize the importance of always taking the time to write up more complete notes.

Fieldworkers should carry a notebook and a writing implement wherever they go to ensure they can easily record observations, thoughts, and

Figure 7.2. Pen and notebook provide a reliable source for jotting metadata or other notes in the field. Fenn creates preliminary logging information for audio recordings of a musical performance by a gospel ensemble. Mzimba, Malawi, 2013. Photo by Lisa Gilman.

contact information, or make quick sketches. Some may want to use their mobile phones but bear in mind that batteries and memory can run out in the middle of something important. Both authors continue to use notebooks, however old fashioned, because of their greater reliability. After the fieldwork activity, ideally on the same day, the fieldworker should take the time to describe what happened in great detail, referring to the jottings as needed. This write-up, which is comprehensive and comprehensible, is what we call fieldnotes. Emerson et al. (1995) explain that in writing fieldnotes, the fieldworker "must construct something out of these bits and pieces of information" that they jotted down. "The description that results must make sense as a logical, sensible series of incidents and experiences, even if only to an audience made up of the fieldworker herself" (49).

Exercise

1. Students go to a public place, ideally one where it is appropriate for every-one to be in the same space writing, such as a building's lobby, a park, or a coffee shop.

2. Students jot down details about what they observe (ten minutes).
3. Students return to the classroom.
4. Students write down their observations in prose based on their jottings (ten minutes).
5. Three to four students volunteer to read their descriptions.

Discussion

- What types of information did different students jot down?
- What was omitted?
- What were differences between students' descriptions?
- Discuss the process of creating prose out of jottings.
- Did the prose accurately represent what students observed?
- Did students elaborate or editorialize what they observed?

The goal of fieldnotes is to write down concrete details and fieldworkers' thinking, rather than to create interesting-to-read descriptions of social life. Note, however, that the process of writing notes "is a highly interactive process of cultural translation" (Barz 1997). Despite your best intentions, you are not writing the full account of everything that occurred but rather noting select details through your own lens. Though interpretation is inevitable, avoid overly flowery writing, attributing emotion to people, or assuming people's objectives. Seek to capture what you experienced and observed with as much detail as possible to enable you or someone else to understand the cultural practice or event at which you were present. If you decide to include information from your fieldnotes in a final product, you can select whether to elaborate on your description at that time.

Garcia et al. (2009, 64–65) explain that when doing fieldwork in digital spaces, fieldnotes may seem less important because "both textual and visual data can be recorded by 'screen save' programs (e.g., Camtasia or Hypercam) that provide a digital 'videotape' of an online environment." The fieldworker can "record their visit to a website and replay it at will, stopping, starting and moving around in the data as needed." However, they emphasize that written fieldnotes are "still essential to help the researcher catalogue, describe, and develop theories from their observations, and to record their reactions and subjective experiences" (65).

Bonnie Stone Sunstein and Elizabeth Chiseri-Strater (2007) recommend that you review your fieldnotes regularly over the course of your fieldwork. As you look them over, ask yourself these three questions: What surprised me? What intrigued me? What disturbed me? Reflecting on these questions and writing down your thoughts about them will help you recognize and deepen your knowledge of the topic.

Research Settings

Now that you have a system for documenting and managing your field-work, it's time to take steps toward doing the fieldwork! In the volume *A Guide for Field Workers in Folklore* published in 1964, folklorist Kenneth Goldstein distinguished between different types of settings where much folklore and ethnomusicologist fieldwork take place. He described the "natural context" as "the social context in which folklore functions in a society" (80). He elaborated that this setting may be highly formal in that it is an occasion that is "organized, required, and sometimes scheduled." These activities include those that are performed on special occasions, such as births or deaths. It can be "semi-formal" as in "those in which folklore performance or statement is expected, but not required." He gives the example of parents telling their children stories before sending them to bed. "Informal contexts" are "those in which such performance is not required, is unscheduled, and is usually unexpected" (81). His example includes someone telling a joke or saying a proverb during a conversation.

Most folklorists and ethnomusicologists try to observe the cultural forms in what Goldstein described as "natural context." The ideal is to observe and participate in the folklore or musical activity without it having been planned for the benefit of the fieldworker and with as little interference as possible from the fieldworker. Note that the presence of a researcher can change the dynamics of a setting, even when it is a so-called natural context. A fieldworker can make performers more self-conscious, cause participants to censor themselves, or influence the audience to be more responsive as they notice that the event is receiving special attention. We will return to these issues throughout this section. Here, we draw on natural context to discuss different types of settings typical for fieldwork.

Ethnographic methods are productive for investigating expressive forms in their natural contexts because of the emphasis on immersion. Ethnographers frequently attempt to immerse themselves in the social environments and events where the cultural form will most likely take place. This is easier for what Goldstein calls "formal" and "semi-formal" contexts in which the activity can be reasonably expected to happen. Informal contexts are more challenging, as fieldworkers should try to put themselves into situations in which the activity is likely, though not guaranteed, to occur. Someone studying jokes within a fraternity might plan to spend time with members of the fraternity in the setting in which they would likely tell jokes. The research strategy would be based on the assumption that if the fieldworker joined them often enough, they would eventually have the opportunity to observe and participate in the joke telling as it would happen presumably with or without the fieldworker's presence. Similarly, someone interested in popular music in Korea might spend time in the natural context where musicians socialize, practice, learn from one another, or perform.

Though the ideal for many is a natural setting, it is not always possible. As Goldstein explains, fieldworkers' observations should be "made in the natural contexts in which folklore is performed. But how can he do so in the limited time at his disposal if he can never even be sure when these natural contexts will occur?" (1964, 87). Timing can be a factor. Fieldworkers are often restricted to a specified time frame, which may not be when the topic of study typically happens. Some activities are restricted to certain individuals or to specific times or spaces to which the researcher might not be welcome. Sometimes researchers might find that though they spend a great deal of time in what they hoped was a natural context, the practice they are attempting to observe never happens. In the example of the fraternity jokes, a fieldworker could spend a great deal of time with the fraternity members without ever hearing the types of jokes he expected to, despite anecdotal evidence. There is not a guaranteed means for ensuring that culture happens when we are prepared to observe it!

In situations where observing in a natural context is not possible, some fieldworkers organize opportunities for the folklore form or music to occur that resemble natural settings (see Goldstein 1964). Someone interested in a certain musical tradition, for example, could ask an individual or group to perform so that the researcher could hear, observe, and record. The fieldworker would be able to hear the music and watch the instruments being played; however, the performance might lack inspiration without an audience, and the fieldworker would learn little about the interaction between performers and audience members. The event might have been more successful if the fieldworker had tried to simulate a typical performance setting by selecting an appropriate location, inviting an audience, providing food, or whatever specific details were typical for that artist or genre.

A thoughtfully organized event can be a successful and productive research strategy, especially if attention is paid to what it is about the natural context that makes it conducive for the activity. Some types of musical and folklore practices are more appropriate for these types of strategies than are others. Activities that involve smaller groups may be more successful, and certain genres will work better than others. Setting up an opportunity for family members to sing songs or a group of youth to tell ghost stories will be more successful than trying to set up a dance competition between multiple village dance teams. Bear in mind that certain types of topics would not be amenable to this approach at all—for example, someone studying musical performance in a ritual, at a large sports event, or in a festival setting would not have the option of setting up an event that replicated the typical context.

As an example of an induced natural context, a student in the United States was interested in studying memorates (stories about people's interactions with the supernatural). She knew that she could not count on hearing these stories during the academic term in which she was doing the research. Knowing that people often tell these stories in the evening at informal social occasions, she invited a group of students from her class one evening. She lit candles in her dark living room, served tasty snacks, and offered everyone a cold beverage. She began the gathering by explaining her project, what her goals were for the evening, and how she was going to use the information. At first everyone sat awkwardly, aware that the event was superficially put together. The host then told a story about having glimpsed a ghost in a hotel. Another student, inspired by her story, tentatively shared a story about a ghost that was believed to be in an abandoned house in his childhood neighborhood. Before he had finished his story, he relaxed and became absorbed in its telling, drawing everyone in to the narrative. Stories then tumbled out one after the other. Each person's story evoked memories that reminded participants of their own stories. The more animated the storytelling became, the more elaborate they were. By the end of the evening, everyone was laughing and discussing the stories, the experience of sharing them, and why so many had been similar—all insightful information for the fieldworker.

This is an example of a successful induced event. Though everyone was well aware that it was organized for research purposes, it was arranged to resemble an informal storytelling event, based on knowledge of what typically happens when people tell stories. The result was an event that was similar to what might occur in a natural context. Although participants were self-conscious at first, they quickly relaxed into the activity much as they would in other situations. The student researcher could not claim to have observed or documented this session naturally; yet, she was able to gather useful information about the storytelling event, such as details about performer/audience interactions, how stories flow one from the next, and participants' meta-commentary about belief in the supernatural. She also had documented numerous narratives whose structure and content she could analyze later.

Collection

Before the shift to processual and contextual approaches to folklore and ethnomusicology that took place from 1960 through the 1970s, one of the main methods used by folklorists and ethnomusicologists was the collection of "texts" (see Paredes and Bauman 1972; Rice 1987; Titon 2008). The goal was to record in writing or audiovisual media folklore or musical texts from practitioners. These "items" were collected for a variety of reasons, including studying form or genre, comparative analysis, tracing movement through time and space, or translation into media for new or larger audiences. Alan Lomax, for example, produced numerous recordings of music that he gathered in the southern United States. Similarly, Benjamin Botkin published collections of tales, ballads, and customs from across the country. Subsequent scholars drew on extant collections in their academic writing. Ethnomusicologists could study collections of field recordings to analyze nonwestern musical structures, or folklorists might study the formal properties of a certain type of material culture or develop theories about how stories spread across time and space by drawing on large bodies of oral literature gathered in the field.

In this type of collecting, the creative forms are removed from the contexts in which they occur. Any future analysis occurs on the decontextualized form, rather than on examining how the form operates within its social setting. From this type of research, little can be said for how people use the form, what meanings it has for practitioners, or how it exists in relationship to such things as economics, social hierarchies, competing aesthetic systems, and so on.

Though many contemporary folklorists and ethnomusicologists no longer consider collection to be the primary objective of their projects, given their attention to process and context, collecting is still part of what some do in the field, so it is worthy of attention. A few examples of the types of contemporary researchers who collect texts include those who are interested in textual or content analysis. They gather texts and analyze details within them to develop an argument about form, meanings, phrasing, or intertextuality. Some interested in history collect oral narratives or song texts and analyze them for content that yields details about realities or ideologies of the past. Others collect texts because their objective is to produce a collection—for example a recording or a publication or website of some type of folklore or music. And, those curating exhibits may collect recordings of texts or objects with the primary objective of showcasing them. Plenty of fieldworkers who are doing more contextually based fieldwork also collect texts, and subsequently produce multiple types of products.

In collection, fieldworkers go into the field where a folklore or ethnomusicological practice happens, find practitioners, and document and record their repertoire. The repertoire could be some type of verbal form (jokes, proverbs, contemporary legends, or nursery rhymes), song tradition, instrumental tradition, material culture, building technique, recipe, or ritual practice. Ideally, they document these as they occurred in their natural setting. They may also solicit practitioners to perform or share the texts in artificial or induced natural contexts. Because the emphasis is on gathering texts, fieldworkers often try to find "culture bearers" or individuals who are particularly knowledgeable and virtuosic in the tradition. Fieldworkers whose primary goal is to collect texts record metadata and relevant information about genre; context; time, place, and occasion where documentation happened; identifying and demographic information about the culture bearers and, if relevant, the larger community represented by the cultural form; information about the researcher; and information about the methods of recording and files obtained.

Observation

Most contemporary fieldworkers' goals include trying to understand cultural forms as they manifest within social life, thus observing and documenting the context in which the form exists is as important as attending to the content. Observation is therefore typically one of the most important fieldwork strategies. Both authors are avid people watchers, and sometimes we joke that we became ethnographers so that we could justify this passion as a professional skill. Though it may seem that observing is something that we do all the time and should require scant instruction, using observation as a fieldwork strategy requires much more dedicated and deliberate attention to details than what most of us do in our everyday lives. Context and process are central to understanding how different folklore and musical forms operate. Fieldworkers should note the many different aspects of the environment in which the practice occurs, in addition to paying attention to the artistic or expressive performances themselves. As will be emphasized over and over, it is critically important to write extensive fieldnotes and sometimes use other types of recording devices to document the details of what one observes.

The term "observation" is limited because it implies a single sensory perception, the visual, as the only and most important way of experiencing and gaining some understanding of a social and artistic environment. Yet, we experience life through multiple sensory perceptions, all of which are important to artistic practice and social meaning. Though we use the term "observation," fieldworkers researching in real life need to be attentive to not only what they see, but also what they hear, smell, taste, and feel—both emotionally and physically (see Bendix 2000; Stoller 1989). Those researching in virtual realms may have access to more limited sensory perceptions, visual and sometimes aural, but awareness that such things as smell, taste, and emotion are part of the experiences of all those participating and interacting in digital spaces can increase the depth and nuance of understanding, as will be elaborated shortly.

Fieldworkers will determine what is most important for them to observe and document based on the nature of the topic they are studying, their research questions, their goals, institutional demands, and limitations. For many projects, it is important to observe multiple events and occasions. Someone studying a form of music who only attends one performance may not realize that the performance was atypical in some way or may be focused on certain details and miss others. Or spending time in a social setting only one time may provide the fieldworker limited experience with a topic, while doing so over the course of several months may enable them to gain a deeper understanding of its significance.

Exercise

Assignment for students to complete individually outside of class: Attend a worship service with which you are not already familiar. Write a three- to four-page detailed description and reflection of your experience. Consider such things as numbers of people present, dress, gender dynamics, class or status differentials, sequence of events, interactional dynamics, use of space, and temporal issues. Briefly reflect on your experience: How did you feel? How were you treated? In what ways was your observation successful? What challenges did you face? What strategies did you use to heighten your observation skills? What strategies did you use to document or remember details? What would you do differently next time?

Following is a discussion of some of the dynamics that are often important to pay attention to and document. It is by no means exhaustive, but we hope that the discussion will inspire readers to think carefully about the breadth of observable phenomena in their own project.

Observation "In Real Life"

People: Because people are at the center of folklore and ethnomusicological production, careful attention to participants is critical. Map the range of participants at the event or associated with the practice. Who is there and what are they doing? For some folklore and musical forms, there is no clear distinction between performers and audience members—for example, in situations where a group of people is playing music together or swapping jokes. In others, performers and audience members are distinct. The impulse of many beginning fieldworkers is to pay attention only to those producing the expressive culture: the musician, storyteller, or person with the tattoos. It is often necessary to expand one's scope to other forms of participation. Who is producing the artistic form? Who organized the event? Who is selling or benefiting from it? Who is the intended or actual audience? When considering who constitutes the audience, it may be significant to consider an audience beyond the event. If a musical performance is being broadcast on radio or television, who is the larger audience? If it is being recorded, who will be the audience of the recording in the future? Will someone post a photograph or video clip on social media for an audience that could expand internationally? Will people discuss the event in person, via text, or through online channels?

In some cases, a topic will involve such things as knowledge or beliefs, and there may not be opportunities for the fieldworker to observe these being shared. Rather the fieldworker will rely on talking to people to gather information. Even in these situations, we recommend thinking broadly and specifically about people's participation. In the case of some types of knowledge, although you may want to focus your attention on the people who have this particular knowledge, you may also want to consider those people who have opinions about it or who are involved in some way other than being a knowledge bearer. For example, if you were interested in the healing property of plants within a community, you could talk to people with the knowledge about the plants' special qualities, those who use them but do not know much about them, and perhaps those who do not believe that the plants are capable of healing.

In addition to documenting the nature of participation, pay particular attention to demographics: How old are participants in the various capacities? What can you tell about their occupations? Depending on the situation, it may be relevant to note other aspects of their identities, such as ethnicity, gender, religious affiliation, race, sexuality, and so forth. As you develop observation skills, test your estimation skills. The authors have often been surprised by the inaccuracy of our estimations. During observation, identifying people in relation to different social or identity categories is inherently problematic because you frequently cannot tell how people identify simply by looking at them.

Exercise

Can be done outside of class or during class time. Go to a public space where there are lots of people, such as a courtyard, concert, or church service. Quickly estimate the breakdown of people that appear to be male or female. Now, count. Does your counting produce something similar or different from your guess?

Assumptions about someone's gender identity might be false; estimating numbers of males and females precludes those who do not identify as either or who identify as both. Yet, we find this exercise to be valuable. In our own experience and in those of many of our students, our estimates about percentages of men versus women in any given group have often been grossly inaccurate. A quick count, even though not exact, provides more reliable information and often brings to our attention how implicit bias contributes to our perception of what we observe. The goal in observation is not to gather statistical information but rather impressions to enable you to begin identifying some details about participants. As the fieldwork progresses and identity categories emerge as relevant to the project, you would use other methods, such as direct questioning, to determine how individuals or communities self-identify. If you are a member of the group being studied or have a high level of cultural competency, you may be more likely to provide accurate information about demographics than if you are an outsider trying to make sense of social cues and norms that might be foreign to you. For example, in the United States, two men holding hands can often be assumed to be in an intimate relationship, while in many African contexts, male platonic friends holding hands is typical and is usually not an indication of a sexual relationship. Knowing that your impressions may or may not be accurate, make sure to provide information about how you came to your conclusions. If you assumed people's sexual identities based on clothing and hairstyles and who was holding hands with whom, note that down.

Dress: Paying attention to what people wear can be valuable for those doing research on creative practices that require specific types of dress or costuming. It can be productive for other types of projects as well. Dress can express a lot about how people identify or issues around gender, wealth, age, aesthetics, political identity, or interests and hobbies. Photography can be very helpful for documenting dress or costume, though it is also useful to note down information to help make sense of dress. A series of photographs of people wearing different T-shirts at a musical performance may need to be supplemented with some contextual information about how many people at the event wore these T-shirts, whether specific categories of people were more likely to wear the shirts than others, and what kinds of people at the show were not wearing the T-shirts. This information would help the fieldworkers interpret the photographs and would also remind them why they took them.

In providing detail about dress, be sure to be specific because fashions constantly change as does naming for different types of clothing items. Specify the style of dress, types of fabric, colors, and ornamentation. Be sure to describe the clothing with specific details rather than using vague adjectives. Consider the description: "The young women were dressed in clothing appropriate for a night out on the town." It gives you little information other than evoking your own thoughts about what young women wear when they go out, which will could be quite different from what the women wore. Compare with: "the group of five women in their early twenties who appeared to be Euro-American wore tight T-shirts in pastel colors (light blue, pink, or white, with no writing or decoration) whose low necklines revealed their cleavage, short floral skirts made out of gauzy fabric that reached mid-thigh and moved when they walked, and colorful canvas sneakers (mostly in bright colors—red, royal blue, and Kelly green) with high white socks that reached to their knees." More descriptive detail is apt to anchor the observation in the reality seen rather than the reality imagined.

Economics: Economic status is often relevant information in research, but in many situations, it is difficult to determine and may be considered an inappropriate topic of conversation. In some contexts, signs of economic class will be displayed in explicit ways. For example, people may be wearing clothing widely known to be expensive, drive upscale cars, provide large amounts of food and drink for guests, pay pricey entrance fees, generously tip performers, or buy art objects. Or the people may ride the bus or walk, wear inexpensive clothing, or not be able to afford entrance fees. In some cases, economic class will be widely known—for example, a highly successful musician may be known to be wealthy or a local potter may be known to struggle financially. In these cases, it is useful to note not only what you know about economic status but also how you determined it.

In the United States, it can be difficult to ascertain class because of a widespread ethos of egalitarianism and a bias toward dominant consumerist culture in which people of different economic levels can access large amounts of credit. It is also not uncommon in the United States for people with money to choose not to exhibit their wealth. Some people may wear old torn clothing despite their financial capability to buy designer brands. Driving an expensive car may be a sign of wealth or a sign that someone is willing to go into a great deal of debt. Regardless, paying attention to what kind of cars people are driving, if any, what they are wearing, and how much money they are spending could give you some insight into class and other economic dynamics. Such observations can also yield insight into people's values.

Gender and sexuality: Determining people's gender and sexuality will differ depending on the context of your research. You may be in a setting where the social norms dictate clear gender differentiation and articulation of gender identities, in which case it can be easy to assume gender based on people's dress, hair, and other aspects of their physical presentation. In other settings, gender can be far more complex if people identify across a broader spectrum of gender identities than the male/female binary offers. Categorizing people as a specific gender identity based on the fieldworker's assumptions is problematic if it differs from how people self-identify. As with other markers of identity, some guessing to get some preliminary information can be useful, but as research progresses the fieldworker should learn how gender is defined and operates within the research setting.

Race/ethnicity: One mistake that is common for people who are part of a dominant social group is to only indicate someone's identity when it does not conform to the dominant one. In our experience teaching, students (especially those who are Euro-American) doing observations in the United States frequently make no mention of race or ethnicity when the people they are discussing appear to be Euro-American or "white," yet they note when someone appears to be African American or Latino. This is problematic because it presumes "white" people as the norm, and people of color as different. To document observations productively, it is therefore important to designate ethnicity for all. If a fieldworker enters a performance hall, and the majority of people appear to be black or alternately white, those are important contextual indicators in the United States. Once again, always be honest about the basis of your categories because one's assumptions about someone else's racial or ethnic identity may not align with that person's own background or self-identification. In the production of final products, be sure that you either provide identifying information based on how people self-identity or that you provide the rationale for your categorizations.

Time: In addition to noting in your metadata and fieldnotes what time of day and which day something takes place, you should also document other temporal dimensions. Is there significance to the time of day in which it occurs? Is it a special occasion? What is the sequence of activities? How long do different parts last? How does the sequence of activities interact with the spatial dynamics? Is someone controlling the sequence? As with other dimensions, be specific. "The song lasted much longer than the other ones" is vague. "Most songs lasted three to four minutes, while the last one went on for ten minutes" provides more concrete information.

Space: Observers should pay attention to the details of spaces used. Think broadly. There could be the spaces in which events take place, where people share their beliefs or feelings about something, where people gather to prepare or reflect on something, or where participants live and work. Some questions to consider associated with particular spaces include: How is this space defined? Does it have a name? How is space relevant to your topic of study or the people involved in your project? Who has access? Is it inside or outside? Is the event framed or announced spatially? For example, are there signs, entryways, gates, doors, or tickets counters that one must pass to officially be within? Is it associated with a particular group or social organization? For example, is it family's house? A community gathering space? A religious institution? A business? A concert hall?

Once you have noted these types of details, examine the space and describe it. How big is it? Be as specific as you can. "Really big" or "really small" are relative terms. In your fieldnotes, find a way to describe the space in a way that you or others would understand. You can use measurements and comparisons to spaces that are familiar to you, for example "as big as a football stadium" or "a small rectangular room roughly twenty feet by thirty feet." Note that in producing the final product, you will have to provide information interpretable by your audience. Those living outside the United States, for example, may have little reference point for the size of a football stadium. How is the space laid out? It can be useful to sketch in your fieldnotes so that you can document how it is laid out and what kinds of activities happen in different locations within it. Photographs are also useful, but it can be difficult to capture and label the overall space, so a sketch and photographs can complement one another.

Exercise

1. Students write a description of the room in which they are sitting (ten minutes).
2. Three to four students read the descriptions out loud to the whole group.

Discussion

- What was included in each description?
- What was omitted?
- How did an individual's physical positioning in the room affect the description?
- Would someone outside the room be able to visualize it?

Pay attention to what types of activities are appropriate in which spaces. Is there an officially marked or unofficial boundary that indicates a space as appropriate to where the artistic practice occurs? This could be a community center, a kitchen, a grassy area in the outskirts of town, someone's porch, or the stage in a performance hall. How is the boundary formed? Consider the difference, for example, between a staged musical performance where there are bouncers keeping the audience off the stage versus an informal gathering where the audience stands around the musicians. It may be appropriate to consider what is happening at the margins. Are there people, things, or activities present in the general locale who are not involved in the activity? What exists or is happening outside the space?

Consider also the physical dimensions within the space. What aspects of the natural environment are present? Are there decorations, symbols, or furniture that indicate information about people, their values, aesthetics, or class dynamics? Are there physical items that were placed there for this event, or are they part of the regular decor? What might these physical items express? How are people interacting with them?

Interaction: Observing interactions between people and various aspects of the physical environment and material culture can yield useful information. Note how people are using spaces: Are there spaces where people are expected to gather? Are there certain categories of people who have official access or are denied access to certain spaces? Are there spaces where no one seems to go, either because there are rules or official dictates or because of informal practice? How are people interacting with their physical environments? Are there things that they touch, hold, avoid? Are there physical objects that are transferred between people? What are these objects, and who is interacting with them and in what ways? If there are decorative items present, are people looking at them? Talking about them? If so to whom are they making their comments? What are they saying?

In observing how people interact with one another, consider what categories or which specific individuals are interacting with whom. What is the nature of the interaction? What seems to be the goal and outcome of the interaction? In what space and in what time frames are these interactions taking place? The physical relationships and interactions between people tend to be culturally specific. It's important not to assume that certain types of spatial relations that seem normal to the fieldworker will necessarily be the norm in the research setting. How closely are people sitting? How close do they stand when speaking? Do people physically touch? If so, in what circumstances? Since there are often ideas about proper gender roles or types of interactions between people of different genders, it may be relevant to note how people of one gender are interacting among themselves in addition to what cross- or multiple-gender interactions take place.

Listen to what people say to one another, and which categories of people say what kinds of things to whom. What can you glean about your topic, how people feel about it, or what kinds of people are most associated with it through listening to what various participants say? If you are new to the environment, listening to people also can be useful for developing cultural competence, or learning what kinds of physical bearing and interactions are appropriate and for whom. You can learn about people's relationships with one another and with the organizations that are involved in the activity. Sometimes people might give one another instructions that are relevant to the project, as when someone explains how to make something or how to play an instrument or corrects someone's dancing. People might express judgments, such as praise or criticism, which could be valuable information about how the topic of study is valued.

Fieldworkers learn a great deal from the conversations and comments that people have in research settings. However, they cannot use this material in research unless they have permission from participants (as will be discussed in later chapters). A useful strategy is to listen and take notes (usually after the fact) to the relevant conversations. This information can contribute to your thinking and knowledge building and might be useful as you develop and refine research strategies; however, *unless permission is granted, fieldworkers should not quote this information.*

Multiple senses/emotion: We cannot give an exhaustive description of everything you should pay attention to in your observations, but do remember to note down information gathered through multiple sensory perceptions. An environment permeated by odors of delicious food will impact participants differently than one with vague smells of waste. What are the smells? Where are they coming from? How do people interact with the odors? Consider the temperature and weather. Are people hot or cold? How does it feel to wear the attire appropriate to the occasion? What does the ground feel under a dancer's feet? Was the music loud and overpowering? Were voices low and subdued? What kinds of emotions were felt or expressed? Consider those of participants as well as your own.

Exercise

1. One student volunteers to perform for the group—for example, sings a song, plays an instrument, tells a story, or reads a poem.
2. During the performance, the audience jots down their perceptions of the emotional experience—their own, the performer, and other members of the audience.

Discussion

- What did individuals perceive about the emotions of others (the performers and audience members)?
- How did individuals' perceptions of others compare to their own feelings?
- What strategies could be used to describe perceptions about emotion given the potential for inaccuracy?

Virtual World

Garcia et al. (2009) provide an overview of the scholarship and methods used by ethnographers doing research in online settings. Some research in virtual realms will occur mostly in relatively static sites useful for information gathering—for example, a website that can be read or a recording that can be listened to or watched. Others may be interactional spaces in which one can do "participant observation" in parallel ways to what one might do offline, as will be discussed in the next chapter. Unlike offline situations, where it is usually difficult to be present in a situation without being seen, online settings often allow for observation without being detected—what some refer to as "lurking." Some ethnographers have found it helpful to lurk first before delving into more active participation. Others recommend active engagement from the outset, but disagreements exist over the ethics of lurking (see Garcia et al. 2009).

As with the offline settings where observing on multiple occasions can provide depth and breadth of knowledge, we recommend that your online observations happen over time. For those of you doing research with social media sites or other online communities, it is easy to spend more time online than you may have to dedicate to it. We recommend creating a reasonable schedule for yourself; what is appropriate will depend on the topic. Consider reviewing relevant sites for thirty minutes a day for one month or two hours a week across two months or some other specified and limited time frame. Your plan should allow you to track and follow the progress of what is going on but also not take too much time and not produce more data than you will be able to review and evaluate later.

By "static," we refer to a variety of online spaces, such as sites intended to provide information. These could be sites of the communities or individuals being studied or sites that provide important contextual information, or anything in between. For example, somebody interested in studying pottery making in a small town in Georgia could use a variety of internet sites to learn something about Georgia, something about the town where the pottery is made, any information about potters that might be available on local websites, or sites associated with specific potters or families.

Control: Doing such research would require careful documentation not only about the content found but also about the nature of the site. Who controls it? Who provided the information? What is the relationship of the people who control the site to the people or communities that produce the pottery? What is the goal of the website? Whether it is intended for other artists, to attract tourists, or to sell the art would greatly impact how and what information was presented. These details will help inform how you interpret and use the information. If you are producing a paper, publication, or other product that requires citations, you will need to provide the name of the website, the URL, and the date accessed. Be sure to capture this information as metadata alongside your fieldnotes so that you can easily find it if you need to cite your sources in the future.

Space: As with face-to-face situations, what you pay attention to when observing in virtual spaces will depend on the objectives of your project. Attending to spatial and temporal dimensions as well as visual and textual details can be useful. It may be important to consider how a space is laid out. How does one page link to another? What is the pathway through which one moves through different sites? What colors are used? How do the colors interact with one another? What images are used? Who or what are in the images? Close readings of each image may be useful as well as how the images interact with one another to produce the whole site. Does the design look professional or amateur? Is it regularly maintained or out of date? What links are there? How does one access those links? Are there advertisements? Are the themes of the advertisements similar or different from those expressed on the site? How can people access the site? Is it open to everyone or closed? If it is closed, what are the criteria for participation? Who grants permission? Is the site built for people to be able to add material or comments? If so, are there restrictions to how this is done? If so, who controls this process, and how is it communicated?

People: If it is a site or platform that allows for multiple participants, observing over time who participates, how they participate, and how people respond to others' participation can yield important information. Observing requires attention to temporal dimensions as well. When was the site created? How can you tell (or not)? When do various participants contribute? When do people respond? For example, if you are observing a social media or news platform, you may note not only *what* people post in response to a post but *how quickly*. If one hundred people post across one month, that may mean something very different than if one hundred people respond within ten minutes of a posting. Pay attention to what people post and how they interact with one another. If somebody posts something critical, followed by twenty people who defend the original post, followed by fifty whose perspectives are similar to the original criticism, that would be important to note.

As with in real life, it can be important to pay attention to demographics. In some virtual spaces, a good deal of information can be gleaned about participants' demographics through the presence of names, titles, occupations or affiliations to a variety of organizations, photographs, or conversation about different topics or themes. Sometimes, this level of detail is not available, but people's email addresses might use names, which could provide some, albeit incomplete and not necessarily accurate, information. In a social media site about African music, for example, people's usernames might give indications about whether participants are from an African country—if the researcher is familiar with name conventions—or from an English or French speaking background. And names might give some indication of gender if naming practices of particular cultural groups tend to be gendered. Yet, determining demographics based on names is inherently limited and will produce inaccuracies because linking names to nationality, gender, or ethnicity may be based in stereotyping or may not account for such things as complex naming practices, intermarriage, or false identification. And, guessing gender based on names often assumes a stricter gender name system than exists and does not account for gender queer and non-gender-binary gender identities. Furthermore, people can intentionally obfuscate their identities online by choosing pseudonyms, assuming an online identity that might differ from how they self-identify or are identified offline.

Researchers also sometimes assume demographic information about online participants based on their preconceived notions about who would most likely participate in a group. As with face-to-face fieldwork, it can be valuable to ask people questions directly about how they identify or to meet with people in person to learn more about the relationship between how they identify in a variety of spaces. The difficulty in determining who is participating in virtual spaces can be frustrating, but it is also indicative of why it is so important for folklorists and ethnomusicologists to study virtual spaces: the internet provides opportunities for individuals to engage in a much wider spectrum of identities and in a broader range of networks, expressive practices, and communities than is often possible in more restricted spaces in real life.

Interactions: As in real-life settings, taking note of interactions can be important. Who are the most frequent participants? How do they participate? What kinds of interactions take place? What kinds of judgments and values are expressed? How do people respond to these? Is there policing of content? Is it official, as in, does someone remove certain content? If so, how do others respond? Or does the policing happen more informally with other participants shutting the people down by telling them the post is inappropriate, or insulting them? Is there a culture of interaction? Some virtual spaces, for example, are characterized as supportive loving spaces whereas others are more vitriolic. Sometimes people post belligerent content on supportive spaces and vice versa or loving comments on aggressive sites. How do these interactions inform your understanding of the people and materials you are studying? Are people ever rejected? Why and how does this occur?

Multiple senses: Paying attention to a variety of sensory perceptions in virtual spaces can be illuminating. The visual is obviously prominent, but many sites now also include aural dimensions. What is the aural dimension? Who produced it? What does it "do" for the site? How does it interact with other dimensions? While touch is not possible, other than touching the screen, thinking about touch can still be significant. Pay attention, for example, to images of touch on the site, for example images of people hugging, people smoothing a ceramic pot, a video of someone beating a drum. Your own experience with touch will necessary inform how you experience and interpret what you see online. As an example, someone who posts a musical creation online may only give access to the visual and audio dimensions of the performance; however, in producing it, she would have experienced touching an instrument or recording paraphernalia, would feel the clothing on her body, and she might have felt cold at the time. All these feelings would have contributed to the audiovisual product that the fieldworker accesses online. Thinking about these dimensions of touch might deepen the fieldworker's engagement with the virtual product.

Emotion is also critical to research in virtual space. What kind of emotions are expressed and how? Look at images and audiovisuals presented. What is the tone of text? How are emoticons, capital letters, bold font, or different colors used? What kind of emotional expression seems to be condoned? Criticized? Rejected?

Relationship between "in Real Life" and Virtual Spaces?

As mentioned previously, many projects benefit from fieldwork in both physical and online sites because so many people and communities participate and interact in both (see Cooley, Meizel, and Wyed 2008). Garcia et al. explain that most internet phenomena have offline as well as online dimensions, and they found "very few research topics that justify limiting the field to online phenomena" (2009, 56). As mentioned already, scouring the internet for any information available about a topic you are studying in real life can be valuable for preparing you for research, developing cultural competency, learning about the topic, and developing contacts. Yet, the value can extend far beyond serving as preliminary research because for some research topics one might find that much of the activity and interaction that happens online integrates with what happens in real life, such that the two domains cannot be separated. A group of musicians who constitute a community in real life might share information, songs, ideas, evaluation on an Instagram site that informs and shapes what they do online and vice versa.

While there are plenty of virtual communities and activities that exist solely online, many also have a face-to-face component. A researcher might be interested in some type of digital artistic practice or in a community that was constituted online, and conduct research online using some of the methods described above. They might find that some of the participants in the virtual community live in proximity to each other and also have face-to-face relationships. Sometimes, virtual communities organize conventions or events that bring together members for in-real-life exchanges. In these cases, considering both the online and face-to-face and how they relate to one another could be valuable.

Even in situations where there is no real-life manifestation associated with your topic, a researcher may still find it valuable to do some face-to-face research. For example, a person researching an online musical scene might find it important to meet with people who participate for a face-to-face interview, observe them as they learn or train in the musical practice, observe them as they produce their music, or interact with them when they participate in online spaces. Or a fieldworker could sit with someone and share the experience of going through a website, listen to their comments and perceptions, and ask about how or why they chose to participate or respond in a particular way.

Conclusion

The nature of your project and your research questions will shape the settings for your fieldwork, whether you choose to collect texts or focus on context and process. Regardless of your goals, focused and detailed observation will yield critical information for understanding the folklore or musical form, how it operates in the world, how people interact with it, and its significance. Systematically writing detailed fieldnotes of all that you observe, experience, and think constitutes the data that will be critical as you proceed through the fieldwork process. We have scratched the surface with our explanation of approaches to observation and what one might pay attention to. In chapter 8, we continue this thread in our discussion of the process and importance of establishing relationships with people involved in the project and inserting oneself into the research situation as a participant as well as observer.

8

PARTICIPANT OBSERVATION

A FIELDWORKER WHO IS OBSERVING may be trying to be a so-called fly on the wall; however, the strategies described in the previous chapter nevertheless involve participation. The fieldworker is involved and interacting with some aspect of the setting using a variety of senses. In this chapter, we cover the method called participant observation, which can refer to this experiential component of the fly-on-the-wall approach, though it more often refers to active involvement in research settings and direct engagement with participants. After defining, we discuss how to introduce oneself, obtain permissions, establish rapport, and build relationships. The rest of the chapter delves into some of the methods associated with participant observation.

Participant Observation

Participant observation is based in the idea that we can learn the most in-depth and relativistic information about a community or artistic practice through active participation. As children, each of us learned our culture through socialization and enculturation, rather than direct instruction; we learned through doing, being, watching, listening, tasting, receiving feedback on our behavior, and so forth (see Dewalt, Dewalt, and Wayland 1998, 265). As we move through different cultural and social spaces throughout the course of our lives, we similarly learn what behaviors are appropriate and what is necessary for belonging largely through our involvement in new environments rather than by receiving explicit instruction.

Participant observation is an extension of this type of learning. To put it simply, it involves hanging out in settings associated with a project, while paying very careful attention to and documenting what we experience, think, hear, and feel. Participant observation may seem like a dressed-up way of referring to what we do anyway. However, when we do fieldwork, we participate and pay attention differently than most of us do in our everyday lives. As Dewalt et al. (1998) clarify, "All humans are participants and observers in all of their everyday interactions, but few individuals actually engage in the systematic use of this information for social scientific purposes" (259). They explain that "living with, working with, laughing with the people that one is trying to understand provides a sense of the self and the 'other' that isn't easily put into words. It is a tacit understanding that informs both the form of research, the specific techniques of data collection, the recording of information, and the subsequent interpretation of materials collected" (264).

Researchers who rely primarily on verbal descriptions or responses to questions, such as surveys, questionnaires, or interviews, obtain important information. However, much of life is not experienced or necessary reflected on or understood through verbal description. Dewalt et al. (1998) explain that "being actively engaged in the lives of people brings the ethnographer closer to understanding the participants' point of view" (261). By being with people on a daily basis and spending time with them while they do things related to the research topic, one can begin to understand something about the participants; how interactional webs are constituted; what is valued; and when, where, how, and why the artistic form is practiced.

The difference between "just" observing described in the previous chapter and participant observation is that fieldworkers are not only watching things happen around them but are also having a phenomenological experience. Think about standing on the periphery and watching a wedding. You see and hear people feasting, laughing, toasting, listening to music, dancing, and arguing. You would certainly obtain a lot of information from paying attention to and noting everything that happened. However, your understanding of participants' experience would be significantly enhanced if you yourself were sitting at the table, tasting the food, laughing, playing an instrument, talking about the ceremony, and feeling goose bumps as you congratulated the newlyweds.

Entering the Field and Identifying Contacts

One of the first things a fieldworker must do is to make contacts with individuals so as to begin to build relationships and gain access to fieldwork opportunities. Marcia Herndon and Norma McLeod (1983) explain that "if the first stage of field work is not successfully negotiated, the second stage—the time of tangible results—may never occur at all" (47). For some, making contacts will be easier because you may already be a member of the group or have prior relationships with members. Or your supervisor may have given you the names and contact information for people whom they want you to meet. For those doing research in a subject in which you have little familiarity, you will need to begin by developing initial contacts. This could involve attending events or going to places (physical or virtual) where people gather or where the creative form is typically practiced, and then slowly establishing relationships with those involved. For other types of projects, the first steps will involve establishing initial points of contact with individuals and then gaining access to activities relevant to the project's goals.

Finding initial contacts can be one of the most intimidating steps, especially for those fieldworkers who may be shy or anxious about introducing themselves to strangers. In our experience, most fieldworkers find that people are far more willing to participate than the fieldworker anticipates. Many folklore and ethnomusicology projects are about topics that are highly valued by individuals or communities. Those involved therefore are often enthusiastic about participating in a project about something they value. Even when a topic may not be about something that is necessarily cherished, many people enjoy that the fieldworker cares enough about them and what they do to take the time to learn about it. Let us be honest: many of us enjoy the opportunity to talk about ourselves. Lots of people are happy to tell stories and share their opinions and thoughts because they enjoy the attention.

For a class assignment, Gilman required each student to conduct an interview with a woman who came from a country other than the United States. Many students were intimated to initiate contact with someone they did not know, especially if they knew little about the woman's country of origin or the circumstances of her migration. They also worried about linguistic barriers. Despite their anxiety, the students were overwhelmingly positive about the assignment. They expressed that they learned a great deal and were grateful that they had been encouraged to step outside their comfort zone. Many of the women interviewed shared that they really enjoyed the opportunity to share their stories. Many felt isolated in the United States because no one, even members of their families, knew much about or seemed to care about their personal histories. One student who interviewed her grandmother told the class that her grandmother cried at the end of the interview. None of her grandchildren had ever asked about her past before.

Doing research with individuals and communities who have an online presence can facilitate this step. Making initial contact through email or other mediated channels can be effective and reduce anxiety because of the social distance afforded these forms of communication. In situations where phone calls are more appropriate, fieldworkers can often find numbers through online sources, newspapers, advertisements, directories, or from other people. In some cases, fieldworkers may not have access to online or phone communication or even any information about who might be relevant to contact. In these cases, we recommend attending events or showing up at organizations' headquarters, offices, or other relevant sites.

For those doing fieldwork in settings that are primarily online, entering the field may entail what we previously described as lurking or becoming an interactive participant in a community. Note that there will often be multiple sites for participating online for a single project. At some point in the process, the fieldworker introduces themselves to other participants and explains their motivation for participating. For some settings, a public announcement for potential participants is most appropriate. For others, sending messages to individuals with whom a fieldworker has already interacted and started to develop rapport, those who seem especially active, or those whose perspective is relevant to the project may be the most appropriate approach.

Fenn conducted fieldwork that explored the culture surrounding the designing and building of boutique guitar effects pedals. Through general internet searching he found a discussion forum that a prominent builder had launched. It was an active and dynamic space, frequented by builders and customers alike and open to the general public. After registering and lurking for a few days, Fenn contacted the builder who ran the space and outlined his project and goals. With her approval and encouragement, he then posted to a general discussion thread a message introducing himself and the project. The community responded positively, asking questions and offering ideas. Fenn was able to arrange several interviews from this initial post and continued to engage with users of the forum throughout the project.

Though potential participants might be willing to be involved once they hear about a project, do not be surprised if they are not motivated to respond to your phone calls or messages initially. The project and timeline might be very important to you; however, the potential participants often have far less, if any, investment. The fieldworker usually must take the initiative and follow up multiple times. Don't be discouraged if people do not respond. It does not necessarily mean that they are not willing to participate; rather, it often means that they were busy when they received the message or did not bother to record contact information. We recommend using direct forms of communication when possible. Sending an email addressed to an individual directly and then following up with subsequent emails, talking to someone on the phone, or meeting the person face to face can be much more successful than more anonymous invitations, such as posting on a listserv or social media site or posting a physical flyer. If you try a variety of methods and still are not successful, review how you are announcing or inviting participation. How did you describe yourself? How did you explain the topic? What assumptions were you making about potential participants?

Exercise

Consider the two introductions:

1. Hi, my name is Sonja. My professor is requiring that I interview a musician and write a paper. Are you available this Saturday morning?
2. Hi, my name is Sonja. I am very interested in Mariachi music because I grew up in a community where many of my friends' fathers played locally. Now, I'm in college at the University of Oregon and am taking a world music class. My professor asked us to interview a musician and write a paper about it. I thought this would be a great opportunity for me to learn more about Mariachi. I am hoping that I could come to an event where you are performing and also possibly interview you or one of the other members of your group. I have a lot of availability this weekend and would be grateful if you had time to meet with me some time.

Discussion

- How might the musician interpret each of these introductions?
- Which of these do you think would be more successful?
- How might you change each of them to be more effective?

Introducing Oneself

In your initial interactions with potential participants, remember that this is a first step in building a relationship. Think carefully about how you want to introduce yourself and explain your topic. Express your own enthusiasm and commitment while presenting it in an honest and engaging way. The goal is for the person to feel compelled to contribute some of their time to help you achieve your goals. Honesty is at the heart of fieldwork. You should be direct with people about both your own identity as a researcher and about your objectives. You should disclose your name, institutional affiliation, topic, and objectives. For those working for universities and other institutions in the United States or doing research in a foreign country, remember that you may have a review board that stipulates how you need to describe oneself.

Folklorists and ethnomusicologists typically prioritize developing or maintaining trusting relationships over obtaining information. Establishing trust initially can be especially tricky for online projects where the fieldworker does not have the benefit of introducing oneself in person, relying on face-to-face interpersonal skills, or relying on other aspects of communication and validation that happens when people interact in a physical environment. Providing information about oneself and links to sites that validate one's identity can be an effective means of building trust.

You should consider how to present yourself in a way that is honest, yet not off-putting. Being vague or inarticulate about your purpose may not entice someone to participate. Some might be put off by their perception of what the fieldworker is trying to obtain from them. For example, one folklore student interested in the cultural activities of a religious institution called the pastor of a local church in Eugene and explained that she was a master's student in folklore at the University of Oregon interested in doing research with the congregation. The pastor responded vaguely and seemed reluctant to meet. It took some sleuthing to find out that to the pastor, "folklore" referred to falsehoods that some people believed to be true. He was reluctant to meet because of his preconceived notions about the student's perspective on his religion. Once the student was aware of this problem, she was able to elucidate the discipline of folklore to him in order to dispel the misunderstanding. She explained that she was not studying the group's beliefs per se nor did she think that they were false. Rather, she wanted to research the cultural activities at the church that had an important role in community formation.

Other students have been intent on presenting themselves as professionals and so have emphasized their academic affiliation and credentials in their initial introductions or have used overly theoretical language. Doing so can be effective in some cases, especially when a contact values higher education or is sympathetic to student researchers. In other cases, this approach can create an immediate dead-end. For example, when a folklore student was doing fieldwork with homeless youth in Eugene, he did little to build trust when he sat down with a group of young men on a downtown street corner and provided his academic credentials. He was much more successful with another group when he presented himself, wearing worn jeans and a flannel shirt, as a person of a similar age who was interested in their lives. Telling them that his brother had recently been homeless, thus sharing the part of his life that had influenced his decision to pursue the topic, helped explain why he wanted to talk to them. He did not hide that he was a student, and he did explain later that he was hoping to spend time with them as part of a school project. However, he waited until after he had established an initial connection and started to develop a trusting relationship. Note the trial and error in these examples. Practice your pitch with classmates of friends, and if one strategy fails, try another,

Exercise

1. Divide into pairs.
2. Each individual jots down ideas of how they would introduce themselves for a current or hypothetical project.
3. Students practice introducing themselves to one another and share feedback.

When making introductions in written form, consider the tone of the writing. Overly academic prose with excellent grammar, scholarly jargon, and professional signatures might repel some people. Adapting the tone of your prose so that it resonates with the writing culture of the people with whom you are communicating might be more successful. Again, we highly recommend sharing or testing your oral and written introductions with peers or mentors prior to making fieldwork contacts.

Consent

Closely related to introducing oneself is obtaining consent. In chapter 4, we explained that some governments or institutions require fieldworkers to obtain permission prior to doing research in a particular setting. We also explained that US-based fieldworkers whose research is associated with federally funded universities may have to develop protocols for officially obtaining permission from participants, and that these protocols have to be approved by the university's Institutional Review Board (IRB). Those of you planning to deposit your materials in a repository will have to obtain the appropriate release forms from participants, as required by the archive. Provide copies of consent to the people who signed them so that they have a record of the agreement and the contact information for you, the fieldworker, and the institution(s) you represent.

Regardless of whether you are obtaining some type of officially recorded consent or something less formal, it is imperative that participants know why you are there and what you are doing and that they have agreed to participate. As you introduce yourself and become more involved, it is your responsibility not only to explain to people what you are doing but also to ask them explicitly if they are willing to participate. For some settings you will be able to obtain permission from every single individual involved. In some cases, however, explaining to every participant will be impossible. At large events, you may be able to observe, and interact with people, but it would not be feasible to explain your project to everyone present. Or even if you could talk to most people, it may not be in a context in which you could effectively present what you are doing. In such cases, there may be someone who is authorized to give permission, such as the manager of a bar where a performance is taking place, the owner of a website, the organizer of a festival, or a community leader. In some situations, fieldworkers can make a public announcement to solicit consent while introducing themselves and the project. When she was making a documentary and wanted to video record at large events, Gilman would often ask to make an announcement at the beginning. In addition to explaining the project, she would distribute consent forms and ask those who did not want to be filmed to let her know. In virtual spaces, a fieldworker can sometimes make a public post about the fieldwork objectives and then make consent forms available online.

Fieldworkers should obtain consent *prior* to recording an activity. Explain the project and ask individuals to sign or otherwise signify their permission before documenting the activity. In some cases, however, it may not be possible or appropriate to obtain consent beforehand. If this happens, make sure to follow through and obtain the permissions as soon after as possible. Keep in mind that the issue of permissions is especially important when one is recording identifying information, including names, images, the names of organizations or places, or descriptive details. If you observe people doing something or overhear a conversation, you can document this information in your fieldnotes and even sometimes present it in your projects without permission as long as you do not include any information that would make individuals identifiable, as we elaborate in later sections. However, if you do provide identifying details, it is imperative that you obtain consent.

Note that consent procedures are culturally specific. The types of documents required by US universities and archives full of legalistic text with signature lines can feel out of place in some settings. Sometimes, participants may not be literate, may not be literate in the language of the consent form, or may be suspicious about signing a bureaucratic document that gives others rights over their information. Ideally, field-workers obtain permissions in the manner most suitable to the fieldwork setting. Sometimes, however, they are required to fulfill their institution's requirements even if it is not culturally appropriate. In these cases, we recommend working with your institution to develop strategies that best meet the needs of all involved. If you are required to do something that does not fit with the fieldwork context, take the time to collaborate with participants to ensure that they understand the consent procedure and most importantly that they are aware that the process is intended to address ethical issues and to protect their rights.

The American Folklore Society (AFS) and the Society for Ethnomusicology (SEM) have position statements regarding research with human subjects that were created in response to the policies of university IRBs. See AFS's "Position Statement on Research with Human Subjects" online at http://www.afsnet.org/?page=HumanSubjects and SEM's "Position Statement on Ethnographic Research and Institutional Review Boards" http://www.ethnomusicology.org/?PS_IRB.

Rapport

Rapport is the word used for the trusting relationship between fieldworkers and practitioners. Rapport building refers to the process whereby fieldworkers and prospective project participants get to know one another, establish trust, and agree on some shared objectives (see Dewalt, Dewalt, and Wayland 1998). In long-term studies, a fieldworker might spend several months in the field establishing relationships prior to beginning the more focused fieldwork. For shorter timelines, rapport is established more quickly. Someone doing fieldwork to gather information about potential musicians to participate in a state's festival will not have the luxury of months of relationship building. Yet, their goal will still be to establish a sense of trust and shared goals with musicians prior to delving into more probing questions. The same is true of a one-hour interview, which may be the only extended contact between the fieldworker and interviewee. In these short interactions, the onus is on the fieldworker to explain what they are doing, demonstrate respect, and establish trust. The participants should feel that they are doing something worthwhile and valued. Rapport should be sincere and reflect a genuine relationship, as much as is possible. The fieldworker can help foster rapport by expressing gratitude, compassion, understanding, and later by sharing the work or benefits from the research.

Dewalt et al. (1998) give examples from anthropological literature of fieldworkers who "can point to a single event or moment when the groundwork for the development of true rapport and participation in the setting was established" (268; see Jackson and Ives 1996). Indeed, many of you may similarly enjoy what feels like a magical moment when you have broken through into being accepted by an individual or group or when you feel that your relationships have shifted from an outside fieldworker into a participating member. Many of you, on the other hand, might find that the process of relationship building develops over time. You might have different relationships with different members of a community, and the rapport-building process might be ongoing and continually shifting. All of these scenarios are normal.

Can you develop rapport with someone with whom you disagree? Much of the fieldwork guides for folklorists and ethnomusicologists are grounded in the assumption that rapport is an obvious goal because fieldworkers should have respect for all the people with whom they do research. After all, why would you not like a musician, storyteller, or tattoo artist? However, the idealization of rapport is based in the romantic notion that all expressive culture and all artists are inherently good and contributing positively to the world. In the past decades, more and more ethnomusicologists and folklorists have selected topics because of their interest in issues of social justice, gender inequities, conflict, racism, economic and political injustice, and other issues that may be controversial. And, of course, these issues have long arisen in research situations even when they were not the intended foci. The difference is that when a fieldworker's main lines of inquiry come out of these types of interests, fieldworkers might approach people fully aware that they could be critical of the topic or participants. This raises the question of whether fieldworkers can develop rapport with someone and be honest when they know that they might provide a perspective that conflicts with that of the participant. Can fieldworkers be critical of the same people who welcomed them into their lives or gave their time to contribute to the success of a project?

There are no easy answers to this question. Some fieldworkers feel that they have to choose topics that avoid these issues. Others feel that their goals as researchers or public cultural workers is explicitly to address difficult topics. Even those who try to avoid these situations, nevertheless, often encounter them (see Patai 1991). The authors' approach in situations where there are ideological conflicts between the fieldworker and participants is often to identify areas of commonality and reasons why we respect individuals even when we may not share all of their perspectives. We build rapport by emphasizing these shared dimensions and then work hard to try to understand participants' viewpoints. In our products, we attempt to present their perspectives respectfully even if we disagree, as we elaborate on in chapter 13. This approach does not eliminate the ethical issues nor ensure that everyone will be happy with the outcome. It does provide a way of thinking through and balancing the need to engage difficult topics and social issues while also being able to genuinely establish rapport and maintain respect.

Exercise

Can be done as an individual or in a group.
Reflect on the following:

1. A Euro-American male student in the United States is doing fieldwork on fraternity rituals and how they forge bonds between young men as they transition into adulthood. He observes during an initial encounter with a fraternity whose members are primarily Euro-American that they often tell racist jokes when they spend time together casually. The fieldworker realizes that these racist activities play a role in forging bonds and thus should be included as a theme in his lines of inquiry.

Discussion

- How should he explain his project to members of the fraternity?
- How should he address or respond to the racist joking?
- What strategies might he use to build rapport?
- What challenges might he face?

2. A homosexual male student is doing fieldwork with a musician whose music the fieldworker loves. While spending time with the musician, the woman continually tells stories about her granddaughter who she believes will go to hell because she's a lesbian.

Discussion

- Does the fieldworker tell the musician about his sexual identity?
- How should he respond to the homophobic comments?
- What challenges might he face doing this project?

In some cases, a fieldworker might choose to discontinue a project because of ethical conflicts or differences in perspectives. We return to this topic in chapter 11, "Issues in the field," in which we emphasize that although the potential conflicts we presented in this chapter are especially obvious, every fieldworker will encounter differences in opinions or values at some point. Each will have to deal with difficult ethical dilemmas that can make rapport-building challenging.

How to Do Participant Observation

As with many dimensions of fieldwork, providing guidelines for participant observation is challenging because it is so individualistic. You will each develop your own approach, and you may find that you do it differently in various settings and for different projects. We provide some guidelines about how to think about participating in a community and its activities, which types of activities might be useful to participate in, and some issues that could arise. Everything you learned in the previous chapter about doing systematic and detailed observation and writing fieldnotes continue to be applicable as you integrate participation into the process.

To begin, as already indicated, participant observation is basically "hanging out." Spending time with a group of people engaged in some type of folklore or musical practice should be fun and engaging. Yet, many of you will be surprised at just how hard and exhausting it can be to "hang out" in the name of research. You may have to stretch beyond your comfort level, do things that you find boring or that you would not otherwise do, or you may find yourself waiting around for hours for something to happen only to be disappointed that it was cancelled or someone did not show up. You may have to stay up later than usual or wake up earlier. And you will probably have to remember details when you are distracted or tired. You may at some point feel too hot or too cold, hungry or thirsty, or confronted with food or drink that is not to your liking. You may feel uncomfortable that you are pretending to be like everyone else when you are really noting everything down for possible future commentary or analysis. Despite these challenges, most fieldworkers find participant observation rewarding. For many of us, each new fieldwork experience is transformative. Fieldworkers often gain something personally over and above the immediate goals of the project and often develop lasting relationships

When to Participate

We will answer this question by thinking first about what type of targeted events and activities would be most relevant to a project and then broaden our recommendation to thinking about what aspects of the context would be important. Many fieldworkers, especially those who have the benefit of time, should participate in a range of activities that will provide them with general knowledge in addition to focusing on more targeted activities associated with their research questions.

Events and Activities

What types of activities and events are relevant to your project? Think both broadly and specifically. For those doing research on some type of music or other performance genre, you may want to participate in performances, rehearsals, organizing meetings, or informal time with the performers. Consider participating in instructional sessions when the performer is teaching or learning the artistic form. You may "hang out" at these sessions or participate as a learner, performer, or if relevant, an instructor. If you are doing research on some type of visual art, you may want to spend time with the artists as they are creating, discussing, exhibiting, selling, or learning or teaching the art form. For those topics that are not as formally organized, spend time in the setting in which the activity typically occurs. Those doing fieldwork on jokes would identify the types of settings in which people tell jokes. If you are doing research on foodways, spend time with people at the times when they are gathering ingredients, preparing the food, or consuming it. Some might do projects on topics, such as folk belief or aesthetics, in which there are no activities necessarily associated with the topic. You should identify settings that would be most relevant to engaging with people about it. Those interested in beliefs about the healing properties of certain plants, for example, might choose to go on a foraging trip with someone gathering plants or spend time at someone's home where they store the plants.

For those doing fieldwork in virtual spaces, identify what kinds of activities happen and which sites are relevant. If you are doing fieldwork on an online network of musicians or artists, where and how do people participate? Do they post things, or do they comment? In this phase of participating, it may be appropriate for the fieldworker to post something and track what kinds of responses they receive, or they may want to comment on someone else's contribution.

For many projects, it is valuable to extend participation beyond the obvious activities associated with the topic to other contextual dimensions. Someone interested in a type of music could select to only attend performances and then interview members of ensembles and audience members. These activities would yield valuable information. Extending participation to the rehearsals and the interactions of the musicians with their fans on social media would yield a range of information that would not be accessible from only attending the performances. During rehearsals, decisions could be made about who plays what parts, discussions over aesthetics and quality often happen, ensemble members might negotiate their relationships with one another, or costuming choices are made. All sorts of details that may be valuable to the research questions specifically

Figures 8.1 and 8.2. When Fenn was doing dissertation fieldwork with a Malawian musical ensemble called the Ghost Face Clan, he joined them at their rehearsal space on top of a hill above the neighborhood they all called home. Chilobwe, Blantyre, Malawi, 2000. Photo by John Fenn.

(Continued)

Figures 8.1 and 8.2. (*Continued*)

or to understanding how the musical practice fits into larger contextual questions will most likely emerge.

In addition to hanging out during activities that are directly associated with the topic, most fieldworkers engage in other activities with the people involved. One can learn a great deal by spending time with people as they go about their daily lives, spend time with friends, work, take care of families, play, or visit sick relatives. This time together can reveal information about how the research topic fits into participants' lives as well as information about their values, social and political perspectives, economic positioning, status within their communities, and all sorts of other things that may be illuminating for the topic. Consider, for example, a hypothetical project about sexist and homophobic jokes told by a group of male friends. If one only did research in the settings where the men gathered socially and told these jokes, the fieldworker might miss that one of the men is a single dad of daughters and is an active leader in his church where he is outspoken about gender equity. This information in combination with what the fieldworker observed in the joke-telling sessions would complicate the interpretation and yield a more nuanced study.

Hanging out in Larger Contexts

It can also be valuable to spend time in the locale participating in the everyday life of the community even when it does not involve interaction with individuals associated with a project. Such things as walking down the street, going to the park, using the bank, buying groceries, standing on a street corner, looking at homes, riding local transportation, or eating at local establishments can contribute to one's understanding of the locale, people, economy, values, and how it feels phenomenologically to be in those spaces. As emphasized in chapter 7, remember to pay attention to all your sensory preceptors. Consider the temperature, how your feet feel walking on the pavement, how the air smells, and what the food tastes like.

For those doing fieldwork in virtual worlds, similarly exploring and participating in sites beyond those that are the focus of your project will yield valuable information. You may find that participants in your project are active on other networks. Spend time with these other networks and learn about them experientially. Pay attention to how those in your project participate in these other spaces. How do your interactions in these different spaces relate to those you've had in the project site?

Participation Driven by Research Questions

Fieldworkers should also select activities for participation based on their research questions. How to identify relevant activities will vary based on your topic; here, we remind you once again that your lines of inquiry should be at the forefront of your planning and fieldwork. To continue the thread of the project about the group of men who tell sexist jokes, you would probably make different decisions depending on your focus. If your main line of inquiry had something to do with the relationship between misogynist joke telling and gendered behavior in other contexts, you would want to participate in both joke-telling situations and other settings where the men engage with gender dynamics. If on the other hand, your research question had to do with joke-telling sessions and the process through which one joke invokes others, you might focus your participation more specifically on settings where joking typically occurs. If you were interested in how jokes exist in variants and travel across time and space, you would come up with yet other contexts for participation.

Exercise

Divide into pairs. Each pair discusses each student's project (if they are working on one) or a hypothetical topic of their choosing.

Are You Welcome?

Part of the ongoing reflection required of fieldworkers is ascertaining whether one is welcome and how one is impacting the environment in which they are asserting themselves. It is normal to feel awkward and uncomfortable. Pushing yourself into uncomfortable moments and encouraging yourself to stay through them is often necessary, especially in earlier phases when the researcher is still developing rapport. Some of you will err toward being overly self-conscious. You might assume that people do not want you around, and you may unnecessarily avoid situations in which no one would have minded your presence. Others will err on the other end of the spectrum, assuming that your presence is accepted in situations where people may have preferred that you not be there. As with any social situation, it is impossible to always be sensitive to the appropriateness of your participation, yet there are some strategies that can be helpful. Prior to attending, gather information about the nature of a research situation, who typically participates, and how they participate. There may be events that are open to broad participation in which you might reasonably expect that no one would mind your presence. There may be other situations that are typically restricted to small numbers or certain categories of individuals, in which case it may be most appropriate for you to obtain permission or to check prior to deciding about whether to attend. Find out in advance if there are norms for behavior. For example, do people dress in a certain way? Are there certain individuals who you should greet or be introduced to? Will you be expected to contribute money or food? Is taking notes or photos appropriate?

As much as possible, your participation should demonstrate respect of the social and cultural expectations for the event. Approach "any particular situation with an open mind and a nonjudgmental attitude." Be aware and reflective about your presence because "a good fieldworker must react to the goings-on with sensitivity and discretion" (Dewalt, Dewalt, and Wayland 1998, 266–67). While you are participating, attempt to put aside your own agenda; pay attention to being where you are, and try to behave and understand what is going on around you respectfully.

Figure 8.3. In her fieldwork on dance and intangible cultural heritage in Malawi, Gilman benefited greatly from her relationship with Professor Boston Soko. He introduced her to people, invited her to events, and explained the cultural significance of what they observed. Here, they are attending the Ngoni Nc'wala harvest ceremony in neighboring Zambia. Chipata, Zambia, 2013. Photo by John Fenn.

Take advantage of your relationships. Many fieldworkers develop a trusting relationship with at least one "insider" or someone who is knowledgeable about the topic or community whom the fieldworker can rely upon to direct them. This may be someone the fieldworker knows outside of the research context—for example, a friend or classmate who is from the community or is a practitioner. It can be someone who is involved in the project more directly. Ask this person whether it is appropriate for you to attend an activity and whether they have guidance for how you should behave. In some cases, someone who is a member may be able to help you gain access.

Be patient. It may take time before you are welcome in certain settings. Doing some participant observation in more public situations where you have access first and moving toward more esoteric events after having developed relationships and trust among practitioners is often the best way to go. Some individuals or groups are frequently approached by fieldworkers and may be reluctant to participate. Accept that you will not be welcome in all situations. Be prepared that there may be some occasions where it is inappropriate for you to participate. Or, though people may say it is okay, you might feel that you do not seem to be welcome. As much as it may be useful to your research, you should respect what seems to be culturally appropriate or the boundaries participants establish.

What to Do When You Participate

What to do when participating will vary depending on your topic, relationship with the people involved, knowledge, and skills. Generally speaking, we recommend participating as much as is reasonable and appropriate. If you are researching a performance genre, you may be able to participate as a performer. However, there may be expectations or culturally bound traditions about who can participate or even be in the audience.

If it is not appropriate for you to perform, consider other ways of getting involved. You could help with logistics, advertising, bringing beverages to people during breaks, or helping them to document the event. Remember that being an audience member is also an active form of participation as is engaging in conversations about events before and after. If your participation is as an audience member, do what audience members typically do: clap, ululate, give tips, laugh, boo, smirk, or post images on social media. If you are studying humor, share your own jokes, pay attention to how people react to them, and note whether your jokes trigger others to tell their own. Share food with people. Ask to learn how to cook or try a new dance step. Often the more you are willing to do, the stronger your relationships will be, the more information and insights you will obtain, and the better your overall project will be.

Learning and Lessons

For some topics, a productive form of participation is learning or receiving instruction on how to do the thing you are studying (see Hood 1971; Kippen 2008; Slawek 1994). As you receive instruction, you might learn a great deal about what is considered most important—for example, the aesthetics of the art form and the process of teaching and learning it—and you will gain greater knowledge about the form. This strategy can be useful regardless of what skill level you have. Someone who already plays an instrument well and is familiar with the musical style will have an easier time joining an ensemble than someone who has never played the instrument or is unfamiliar with the music. Both will gain something from participating directly and in receiving guidance. Bear in mind, however, that "the responses of the teacher may be quite different toward an ethnomusicologist [or folklorist], or other outsider, than toward native students. Thus, if one of the goals of such instruction is to learn how a genre is taught within a culture, great care should be taken to establish any difference between the way an outsider is taught and the way an insister is taught" (Herndon and McLeod 1983, 80). This caution can be extended to any topic. Imagine you are learning to cook something within a community that is foreign to you. An insider may receive much more critical feedback about seasoning or texture, while an outsider might be directed based on the cook's assumption about the fieldworker's food preferences or taste palette.

Figure 8.4. Folklorist Cuixia Zhang's husband Gu Chengjie teaches Gilman how to make dumplings. He was very generous with his praise, despite the obvious superiority of the ones he made! Kunming, China, 2017. Photo by Cuixia Zhang.

Impacting the Situation

Many of you will be concerned that your presence and participation may impact the situation, wondering if what you have observed and experienced would have been different without your presence. It is true that fieldworkers affect what happens in a research situation. As mentioned previously, if you feel that your presence would change the environment so much as to make it impossible to do the research, you should reconsider the topic. In many cases, however, though a fieldworker's presence may affect the research setting, it may have less impact than they assume. Remember that social situations are inherently fluid and dynamic. What happens depends on who is present and what they do. Your presence may have an impact on what might have otherwise happened, but so would any number of other factors. There is typically no fixed way that things should have or would have been without you; rather what happens is dependent on the situational context of the occurrence. If your presence had an impact, you should be aware of the effect that you had, be honest about it, reflect upon it, document it, and share this information in your presentation of the materials. Often, this reflexive process yields deep insight.

Conclusion

This chapter built on the previous one in its discussion of the strategies associated with fieldwork, and the importance of social relationships and participating in the fieldwork process. Hanging out in many different settings, interacting with lots of different participants, and engaging in a variety of activities, always with the explicit permission of participants, will yield valuable insights. Keep your project goals and lines of inquiry in mind to ensure that you focus your activities as necessary to achieve your objectives. Always systematically document your experience through fieldnotes and other media. Remember that sometimes you will not be able to do what you had hoped and that unplanned for opportunities can be even more illuminating than those that were planned. And finally, as Dewalt et al. (1998) advise, realize that "everyone will make mistakes" and know that "most of these can be overcome with time and patience" (267).

9

INTERVIEWING

THIS CHAPTER IS ABOUT RESEARCH strategies that involve interacting verbally with individuals or groups with the explicit intent of gathering information. The strategies include informal conversations that happen "in real life" or virtually and interactions that are more explicitly framed as interviews, interactions with a single individual or situations where multiple individuals are brought together to answer questions and discuss a topic. In ethnographic fieldwork, interviews are usually used in conjunction with other methods, though on occasion they can be used on their own. There are many ways to design and conduct interviews and thus many different types. We will focus on how to use informal conversations and open-ended interviewee-driven interviews as research data. We also provide some information about follow-up, group, and feedback interviews because these are methods that are commonly used in folklore and ethnomusicological projects.

Informal Conversations

A big part of the experience of participant observation and where much insight can be gained are the informal conversations a fieldworker has or overhears while in the field. Informal conversations are one of the most valuable ways to learn about a topic, build rapport, and explore research questions. A conversation does not have to be explicitly structured as an interview to contribute to your project. While interacting with someone in person or virtually, something might come up, you might overhear a conversation or read something, or you might direct an interaction toward something associated with the project. When participants are aware of the fieldworkers' objectives, they often welcome these discussions and understand that they comprise part of the fieldworkers' information gathering. Always keep your lines of inquiry in mind. Remembering what you hope to learn from particular individuals can help you use this strategy effectively. You can raise topics that will help you answer research questions and lead to the project's objectives. Be sure not to overdo it. If you are hanging out with people and constantly expecting them to talk about your topic, you may find that they lose interest in spending time with you.

Obtaining consent can be confusing when the fieldworker is using informal conversations as data. It is unethical to record a conversation using audio or video recorders without participants' knowledge. If informal conversations are important to your information gathering, be honest with participants and explain to them that you are always doing research. Be explicit that you will be learning from both your informal and more formal research activities. Writing down fieldnotes about conversations for you to review in the future usually raises minimal ethical concerns *as long as you do not quote them without permission.*

You might have informal conversations with people you do not know. You might overhear something that is relevant in a conversation of which you are not a part. Or you may be part of a conversation that is relevant to your research, but it would be inappropriate to interrupt to explain that your involvement in the interaction is in your capacity as a fieldworker. Whether you could use this information is a big question. Some would say that you cannot use it because your research intentions were not disclosed. Others would suggest that you can write it down in your fieldnotes for future reference. These informal conversations could have a big role in shaping your understanding without being referred to or quoted explicitly. And, something overheard could inspire interview questions. If it is important to quote or to refer to an informal conversation explicitly in the future, then the researcher should think carefully about how to do so. If you want to provide the information and attribute it to the person who said it, you must obtain consent to do so. For example, if a researcher has been working closely with a musician, it may be easy for the researcher to present something that came up in conversation to the musician and ask for permission to use it. Another option is to present the information anonymously—for example, "in a conversation with members of the community, some stated. . . ." Be sure, however, that you do not provide information, such as names, physical descriptions, or idiosyncratic information about the person's social position, relationships, or occupation or that would make the person identifiable.

The *Smithsonian Folklife and Oral History Interviewing Guide* is an excellent and accessibly written resource about the basics of interviewing. It is available at no cost on the website of the Smithsonian Center for Folklife and Cultural Heritage (Hunt 2016).

Interviews

We cannot emphasize enough how important and central participant observation is to fieldwork methods. Gilman regularly teaches a fieldwork class and is used to students coming to her office, discouraged because they have not done any fieldwork. It frequently turns out that despite their frustration, they have done a great deal by spending time in relevant locations, attending events, lurking on internet sites, and having informal conversations with people. What they have not done is carried out formal interviews, which is what they perceive to be the *real* research. When it comes to fieldwork, this perception is inaccurate. All the activities the student has already done will produce a wealth of information; what they have already done counts as "data"—that is, as long as they have been systematic about maintaining detailed fieldnotes!

Interviews are valuable because they provide opportunities for focused conversations related to the research goals. Furthermore, people sometimes will discuss topics within an interview frame that might never come up in informal situations, such as those that are taken for granted, taboo, or typically silenced in participants' communities (Shuman 1986). Interviewees sometimes take on expert status in an interview, and these occasions can "afford tellability that might otherwise be restricted" (Modan and Shuman 2011, 14). For many projects, it is best to wait until you have started participant observation before delving into the interview phase. Doing so allows you to develop rapport before expecting anyone to share more personal details. It also enables the fieldworker to gain a deeper understanding of the topic, and thus develop better interview questions based on what has already been experienced and observed. For some projects, fieldworkers will begin interviewing early, often because of deadlines or expectations from instructors or supervisors.

Scheduling a Face-to-Face or Virtual Same-Time Interview

When you schedule an interview, explain the project, goals of the interview, and time expectation to the person you hope to interview. They should have some idea of the expectations before they agree to it. Sometimes potential interviewees request to be given the questions that will be asked in advance, which is fine to do. However, if you are planning to do an interviewee-driven interview, it may be more productive to give some examples that provide information about the scope of what you are seeking rather than giving a specific list of questions.

Where to Hold a Face-to-Face Interview

Be sure to find a place that is available and accessible to you and the person or people being interviewed. Ideally, it should be a place that is easy for the interviewees to get to so that you are requiring minimal effort on their part. If they need to take a taxi or bus, you should offer to pay for the expense, especially in situations where the interviewee has fewer resources than the fieldworker.

The location should be one that is relaxed, a place where you can spend the time without worrying about the appropriateness of being there and where there will not be too many distractions or interruptions. Make sure it is safe for everyone involved. If you do not know one another, it may be more comfortable and safer to be in public where others are present. Bear in mind that some public places are more welcoming or comfortable for some people than others, so be sure to be deliberate about identifying a place that you think will be welcoming for everyone involved. Though being in public may feel safer for some individuals and topics, in other cases finding a private space could be necessary. If the interview might delve into personal topics or emotionally difficult ones, identify a place that affords privacy while also ensuring everyone's safety, including your own. If you plan to record the interview, take into consideration whether recording or photography would be appropriate or possible. Would recording be allowed? Do noise levels make it possible to record audio? Would the light situation work for video? If you need electricity, would you have access?

Though we may think of interviews as framed interactions that should occur in comfortable places where people can sit together and talk with minimal distraction, for some projects and for some individuals, other kinds of interview contexts can be productive. Many folklorists and ethnomusicologists interested in process and aesthetics have found that it can be useful to interview someone while they are engaged in the creative form they are studying, for example, while they are making a basket, building an instrument, cooking, tattooing, designing a costume, or planning an event. Similarly, some have found that organizing the interview around some type of activity or examining something relevant to a topic can be useful. Some examples include asking a musician to listen and comment on a recording or having someone look at and respond to photographs.

Figure 9.1. Gilman video recorded an interview with a member of the Crochet 4 Community group at the Oregon State Correctional Institution while he made a hat. Salem, Oregon, 2011. Photo by Shelise Zumwalt.

Where to Hold an Online Interview

There are many ways to conduct an online interview, from using asynchronous media—for example, crafting a set of questions that is sent via email or is made available through an internet survey tool—to synchronous technologies, such as widely available video communication applications. Place is not a factor for most asynchronous interviews because the interviewer and interviewee have a lot of control over where they decide to create the questions or post their answers. Place may be more of an issue for certain types of synchronous interviews. For example, if the interviewer is sending questions or materials for consideration with the expectation of receiving immediate responses to which they can post the next question or material, then thinking carefully about place could be important. Both the interviewer and interviewee should ideally be in a location where they can focus and where they feel comfortable expressing themselves without worrying about interruptions. In some cases, they might want to make sure that no one comes and reads over their shoulder or otherwise sees the interview. In other cases, having other people around might be productive if their insights and perspectives can add to what the interviewee can or is willing to share.

If the online interview is conducted using audio or video, then both the interviewee and interviewer should select locations that are fitting for issues of privacy, noise levels, and time constraints. It might be suitable to use audio or video in a public place, such as a library or cafeteria, but there may be limits on how long it can be used. In preparing for the interview, think about what would be the best setting available to you and communicate your preferences explicitly to the interviewees so they understand the expectations and can find the most appropriate place.

Time and Face-to-Face Interviews

Schedule interviews at a time when you and the interviewee have adequate free time so that the interview can proceed in a relaxed manner and no one is hurriedly trying to get through it because of other obligations, the place is about to close, or the children are about to come home from school. We usually tell people that the interview will last around one hour, but that it may take longer. If you are interviewing with the help of a translator, allow for more time so that there is the opportunity for translation and additional explanations. As the interviewers, we always try to make sure we have two to three hours available. When interviews do extend beyond one hour, it is often because they are really dynamic and about especially interesting and relevant information. Interrupting someone's thoughts because of our time constraints can be interpreted as rude. And, you cannot count on the person necessarily making time again, that they would have the same inspiration to talk, or that the same information would emerge in a subsequent interview.

As with place, be attentive to restrictions or culturally acceptable ideas about time. If the interview is with young people, think about when they need to be home, at school, doing chores, or sleeping. If the interview is with someone who works or is responsible for preparing a family meal, suggest times that would be convenient to their scheduling needs. Always remember that the interviewees are generously offering their time; the fieldworker should be the one to be the most accommodating and considerate of their needs.

Time and Online Interviews

For online interviews in real time, the types of consideration described for face-to-face interviews are as relevant in terms of making sure that both parties have planned for enough time and that it works for everyone's schedules. Asynchronous interviews have the advantage that they can be carried out at the time convenient to each party. People who might not have time for a lengthy face-to-face interview may be able to participate and provide important insights into the project if given the opportunity to do so on their own schedule. However, it can also be challenging in that unlike in real life or a scheduled online interview, the interviewee may not respond in a timely manner or may answer a few questions and then disappear. The interviewee may also be participating at a time and place

Figure 9.2. Myra Tam translates during a group interview by the ChinaVine fieldwork team with artist He Xue-Sheng. Song Zhuang, China, 2009. Photo by John Fenn.

where they have a great deal of distractions or are otherwise engaged. Communicating explicitly about the expectations of an interview can help mitigate potential problems.

Sharing Cookies or Paying for Tea

If you are conducting an interview in a place that requires purchases, such as a restaurant, coffee shop, or bar, the fieldworker should typically pay for any costs. Some of you may be on a low budget, so take this into consideration when choosing a location. Will you have to buy something, and if so, can you afford it? Sometimes, the interviewee will offer to host. Follow what is culturally appropriate for the context of your project, and always err toward being as generous as possible. If you are holding the interview at your home, we recommend treating it as you would other social occasions. Consider offering something to drink or eat as is appropriate to the time of day. Do not worry that sharing food will overly impact the interview because it is quite common in many cultural contexts to talk over food.

If an interview occurs in the home of the interviewee, in many contexts, you can arrive empty-handed without raising attention since the interviewee knows that you are coming for the interview. They might welcome you with something to eat or drink, which you should accept graciously. In some cases, it might be appropriate to bring something to their home to express your gratitude or to follow local customs. As with all dimensions of fieldwork, do your background research to determine what is culturally appropriate.

What is an Interviewee-Driven Interview?

The basic premise of any interview is that it is an interaction that is framed as a special kind of communication event where one party in the interaction asks questions that the other answers. In unstructured or semistructured interviewee-driven interviews, the interview frame exists but it is less structured than are interviews where the interviewer asks a predetermined set of questions in a set sequence. Instead the researcher comes to the interview with some key questions or ideas about the types of information they hope to gather. They then ask open-ended questions that invite the interviewee to reflect upon, tell stories, or share ideas. The researcher listens to each response and then asks questions based on details provided in the answer. While following the threads of the responses, the interviewer keeps track of the information that they were hoping to obtain and guides the interviewee toward those questions while maintaining the conversational flow. The emphasis is *listening* rather than making sure that a set of questions is answered. In the discussion that follows, we are assuming a face-to-face interview. Similar strategies can be used for phone, online video applications, and text-based communication systems.

Many of us find this listening-driven strategy productive because folklorists and ethnomusicologists are usually trying to learn about how a cultural practice fits into social life and what roles and meanings it has for individuals. Following the train of thought and narrative trajectories of interviewees rather than using a predetermined list of questions allows the interviewee to share what they find to be most important and relevant, rather than what the fieldworker assumes might be most significant. If a fieldworker comes with a preestablished list of questions and only asks those, they might learn more about their interests than they do about the perspectives of the people they are interviewing. This strategy also allows for more sharing of power in the communication than some other types of interviews because the interviewee has the opportunity to shape the conversation by initiating topics, determining foci, or asking the interviewer questions.

We often compare this type of interview process to a conversation one might have with a close friend in which the aim is to find out about something that happened. Note, however, that how we engage in conversations is culturally specific, and that people in different communities have different ways of communicating (see Briggs 1986). The description here is based on a conversation pattern common in many communities in the United States. As you develop linguistic and cultural competency, you should adapt this technique to the setting in which you are researching.

As an example, consider a conversation between two friends (A & B) about a family argument that Friend B had. Friend A really wants to know what happened. While the two may be having a conversation about a variety of topics, Friend A may do most of the questioning and may keep the conversation focused on the conflict. Friend A could ask questions about specific details and invite and listen to long detailed answers. Friend A might start the conversation by asking an open-ended question, such as "Tell me what happened on Friday night?" or "I heard that you and your brother had a fight?" These questions would serve to frame and focus the conversation on the topic of the argument. Friend B might provide a detailed description of the argument and then sit back and sigh. Friend A, having listened carefully, might perceive that details were missing that would enable a better understanding of what happened. Friend A would then ask a follow-up question that would build on part of the story Friend B had already shared. Friend A might say, "Wait, so I get that you started fighting when you got in the car, but what were you fighting about in the first place?" Though the conversation is a dialogue, the frame shifts to a conversation in which one person is trying to get information from the other. Being familiar with this conversational frame, the "questioner" knows that in order to be a good friend and to elicit as many details as possible, they need to listen carefully to each explanation. Each subsequent question should elicit information to get Friend B to fill in gaps, elaborate, or continue the narrative. Sometimes the conversation may pivot to other topics, but eventually the questioner redirects the conversation to obtain the information they want.

Fieldworkers use a similar communication process when conducting open-ended interviews, with the exception that the interaction is explicitly framed as an interview rather than what we described above. Both parties have agreed to come together to talk about a particular topic with the shared understanding of who is the questioner and who is the respondent. The idea is the same. The interviewer asks a question or provides a conversational prompt, listens, asks follow-up questions, listens, asks for elaboration, and so on. Though this may sound quite simple, the job of the interviewer is challenging. The interviewer should keep track of what information they are hoping to gain while listening attentively to what they are hearing. Their follow-up questions should build from a response at the same time as they might veer the conversation to the information they are specifically hoping to get. Doing this type of interview effectively takes a lot of practice.

How structured an interview will be depends on the goals of the project as well as the goals for a particular interview. Sometimes in the early stages of a project, we focus primarily on open-ended interviews. As the project progresses or when we do follow-up interviews with the same people, we may need to get more specific information or fill gaps from the earlier interviews. We then shift to more structured interviews with an explicit set of questions to be answered, sometimes in a set sequence. On the other hand, for some projects, it might make sense to start with a survey or more structured interviews at the beginning while one is trying to gather enough information to create a foundation for the project, and then move toward less structured interviews later.

Beginning the Interview, Recording, and Consent

Always begin an interview by taking a few minutes for introductions, small talk, and making connections. This is important for setting the mood, building rapport, and ensuring that everyone is aware and comfortable with what is about to happen. The interviewer often sets the tone. Even if you are nervous, try to engage and relax. Sharing a joke or talking about current events can sometimes help everyone feel comfortable.

Before you launch into your questions, be sure to thank the person for their participation and explain again the reason for the interview and your objectives—even if you did so prior to meeting for the interview. Be as honest and clear as possible about your topic and goals without taking too long or going into too much detail. Make every effort to use language that will be understood by the interviewee, avoiding jargon that they might not know or might find off-putting. Be sure to ask the individual if they have questions or concerns and take time to address these. Explain that they do not have to answer any question that they choose not to and that they can stop the interview at any point. Let them know that they are welcome to ask you questions or inquire about your motivations for pursuing certain lines of inquiry at any moment during the interview.

If you are interviewing with a research assistant or translator, you each should introduce yourselves. If you do not know the language of the interviewee, make sure that when asking questions, you face the interviewee and direct your comments to the interviewee and not the translator. This will help establish rapport, and you will be communicating directly to the interviewee through your tone of voice, facial expression, posture, and gestures.

If you are planning to record the interview, using fieldnotes or audiovisual recording, ask permission to do so *before* you turn on any equipment or start to jot down information. Ideally, you should obtain permission before bringing out any recording equipment, though this might not be efficient if you need to set up the equipment and make sure it works in advance. Be explicit and honest about how you plan to use the recordings in the future. If the person is uncomfortable, take the time to answer their questions and concerns. If they still do not feel comfortable or object, then *you should not record.*

Many university Institutional Review Boards (IRBs) require field-workers to obtain consent prior to an interview. This can involve the interviewee giving verbal permission or signing a formal consent form. Explain that by providing consent orally or on a recording, the participant is giving permission to use the material, and that you will respect how they specify that they want to be identified or any restrictions they put on its use. We recommend that you do not bring out the form until you have had a conversation about your goals and what the interviewee is agreeing to sign. If you are using a form, be sure to bring two copies, one for you and one for the interviewee. As mentioned previously, this will ensure that the interviewee has a record of the agreement and has your contact information as well as that of relevant institutions, such as a university, arts organization, or archives. As we discussed in the previous chapter, obtaining signed consent in folklore and ethnomusicology fieldwork situations can seem awkward given the informal nature of the relationships that often characterize our projects. In our experience, as long as we are respectful and clear about the reason for the form, participants have been willing to sign the form and often appreciate our concern for ethics.

Sometimes, especially when our research topics elicit personal or sensitive information, we suggest waiting until the conclusion of the interview to obtain consent. Asking for permission before the interviewee knows what information they shared can sometimes seem inappropriate. Waiting until after the interview ensures that the interviewee knows what they have said and what they are agreeing to let you use. It also enables them to specify whether there are details they do not want made public. Even if you do obtain consent at the beginning of the interview, always review the consent procedure at the end after they know what they have said. Ask if the interviewees still agree to the terms of the consent form and whether they have any additional restrictions to how their information could be used.

What to Ask

In preparing for this type of interview, the fieldworker creates a set of prompts or topics about which they want to elicit information. Below is a list that Gilman used for her interviews with US veterans for her project *My Music, My War* (2016).

- History of military experience?
- How prepared for music for deployments?
- Content of playlists?
- When listened to music?
  - Music during work time?
  - Music during leisure?
- With whom listened to music?
  - Private versus collective listening?
- Music and gender?
  - Articulations of masculinity?
  - Relations of men and women?
  - Experiences with homosexuality?
- What happened when returned?
- Memories tied to music?
  - Trauma and music?

Notice that this is a list to remind her of the information she hoped to obtain rather than the specific questions she would ask. During the interview itself, Gilman asked questions to elicit details about these topics. For those who are nervous about crafting understandable questions spontaneously during an interview, you can craft questions in advance. However, be prepared to use these flexibly. You may find that you ask some of the question verbatim, but that you deviate for others in order to follow the flow of the conversation.

Guidelines provided in *Folklife & Fieldwork* (Winick and Bartis 2016, 17)

Keep your questions short and avoid complicated multipart questions; the interviewee can only answer one thing at a time.

- Never ask questions you don't understand; if you're pretending to know more than you do, your interviewee will probably see right through it!
- Avoid questions that can be answered with a "yes" or a "no"; you want their answers to be full of stories and explanations.
- Avoid leading questions or ones that already suggest an answer; your interviewee may give you the answer you seem to want instead of the answer they think is true.
- Don't begin the interview with questions about topics that are controversial within your interviewee's community; it's best to have a rapport with

the interviewee before tackling more controversial subjects, and controversy can sometimes cause an interviewee to stop talking altogether!
- Don't worry about pauses. You may be asking about a topic the interviewees haven't thought about for many years. Give them time to reflect and formulate their response.
- Somewhere between twenty and twenty-five questions is usually a good number for an interview of about an hour. With this in mind, finalize your list. (If you have a lot of questions, bring them all but be aware you may have to schedule a second interview.)

In order to establish the interview frame and ensure that important demographic information is collected, we recommend starting an interview with a set of focused questions to gather metadata and document demographic and other specific information about the interviewees and their engagement with the topic. These could be questions about the interviewees' full name, age, demographic information, place of residence, nationality, and so on. In addition to these questions, most of you will want to include some more specific questions relevant to your project. If one is interviewing a musician in a band, for example, the name of the band and instruments played might be relevant. If one is interviewing a youth about children's hand clapping games, the name of the school the child attends or the neighborhood in which they live could be relevant. In Gilman's research with US troops, she collected information about the branch of the military in which the interviewee served, their years of service, their rank, and their job in the military in addition to their name, gender, age, nationality, ethnic identity, and place where they grew up. She knew she might need this information as metadata and to contextualize and interpret the interview later. She also found this information invaluable during the interview itself, which is why she collected it at the very beginning. Knowing at the outset that someone had served at a particular rank in the navy at a specific time enabled her to ask open-ended questions that were appropriate to that individual's personal history.

We recommend gathering more information than you think you will necessarily need. You cannot always predict how you will use your data or what contextual information will be necessary in the future. Being thorough and detailed at this phase can save a great deal of time and headaches later. Each fieldworker should think carefully about what kind of information they need and try to gather it at the interview. You should never assume information about anyone, and it can be difficult or even uncomfortable or inappropriate to obtain the information afterward.

The beginning is also a good time to obtain the interviewees' contact information. We often ask the interviewees to write down (if they are literate) their full name, title (if relevant) and contact information. This ensures that we refer to them correctly during the interview, have the correct spellings, and that we do not forget to collect this information at the end of the interview. It is a good idea to obtain as many different types of contact information as is possible to best ensure that the interviewer can send a note of thanks after the interview, follow up with the interviewee, contact them for feedback interviews, ask for permission for additional uses of the material, and most important, provide them with copies or access to the products in the future. Depending on what kinds of communication media are used by participants, consider noting down phone numbers, email addresses, and mailing addresses in addition to web addresses or information about social media participation. Do not expect to rely on whatever means of communication was used in making initial contact. People tend to change addresses and numbers over time. They may discontinue using a particular medium, or it may no longer exist in the future given the rapid changes in communication technologies. You should also provide them with your full name, title, affiliation, and multiple forms of contact information.

Starting the interview with these detailed questions helps to shift the event from informal talking to the interview frame. It also can contribute to developing rapport. However, some fieldworkers might find that asking these questions up front does not work well because they can be off-putting or create too much social distance. All interviewers eventually figure out what works best for them, and they often shift strategies for different interviews. Practice is the best way to develop your own personal style. Each interview will serve as practice in and of itself. We also recommend practicing with people you know so that you start to feel comfortable with the format, listening, and asking questions prior to doing so for your project.

After these structured introductory questions, we recommend that the first interview question be open-ended to give the interviewee the opportunity to tell you something about themselves and their engagement with the topic. In Gilman's research about veterans' musical listening, after having asked for the specific details mentioned above, she began with an open question: "Can you tell me about your service in the military—for example, when did you join, how long did you serve, and where did you serve?" This question usually elicited important information for her project and yielded lots of details from which she could build in her subsequent questions. It also gave the interviewee a great deal of control and freedom about how they wanted to respond and often elicited interesting stories. It was also a very broad question that could easily have taken hours to answer. Her objective in asking this huge question was for the interviewee to provide her with background information and set the tone for the interview so that she would know enough to be able to ask more directed questions. Once the person came to a stopping point, she directed the conversation with subsequent questions that elicited the type of information she wanted. For example, if it came up in the answer that the person had joined the US Army right after graduating from high school, she could then ask an open-ended question about how they would describe their musical listening in high school prior to joining the army.

Adapting for Email or Other Asynchronous Interviews

Often when we do an interview by email, the interviewer and interviewee may be participating at different times from one another, making it inefficient and less effective to do the kind of questioning that relies on one question being asked at a time. When doing an email interview, you can adapt the above strategy by beginning with the same fixed demographic/specific questions, and then asking four to five open-ended questions that cover the scope of your project. Asking more than that in one email can be overwhelming for the interviewee and gives the interviewer less opportunity to ask for expansion or clarification as they receive the information. After obtaining the responses to the first set of questions, the interviewer can follow up with another three to five, building on details in the responses as they would in a face-to-face interview. At some point in the process, switching to another medium of communication for part of the interview can be productive. We recommend the website www.ethnographymatters.net for additional resources about conducting online interviews.

Crafting Open-Ended Questions

In asking open-ended questions, the goal is to elicit a story or longer answers with lots of details rather than short ones that dead end.

Consider the two prompts below:

1. Who taught you to make instruments?
2. Tell me how you learned to make instruments.

The first is less open-ended than the second. It could elicit an explanation of how the person learned to make instruments and who their instructor was. It could also elicit a one-word response, such as "my mom," or "Elijah," which would then require the interviewer to follow up with a broader question. The second one, by contrast, would elicit a more detailed narrative that should provide both important details to the project and enough threads for a number of follow-up questions. If the interviewer was interested in the identity of the instructor and that detail did not come up, then they could easily ask a follow-up question about who specifically taught them. They could phrase the question in response to something already said, such as "You shared that everyone in your family made instruments and that you learned from older members. Was there someone in particular who taught you?" They might answer "my mom." This one-word response could then elicit a follow-up question about the person's relationship with their mother or gender roles in this instrument-making community or anything else relevant to the project.

In developing the open-ended questions, be sure not to include the answer in the question. The idea is to ask a question that does not presume the response and that will elicit a long answer and even a story rather than a short one or two-word response.

Consider the two examples below:

1. Why do you like making instruments so much?
2. How do you feel about making instruments?

The first question presumes that the interviewee likes making instruments and that they like it "so much," which may or may not be how the interviewee feels or would describe their attitude toward their craft. The second question is better because it allows the interviewee to describe for themselves and in their own words how they feel about making instruments. Consider the prompts below, in which the assumption may be less obvious:

1. Tell me how you first became involved in instrument making.
2. Tell me what it was about instrument making that inspired your passion.

Both of these are broad questions that invite a person to share something about their life and what led to their instrument making. The first does not imply anything about the individual's relationship to the craft other than that the interviewer knows that they make instruments. The second question would probably invite a long answer, but it presumes that the interviewee is passionate about their craft, which may or may not be true. The word "passion," is also a value-laden word that can mean many different things to different people. This question would be most appropriate if the interviewee had used the word "passion" in their self-description, which then could elicit a second question. If in answering how they felt about their craft, they said, "I've always been really passionate about making instruments," then the interviewer could ask what it was that inspired the passion or what they meant by "passionate."

Listening

Listening is crucial for this interview strategy. In their essay, "Learning to Listen: Interview Techniques and Analyses," Kathryn Anderson and Dana C. Jack write about effectively doing oral history interviews with women; we have found many of their insights to be invaluable for doing research with people of all genders. They recommend a "shift in methodology from information gathering, where the focus is on the right questions, to interaction, where the focus is on process, on the dynamic unfolding of the subject's viewpoint" (1991, 23). Anderson and Jack provide many useful strategies for improving listening skills. We recommend you read their essay in full, here we share only some of the strategies.

According to Anderson and Jack, the best interviewers pay attention to emotional expressions as well as verbal ones. They recommend listening carefully for silences, nonverbal expressions, and emotionally laden language. Do not assume the reasons for the emotional expressions; rather, listen for them and ask for elaborations or clarifications as appropriate. Doing so often elicits the most important and thought-provoking information.

Anderson and Jack summarize three ways of listening that can sharpen one's awareness of the feelings that might lie behind an "outwardly conventionally told story: (1) listening to the narrator's moral language; (2) attending to the metastatements; and (3) observing the logic of the narrative" (1991, 24). The authors explain that "incorporating these insights has helped us learn how to remain suspended and attentive on a fine line between accomplishing our research goals and letting the subject be in charge of the material in the interview" (24).

One of the most effective ways to build these fine-tuned listening skills is to listen to your interview recordings and review your interview transcripts. Note instances where you feel that you did a good job, really listened to your interviewee, allowed for pauses, and followed their train of thought. Pay attention to silences, expressions of discomfort, metastatements, references to emotions, and laughter. What do they seem to be expressing? What assumptions are you making? What was your response or next questions? What might you have done differently? The more you practice, always reflecting on what worked and what could be done better, the better interview skills you will develop.

Go with the Flow

Describing this process makes it sound more complicated than it is. Remember our earlier explanation that it is similar to a conversation with a friend in which you are trying to elicit specific information. The conversation might proceed with a focus on the desired topic until you feel that you have obtained enough information to understand what happened, support the friend, or whatever else motivated your interest. Similarly, in an interview, the job of the interviewer is to be an engaged and attentive listener who asks follow-up questions that proceed from the answers given. This process continues until either there is no more time, or the interviewer feels that they have obtained all the information they hoped for and the interviewees feel that they have shared everything they wanted about the topic.

As with all aspects of fieldwork, try to relax and be flexible. All too often, the interviewer is so intent on asking questions that they miss important information or forget to pay attention to what is most important to the interviewee. Remember that the objective of folkloristic or ethnomusicological ethnographic research is to try to understand people and their engagement with expressive practices from their point of view. Relinquishing control and allowing the interview to emerge collaboratively with an emphasis on the interviewee sharing with you what they think is significant can be gratifying. That said, a fieldworker should also keep their objectives in mind and redirect or refocus the conversation when it has veered too far off track. Overall, enjoy the discussion because every interview is an opportunity to connect with and learn from someone who is willing to share something.

Exercise

1. One student agrees to be interviewed about something of their choosing [let the interviewee select topic to ensure appropriateness], and another student volunteers to be the interviewer. Set up two seats in front of the room.

2. The interviewee leaves the room.
3. The remaining students devise four questions to elicit the information about the topic.
4. The interviewee returns, and the interview is conducted in front of the class. During the interview, the students in the audience jot down notes about strengths and weaknesses.

Discussion about the interviewer

- How did the interviewer feel about the process?
- What strategies did they use to elicit information?
- How could their information-gathering have been improved?

Discussion about the interviewee

- How did the interviewee feel about the interview?
- Did they provide the information that was hoped for?
- What did they express outside of their verbal responses?

General question

- How did the setting of the classroom impact the interview?

Final Questions, Consent, and Other Contacts

We recommend ending an interview by asking if the interviewee has anything more to share or has any questions for the interviewer. Then ask the interviewee to reflect on the interview and let you know whether they feel comfortable having you use what they have said. Be specific about your plan and be sure to consider all the possibilities for future uses (even if you explained them before the interview). Uses could include placing transcribed quotes in a publication, using parts of an audio recording in presentations, referring to details in a blog, integrating footage into a video, selecting bits of transcribed text for an exhibit, or depositing recordings and transcripts in an archive. Sometimes interviewees consent to having their information shared, but do not want their names used or want specific details omitted. Be sure to document this information carefully so that you can respect their wishes. Review how they want to be identified: full name, first name, pseudonym, or anonymously. If the interviewee signed a consent form before the interview, confirm with them whether they have changed their mind now that they know what information they have shared.

We also recommend asking the interviewee whether it would be okay for you to contact them with any follow-up questions or a second interview. In addition to obtaining the desired information, asking this question when you are together can help alleviate anxiety on the fieldworker's part about inconveniencing the person should you need additional information. This question can be illuminating because sometimes interviewees express enthusiasm for the project and share their interest in contributing to it in the future, in which case you know that they will probably be generous with their time and information as the project progresses. On the other hand, it could also give them an opportunity to express reservations or concerns.

If the fieldworker is still in the process of trying to identify other participants, ask for recommendations of others to interview. This process is called snowball sampling: one contact connects the fieldworker to another who leads them to several more. If they do have suggestions, be sure to obtain the full names and contact information at that time so you do not have to track down the person again. If appropriate you might ask the interviewee if they would be willing to make the introductions.

You could also ask about relevant events or activities that you could attend. Be sure to note down all the details about time, place, cost, and whether you would be welcome. In addition to eliciting information about opportunities, these questions also communicate your interests and enthusiasm. In our experience, we have often received invitations as a result of these questions that have led to interesting fieldwork experiences.

Expressing Gratitude

Always end an interview by expressing gratitude and being explicit that you gained a great deal from the experience. Remember that the person took time to participate and has generously responded to your questions. Sometimes interviewees will be self-conscious and will ask if they have responded well or will apologize for not being articulate or otherwise not being "good." Sometimes those who are the most self-conscious have shared some of the most articulate and insightful information. Regardless of your assessment of the value of what was said, assure them that the interview was helpful and that it contributed to your knowledge and understanding. We recommend sending a thank you message after the interview. Taking a moment to send a card, email, text, gift, visit, or whatever else is appropriate for the cultural context can go a long way toward letting the person know how much you appreciate them and making them feel that their time was well spent. It also contributes to rapport building and can be important to your success in interacting with this and other individuals in the future.

Follow-Up Interviews

Fieldworkers often find value in doing multiple interviews with the same person. Sometimes time constraints during the first interview limited the amount of information covered, and a second interview is useful for continuing the conversation. Frequently, as research progresses, new themes or questions emerge as important. Or, in the process of creating a final product, more information about a topic or from an individual becomes important. Depending on the nature of the project and the information needed, follow-up interviews can happen in person or using other media.

Follow-up interviews can take many shapes. While we may have been interested in learning about the individual and the topic in a broad way in the initial interview, we often create more structured questions for follow-up interviews aimed at obtaining clarification, more information, or eliciting stories. We usually review interview recordings or transcripts carefully first to ensure we remember what an individual shared already and to make sure that we develop questions based on what we already know.

Group Interviews/Focus Groups

Interviewing more than one person at a time can be an effective strategy for gathering information from multiple people in a short amount of time. It can also be productive when interviewees' answers inspire stories and answers from one another. For example, an interview with only one musician will yield information that the individual recollects or is willing to share during an interview. An interview with members of a musical ensemble, however, could elicit a wider range of information. One person might add to another's memories, interviewees might correct one another, or one person's answer might remind someone of a funny story. Much can also be gleaned about social relationships and hierarchies during group interviews as well as cultural modes of communication and information sharing. Pay attention to who answers first, who interrupts whom, who tells the stories, who makes the most jokes, who rephrases the questions, who corrects whom, and so on.

Some topics lend themselves well to group interviews because individuals might be more likely to talk about certain topics when other members of their communities are present. In Gilman's research with combat veterans for the documentary *Grounds for Resistance*, she had conversations with participants about trauma and post-traumatic stress disorder (PTSD) when the camera was not on. However, it was challenging to find an appropriate way to video record interactions about this topic because it was sensitive and emotional. With the help of participants with whom she had good rapport, she eventually brought together a group of veterans to discuss their struggles with PTSD, which she was able to record. Because they were used to talking about these emotionally laden experiences with one another, she found that despite the camera, participants were willing to share their experiences. The result was much more informative and powerful than would have been attempts to video record interviews with individuals.

Conversely, group interviews sometimes can be limiting. Some individuals might dominate for any number of reasons. Status differentials can contribute to some individuals participating more than others. Some people may be shyer or may not feel comfortable sharing their perspectives in front of others. And, if the interviewer does not already have a relationship with participants, it can be harder to develop rapport with a group than with one person. If a group interview does not yield the desired result, one can often follow up with interviews with individuals. In such situations, we recommend being positive about the group interview and explaining that you want to talk to individuals to clarify or expand on things said during the group exercise, rather than indicating that the group interview failed.

Feedback Interviews

Feedback interviews refer to opportunities to share research data and findings with participants in order to receive feedback, obtain additional information, and formulate further ideas and analyses. In the following quote, Ruth M. Stone and Verlon L. Stone (1981) explain the value of using feedback interviews.

> Given our concern for the meaning constructed by the participants in a music event, we find that the feedback interview offers some fruitful ways of getting at this problem. For example, the research can begin with two assumptions: (1) affective and nonverbal behavior are human modes of communication, and (2) these behaviors, as well as much cognitive and verbal behavior, operate on a nonreflective level. To study these behaviors, the researcher attempts to make communication that takes place on a nonreflective level problematic so that the participant has to bring it into awareness in order to think about or discuss it. (221)

Stone and Stone refer to strategies to inspire participants to put into words meanings associated with music that might not be at their level of awareness. Feedback interviews are useful for those interested in meaning-making more generally and for obtaining other types of information. Some examples include:

- An interviewer provides an audio recording or transcript of an interview to someone they interviewed. They meet to discuss the interview

- A fieldworker shares still photos with participants and asks about details in the images
- A fieldworker shows video footage of an event to the event participants and asks them to explain and reflect on what is occurring in the footage.
- A fieldworker plays an audio recording of a musical performance to the musicians and asks them to explain
- A documentary filmmaker shows a rough cut of a video to the people in the video for their feedback and input
- An author shares an essay, book, or other written document to the people featured in it and invites feedback
- A cultural worker creating an interactive online exhibit meets with participants to explore the exhibit and elicit feedback
- A museum worker invites participants to view an exhibit prior to its completion and invites feedback

In the first examples, the fieldworker invites the feedback on the raw data before drafts of final products are created. Note that there are many ways of eliciting information. One can take advantage of the capacity of the technology used to record the fieldwork activity. In sharing raw data, for example, the fieldworker could slow down playback or move through the data frame by frame in order to elicit explanations about details that would otherwise not be addressed. One can ask questions about visual, audio, interactive, or emotional dimensions. Documenting what happens in a feedback interview with recording technology enables a fieldworker to review the interview later. In addition to the participants' verbal descriptions and explanations, emotional, kinetic, or interactive responses are often important (see Stone and Stone 1981). This process of soliciting feedback can be invaluable for increasing participants' opportunity to participate and clarify their perspective, increase the fieldworker's understanding, build rapport, and address problems and inconsistencies. Charles Briggs (1986) importantly reminds us that the material obtained during the feedback interview should not be used to replace the original material, but rather should be used in dialog with it. Do not change or get rid of the original documentation of the fieldwork activity, but rather keep both the original and the documentation of the feedback activity and consider the combination as your data.

The last examples are different in that they provide opportunities for participants to contribute their perspectives and insights to the creation of the final product, which allows for collaboration between the fieldworker and participants, often producing far more nuanced end products. These last examples can also lead to complicated power dynamics between the researcher and researched in terms of who has control over the focus of a final product, who gets to select what is presented and how, and who has interpretive control, a topic we return to in chapter 13.

Figure 9.3. Folklorist Kelley Totten shows a member of the Oregon State Correctional Institution's Crochet 4 Community group a photograph she took to find out if he would approve its use in the "Hooks, Yarns, and Bars" exhibit the team was planning. Salem, Oregon, 2011. Photo by Shelise Zumwalt.

Exercise: Feedback Interview

If video equipment is available:

1. One person (can be instructor) videotapes three to four participants in a class or workshop doing an activity together for five minutes. (Suggestions include singing a song, sharing jokes, or one person teaching the others a children's game.)
2. Show the footage to the group.
3. One or more participants asks those who were involved to explain what was documented in the video. Some possible questions would be about the tonal quality, what someone was thinking at a particular moment, evaluation of quality of performance, or the meaning of a word.

Discussion

- What is the value of this method?
- What are its limitations?

If video equipment is not available (this is also good exercise to do in addition to the one above):

1. Divide into pairs.
2. One person interviews the other for five minutes on a subject agreed upon by both participants.
3. The interviewer writes a description of the interview.
4. The interviewee reads the description.
5. The interviewer asks the interviewee questions about the documentation. Some possible questions would be about accuracy, feelings associated with things that were said, and meanings associated with value laden words.

Discussion

- What is the value of this method?
- What are its limitations?

We encourage you to experiment with different types of feedback interviews and reflect on their value. For more information about using feedback interviews, see Stone and Stone, 1981; Stone and Stone-MacDonald 2013; Borland 1991; Briggs 1986; Lawless 1991.

A Brief Comment on Surveys

Ethnographic research has typically focused on direct interactions between fieldworkers and the people whose practice they are studying rather than using questionnaires or surveys, which are often intended to produce quantitative rather than qualitative data. However, these research tools can be effective for certain types of research projects and are often used in combination with the more typical fieldwork methods.

A survey is an instrument used to gather information from a large number of individuals who all answer the same set of questions. Surveys can be useful for gathering demographic information; contextual information about a practice; identifying patterns in attitudes, participation, or practice; and insights into values or aesthetics. Sometimes in the early phase of a project, fieldworkers distribute a survey that helps launch the project. At the end of the survey, they can include questions about whether the person would be willing to participate in a follow-up interview or if there are upcoming events relevant to the topic. The survey results provide the fieldworker with some preliminary information and it can help them determine whether to contact the person for a more indepth interview. It can also be useful for identifying a potential focus for a project. Much has been written about developing survey questions, so we will not replicate that information here. If you are interested in designing a survey, we recommend that you look at available instructions and tools to guide you (see Weller 1998).

If you are doing research with people who have access to the internet, free or inexpensive tools exist that can be used to create online surveys and to organize and analyze responses. Tools exist for both quantitative and qualitative questions, and a combination of the two can be useful. We do not provide the names of specific programs because of the rapidity with they tend to change. A few minutes searching "free survey tools" on a search engine should produce some options. Reviews about the efficacy of different programs are also typically available online.

Conclusion

We have provided a great deal of information about gathering information learned through informal conversations, conducting open-ended interviewee-driven interviews, group interviews, and feedback interviews. There are many other interview techniques that can be equally valuable in ethnographic research. For the novice we encourage focusing your energy on one or two interview methods and then broadening your scope to others as you develop competency. No one is a perfect interviewer and no interview is flawless. Interviewing is one of those skills that fieldworkers continue to develop, adapt, and change over time. We recommend you listen to recordings of yourself in interviews and reflect on what strategies you used, how well you listened, what you did well, and what you could do better. As you do so, be easy on yourself. Be critical, but do not get discouraged. You will probably be your own biggest critic. Remember that the goal is not to ask beautifully crafted questions but to elicit thoughtful answers. If you received insightful responses even though you feel that you bumbled, be assured that you were successful.

10

DOCUMENTATION

IT IS CRITICAL THAT FIELDWORKERS be conscientious and systematic about writing fieldnotes while they are in the field. This can often be an exhausting enterprise. At the end of a long day of participating and observing, trying to fit into various cultural situations while paying attention to everything and anything, the last thing you might feel like doing is spending several hours writing up everything. However, if you fail to do so, it likely that you will wake up to another full day, at the end of which you will also be exhausted. If you wait until you are no longer in the field, you may be overwhelmed by the amount of what you need to record, no longer have time to dedicate time to your research, and your memory about details will have already started to fade. Push yourself to keep up with note taking.

For most projects, it will be valuable to document using other means as well. While we cannot provide guidelines for everyone and all potential fieldwork projects, in this chapter we explore strategies for developing a cultural documentation approach that best suits your project. First and foremost, however, we want to emphasize that fieldwork is primarily about the relationships, experiences, and interpretations rather than the use of technology—so make decisions about recording technology carefully and only use it when necessary, relevant, and appropriate. In other words, be wary of privileging the technology over the fieldwork.

As R. Stone and V. Stone caution, "Many researchers hope that their use of technological media will help them to be more objective in their studies. We question this notion. Humans operate these machines and humans analyze the data thus collected. These devices cannot, therefore, be more objective than their users" (1981, 218). Fieldworkers sometimes mistakenly think that documenting using recording technology produces an accurate record of what transpired. However, be aware that all documentation is inherently subjective and selective. The person with the recording gadget decides what to record and what not to, where to direct the recording, and what and how to frame an image (for visual media). Folklorist and filmmaker Sharon Sherman makes the important point that "Film is always a construction . . . Even the placing of the camera for a film consisting of a single "take" (uninterrupted shot) is a manipulation. The camera reflects the filmmaker's view" (1998, 207). Furthermore, the subjectivity of these media extends to the audience who will interpret what they see and hear based on their own biases, perspectives, previous knowledge, and expectations.

Making Decisions about What to Document

As we have been discussing, culture constantly happens, and folklorists and ethnomusicologists encounter a continuum of cultural phenomena from processes to products. Here, we explore in more depth ways this continuum manifests with regard to a range of forms, settings, and contexts. First, we will consider the example of a song and the various settings in which it could be encountered in the field. The song is part of a somewhat scripted performance put on by a community annually to celebrate an important day in the calendar. Each year community leaders come together and ask a certain group of musicians to perform music at the beginning and end of the performance, with the middle of the event taken up by short skits based in traditional narratives about the day. All the performers are volunteers, culturally engaged members of the community, but with other responsibilities and demands on their time beyond preparing for the event. While they do not have rigorous rehearsal schedules, they nonetheless gather a few times beforehand to go over the material. The group of musicians are welcoming a new member, a young musician or someone who recently moved into the community who does not know the tunes. The activities associated with learning and preparing are on the "process" end of the continuum. These are the sessions where the new musician learns the chords, melody, and lyrics to a song; the appropriate style of performance; the cues from other musicians; the place of music in the larger performance; and myriad other culturally grounded expectations that structure the overall event.

The final performance falls toward the other end of the continuum as a product: the "result" of effort and investment by community members that is culturally framed as the focus of attention. Let us assume that the event—the final step in a process of planning, rehearsing, and annual meaning-making for a community—is the focus of a fieldwork-based research project. Documentation of that event across textual, audio, and visual means might be an obvious choice for a fieldworker to pursue. Assuming that the fieldworker has obtained consent from participants, they could plan to make video recordings and photographs during the performance, while also jotting down information to write up into fieldnotes. At a later date, transcribing from audio or video recordings the spoken or sung performance would produce textual documentation for analysis, supplementing the fieldnotes. Additional textual documentation could include transcriptions of interviews with event organizers and community members who participated as attendees or performers.

Though a tendency might be to only document the final event, it may be valuable also to document preperformance activities and meaning-making to understand the full context. Note that community members and performers could have other views: they may consider rehearsals to be unfinished, rough, or embarrassing; the preperformance time may not be meant for others to see or hear; or they may not perceive value in anything other than the final performance. A fieldworker should be sensitive to whomever they are working with, but also attentive to their own research and documentation interests. Be prepared to explain why and how you want to document in ways that engage the trust of community members while aligning with the goals of your fieldwork project. Such dialogue and rapport are as much a part of the consent procedure as they are part of the documentation process.

Think carefully and make deliberate choices about documentation. Some research questions may make it important for you to attend rehearsals but may not necessitate the use of audiovisual documentation. In this case, fieldnotes may be adequate for recording your observations. If you are interested in social dynamics, the process through which a song is learned, or how participants discuss aesthetics, it could be useful to video record a rehearsal so that you can review and analyze it later. In this case, it would be important to explain to participants why you want to video record and to explain that you will not be showing this footage to others but will only use it for your own review. If, on the other hand, your interest in the rehearsal is the different clothing choices performers make during rehearsals versus during a performance, then photography rather than video might be the most appropriate. Your goals would also impact your choices. If you are making a documentary video, you would want to video much more than you probably would if your goal were an essay or dissertation; and if you were producing an exhibit, photography and sometimes video would be important for your end product as well as for documentation and analysis purposes.

The above example presents an abstract setting within which several documentation strategies were possible. To make such planning more concrete, let us consider a more detailed scenario: a fieldwork project exploring traditional pottery in a rural east African community. The cultural context is multifaceted, so choosing what to document should connect to your primary research interests. In this case, your interest could be in the pottery itself—a focus on a cultural product that attends to the process of creation, the materials involved, and the uses of pottery by residents. Or, you might have a broader interest in the way that the tradition of pottery intersects with other components of social and cultural life, such as food-ways, storytelling, or gender dynamics. This second option is a broader focus compared to an emphasis on the objects, and it is important to point out that these two foci represent a wide spectrum of opportunities within a fieldwork project. There are myriad options for this topic, but we will stay with these two to explore ways to design documentation strategies in appropriate scale to your primary research objectives.

Within the first example, the materiality of pottery is the primary focus. We will consider two distinct research products: a documentary video and a written dissertation. Documenting material culture often involves recording information about the process of creation—and this can be done with both still and video photography. How much process you choose to document depends on numerous factors, but for this example we will start with the gathering of materials traditional to the pottery: local clay and plant materials (for decoration). Short video clips and dynamic photographs would link the human activity to the surrounding environment, establishing connections between cultural and natural resources. A mix of tightly framed shots featuring details and more wide-angle shots establishing context would provide you a range of visually diverse narrative elements. Shots of people resting or socializing in between moments of working on gathering materials would further delineate context. For either a documentary video or a dissertation, such visual material could be valuable to the method of observation; the documentation feeds description and analysis for a dissertation, while it might form the core of a scene in a documentary video.

In addition to the visual documentation, a notebook would enable you to jot down place names or the words used to identify the materials. You should also write down the date, time, and names of anyone that is there—this is part of the metadata! Wait—someone starts to tell a story about the place where they are digging for clay. The video camera is not on, so you are not recording the story. Others in attendance are laughing, underscoring its relevance to the activity. Make a note to ask about the story at a later point, maybe including a question in an interview you have already planned with the potter. On the short walk back home, gossip or

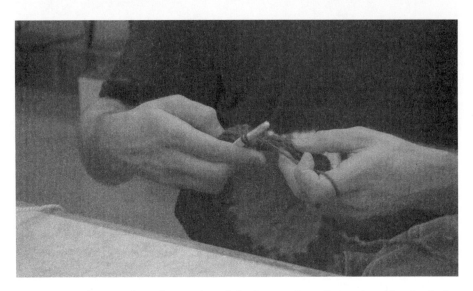

Figure 10.1. Close-up shot of a member of the Oregon State Correctional Institution's Crochet 4 Community group in the process of making a hat. Salem, Oregon, 2011. Photo by Shelise Zumwalt.

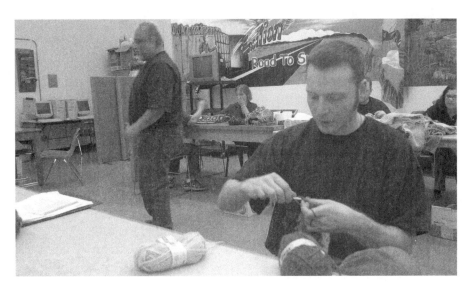

Figure 10.2. Wide-angle shot that shows the room, other people, and additional contextual details about the setting in which the member of the Oregon State Correctional Institution's Crochet 4 Community shown in Figure 10.1 was crocheting. Salem, Oregon, 2011. Photo by Shelise Zumwalt.

joking emerges—but appears to not be related to the gathering of materials beyond the fact that several people are socializing in this moment. Make a note as it could be of interest later.

The next step in the process of making a pot is the creation of the vessel. The potters gather where they usually do and begin preparing the raw materials. Some work with the clay while others process plant materials to make paint for decoration. Again, you could go with still or video documentation—depending on the needs of your final product. A mix of tight- and wide-angle shots in either format will provide you with a range of detail and context. If shooting video, pay attention to sound. Are many people talking? Did you plan accordingly for the correct kind of microphone? As you move around the area where everyone is working, trying to document the right "stuff" for your project, you notice that someone has grabbed a special tool for a step in the process. You had not thought about the importance of tools up until this moment! Are they part of the material culture your project explores? It might be easy enough to take a few photos or minutes of video featuring the tool, as you are already documenting in the moment. It could be worth it to make some isolated images of the tool (or someone holding it) after the work is done.

Across the documentary video and dissertation projects, paying attention to emergent aspects of the fieldwork and being agile with your documentation might provide you with great opportunities for enriching your outcomes. But there should be limits, especially since in the digital era it is possible to continuously document. For example, it would not be difficult to wear a body-mounted action camera (e.g., GoPro) that recorded constantly. Toward what end would you want to do this though? Would such video documentation augment more traditional ethnographic video? Would you capture some aspect of the process that is otherwise inaccessible?

Another possible extension of documentation might be into other elements of material culture. The potters at work might sit on small stools or lay the unused clay on a short table. Should you document those objects as "tools" or key components of the pottery tradition? You would likely have to make a decision in the moment and could end up snapping a few photos of a stool or a potter sitting on it. When writing fieldnotes, provide yourself with a reminder of why you took images of the stool and write down any information you may have gathered about it: this is metadata as well as contextual information.

Maybe the vessels now sit for a few days to air dry, and you have arranged interviews. With the documentary video project making a visual recording of the interview might be your preferred option—though audio recordings would also be useful in video pieces. For a dissertation you should ask yourself whether a video or audio recording better serves your research goals. Keep in mind that if you intend to make a video recording, you should have a methodological rationale: what does video provide that audio doesn't when it comes to your main research questions, and what role do interviews have in addressing those questions? Not only do video files require more hard drive storage space but using video equipment during an interview can be cumbersome or distracting, especially if you are working solo in the field. In planning to use video for interviews in a project focused on something other than a video-based product, having explicit methodological reasoning to support your choice will enable you to take all factors into consideration. Keep in mind that, as always, notes written down during an interview are valuable components of field documentation—even when you also use audio or video recording.

For the project discussed above across documentary and dissertation-type products, the focus of fieldwork was the pottery itself. Strategies for aligning documentation and methods therefore emphasized the pottery and processes associated with it. A broader approach would seek to place pottery in a context, foregrounding documentation of cultural phenomena such as foodways or community events in which pottery may play a role, as well as social systems intersecting with the pottery tradition: gendered work, class distinctions, or economic patterns imbricated with pottery. The scope of this project would entail different considerations when compared with a tightly focused approach to the pottery itself. While some of the methods and documentation approaches would be the same, the ways you would employ them with regard to how, when, and what you document could shift.

Let us consider the process for making traditional pottery again, but this time with an emphasis on understanding how gendered roles or expectations around work play out. While you may want to photograph the process of gathering materials and creating pottery, your attention should shift away from a focus on materiality to a focus on who is doing the work at any given stage. Photos or video would feature the people involved, as well as the raw material and other objects. You could include more wide shots that document context and social interaction, with fewer detailed images of making pottery. Via video, audio recording, or fieldnotes you might document the verbal interactions—stories, jokes, gossip—that emerge in the social setting of pottery creation. This documentation would enable you to seek patterns or meanings during analysis (see chap. 13), such that you could generate ethnographic understandings of connections between material culture, verbal traditions, and the broader tapestry of cultural identity in a community.

Moving beyond the process of making pottery, a context-focused approach might lead to exploration of uses for traditional forms of pottery in the community. Documenting foodways through interviews, recipe collection, photography, and fieldnotes would help contextualize pottery traditions. Further exploration of how pottery might be disposed of (or repurposed) when broken or dispersed when an owner dies or otherwise no longer has use for it, could lead to an even deeper understanding of the many domains of daily cultural life that pottery inhabits. Interviews are a key method for gathering this type of complex cultural information, with either audio or video documentation or notetaking being options. Photographs could come in handy, for example, if you were depicting a series of pots that someone described to you along a continuum of "usable" to "broken." But video would work better if you were documenting the physical practice of destroying pottery (ritualized or otherwise).

In addition to prose, notes for this project might include charts or diagrams illustrating the options for disposing of broken pottery. Yet another form of visual documentation, drawing or sketching can allow you to articulate details and observations from a perspective that is part fieldnote, part photograph (Taussig 2011). Finally, your fieldnotes could include physical measurements of full pottery vessels, the relative sizes of broken pieces, and even the spaces or buildings within which the potters work. Architectural measurements have long been a feature in folklore and ethnomusicology fieldwork, especially when the physical spaces have meaningful connections to the cultural practices and forms under consideration.

We have emphasized the importance of being flexible while doing fieldwork, advice that applies as much to documentation as to other aspects of the process. For example, we noted above with the first scenario that detail-oriented, close-up photography of pottery would serve a focus on the cultural object. But imagine that you are pursuing a more contextual approach with audio recorded interviews and still photography as your documentation tools. During an interview a potter tells you that in her family's tradition there are fine etchings put into the clay around the middle of a vessel while it is wet. She goes on to narrate the reasons for these etchings, and you see a connection to aesthetics and identity that had not been apparent before. You had not been shooting close-up images of pottery, but now such visual documentation takes on value in your project. She agrees. You decide that it makes sense to alter your approach to fieldwork by documenting family oriented aesthetic choices through photography and new interview questions (see Collier and Collier 1986).

As you document, it's important to keep in mind that beyond the final products you plan to produce you may need to have images for promotional materials, book or video covers, and for public presentations. Make sure to create aesthetically pleasing images of individuals, locations, events, and objects with these purposes in mind. Such images are certainly part of your larger body of documentation but might be a bit more staged or intentionally designed than the bulk of your visual materials. Furthermore, participants in your project might appreciate these images, especially in settings where they have limited access to audiovisual recording technologies.

Documentation: Thinking through Scenarios

Below are three hypothetical scenarios for fieldwork research in folklore and ethnomusicology. We intend these scenarios to accomplish three goals: (1) serve as generalized backdrops for examining the varied forms, settings, and contexts that folklorists and ethnomusicologists encounter in fieldwork; (2) provide illustrations for the ways in which planning a fieldwork project involves matching documentation strategies to research questions and methods; and (3) demonstrate the need to balance planning and preparation with flexibility and fluidity. There are many ways to approach fieldwork and documentation for each of the scenarios, and we encourage you to explore documentation strategies from multiple angles. To get you started we have provided two primary research questions for each scenario that can help you begin matching documentation approaches to research questions and methods. Each of these primary research questions lead to or depend on secondary or supporting questions—as is the case with any fieldwork research project.

The scenarios are intentionally open-ended. Whether in small groups or on your own, draw on the scenarios as exercises rather than blueprints. Reading through the scenarios will not tell you what to do in any situation but will instead give you practice designing approaches to documentation. In using these scenarios as exercises toward planning fieldwork, feel free to modify the questions or add new ones to more accurately align with the tone, scale, or scope of your hypothetical project.

Scenario 1: Instrument Builder

In a small community about halfway between two urban areas lives a builder of musical instruments. While not unique to the region, these instruments are identified with the area and feature in several different styles of music. She has been building these instruments for over two decades, having apprenticed with an uncle, who learned the craft from a local elder who passed away several years ago. The instruments are prized possessions for local musicians as well as aficionados in the national community favoring the styles of music featuring the instruments she builds. Her workshop is in a separate building on the family land where she lives with her husband and two children. Building instruments is her sole source of income, and her husband helps her run the business. He also works full time in a nearby town.

The research questions guiding this hypothetical project include:

A. What are the steps and materials involved in building one of her instruments?
Subquestions/interests: what are involved with the choice of materials? What are the tools used? Who are the clients?

B. What innovations or changes to the instrument design has she developed in her practice?
Subquestions/interests: what was the learning process in her apprenticeship? What does she do that is "traditional"? How have any of her innovations or changes to the instruments been received?

Discussion (can be done as a group or by individual).

1. What research methods would be best for pursuing this project?
2. What documentation strategies would be best for each method you identified?
3. What challenges might you face? (Consider such things as appropriateness, technical issues, and ethical considerations.)

Scenario 2: Family Lore at a Gathering

Every spring, a couple living in a semi-urban area where one of them grew up hosts a family gathering that involves three to four generations including themselves, their parents/uncles/aunts, their kids/spouses, and their grandchildren. The centerpiece of this gathering is a meal that involves family recipes that are core to the nuclear family as well as "imported" via marriages. The food is both potluck (prepared at other homes) and collectively cooked at the gathering place. In addition to the food, there are other activities and traditions that everyone looks forward to in the weeks leading up to the gathering. The 85-year-old maternal uncle of one of the hosts always tells a story connected to the local community; he grew up in the area and made his living as a logger, but also spent much time in the surrounding forests engaged in outdoor recreational activities, such as hunting, fishing, and hiking. These stories are usually quite humorous, and generally have some sort of morale to them. Additionally, many of the family members are musicians, and there is no shortage of instruments at the gathering. Over the years, a "family songbook" has emerged as people contributed tunes and sing-alongs to the collective repertoire; two years ago, someone produced bound photocopied versions of the songbook so that more people could join in with singing and playing along. The kitchen itself is an active zone of performance with teasing, teaching, and telling tales driving the participatory production of the meal's core dish, a meat stew that is a special family recipe. Finally, when everyone gathers around to eat together, there is much ritualistic toasting, joking, and trading of tall tales.

The research questions guiding this hypothetical project include:

A. What roles does performance play in the gatherings with regard to family tradition?
Subquestions/interests: What genres of performance occur? In what spaces does performance occur? Are there gendered or generational expectations or considerations with performance?

B. What family foodways are involved in this gathering?
   Subquestions/interests: What are the roles, and how are they filled: who cooks, cleans, serves, toasts, or otherwise contributes to the flow? How are dishes decided upon? How are recipes traded, shared, and modified?

Discussion (can be done as a group or by individual)

1. What research methods would be best for pursuing this project?
2. What documentation strategies would be best for each method you identified?
3. What challenges might you face? (Consider such things as appropriateness, technical issues, and ethical considerations.)

Scenario 3: Festival and Local Heritage

An urban area is the site for a community-driven festival every summer featuring a range of regional musical acts, with an emphasis on local roots music performers who gather on dedicated stages, in workshops, and at informal jam circles over the three-day event. The city government works with a local nonprofit that functions as the event promoter; the city parks department helping to provide space and facilities. The nonprofit organizes food vendors from the community and attends to other aspects of festival production such as sound, marketing, ticketing, and booking. This nonprofit grew out of a small group of community members who began the festival over twenty years ago. All the nonprofit staff and board are strong participants in the festival activities; almost all of them are musicians who play in the acts on stage or in the jam circles.

The instrument builder from scenario 1 plays a role in the festival. She lives outside the urban area that hosts the festival, and some of the musicians use her instruments. While she does not sell many instruments at the event, she has a booth that functions as an instrument repair clinic. She charges nominal fees to do small repairs, but thoroughly enjoys chatting with festival goers and music enthusiasts. The family from scenario 2 also figures into the festival, running a food booth for the past decade. At this booth, family members from all generations pitch in to prepare and serve their signature dish from the annual gathering. Many of the family members also play in the jam circles and attend the musical workshops. Finally, one of the family members is a founding member of the nonprofit that promotes the festival.

The research questions guiding this hypothetical project include:

A. In what ways does community or local identity manifest through the festival? How is identity enacted in performance, food, or other culturally framed means? Subquestions/interests: How does the instrument builder (scenario 1) or the family food booth (scenario 2) figure into the sense of "local" culture? In what ways is the event place-based? What is the organizational culture of the event?

B. In recent years, how has the web presence of the festival grown to be a key cultural component of the event?

Subquestions/interests: How do event organizers or participants use web-based platforms for communication or self-documentation? What is the role of mobile computing before, during, or after the event, especially as a means of community formation?

Discussion (can be done as a group or by individual)

1. What research methods would be best for pursuing this project?
2. What documentation strategies would be best for each method you identified?
3. What challenges might you face? (Consider such things as appropriateness, technical issues, and ethical considerations.)

Experimenting with Documentation

Prior to going into the field, we recommend taking the time to experiment with different documentation technologies. Learn to use cameras, video equipment, audio recorders, and fieldnotes by documenting occasions to which you have access and where it is appropriate to use these technologies. You might try documenting a meal with friends in a private home. We recommend not just using the recording capabilities found on smartphones but employing the equipment you would use for your fieldwork. Such exercises will enable you to become familiar with your own gear, and you will also start to gain understanding of how documentation in various forms unfolds in living contexts.

Choose a focus and use a combination of strategies. Reflect on how using the technologies impacted your own experience of the meal (or another event). Did recording in some capacity distract you from paying attention to or participating in various parts of the event? Did it bring your attention to details that you might otherwise have overlooked? How did the participants feel about having you document them? Did they say anything or behave in different ways than they might have otherwise? After the event, look through your images and video; listen to the audio, and read your fieldnotes. What information were you able to record? What is missing? Are there biases? What might you do differently next time? What would you do differently if you had a different focus? Reflect on whether the experience would be different if you had not known the participants as well.

Exercise

Assignment for students in groups outside of class.

1. Divide into research teams of three to four members.

2. Identify an event or occasion to which you have access and where this assignment would be appropriate.
3. As a group, select a focus or hypothetical research question.
4. Observe and document 20 to 30 minutes of the activity or event.
5. Each individual on the team documents using a different medium:
   - Fieldnotes
   - Photography
   - Audiorecording
   - Videorecording
6. Each member reviews their documentation.
7. The team gathers to discuss with the team members the pros and cons of different technology used. Consider also the ways in which approaches complement one another and ways in which they detract/contradict one another.

Documenting in Digital or Virtual Spaces

The preceding sections assume fieldwork in physical spaces, though some of the suggestions or issues apply equally to fieldwork in digital or virtual environments. There are some considerations that only apply to documenting online or virtual components of a project, including hybrid fieldwork projects navigating a combination of physical and digital spaces. For the most part the issues and suggestions discussed below pertain to established and emergent modes of digital communication or creativity. Given the pace at which change happens technologically and socially with such modes, it is best to apply the following as suggestions for thinking about a given situation rather than as universal solutions.

If you plan to interview through a video call platform, explore how you can record it. In some cases, the platform you use may have built-in recording capability, or you can install a plug-in or add-on piece of software that will enable both audio and video recording. In other cases, you may have to operationalize a recording feature in the system software of your computer or use a separate program to record audio and/or video.

Interviews that you conduct over email or other text-based electronic formats, such as SMS, should add to your fieldwork documentation in concrete ways. Exporting email conversations to nonproprietary file formats, ideally with searchable and editable text, will allow you to draw on the materials while also archiving them outside of your email program. Saving exchanges as threads or conversations helps preserve the context for an email interview, including time and date data. Archiving them external to the system you use for the communication is a safeguard—important if a client or web-based email system experiences technical difficulties, putting at risk any interviews you had been storing only in that system.

Similarly, as communication with fieldwork participants increasingly occurs through SMS or other mobile messaging systems, fieldworkers should seek means for exporting and storing conversations other than on the mobile device. This is especially important if the conversations function as interviews, or even follow-up questions to more formal interview sessions. Other channels for communication and interaction, such as social networking sites, may become means for you to interact with participants in your fieldwork project and you should investigate ways for capturing meaningful exchanges as part of your field documentation.

The preceding discussion of considerations for documenting mediated interviews or communication with participants assumes you have already received consent from them. Ensure that each person you work with through any of the above means understands that you intend to create documentation and use it to support your project. While there may be more explicit culturally framed expectations around taking photographs or video recording an interview, your ethical responsibility as a fieldworker does not diminish when you rely on omnipresent systems such as SMS to enrich your fieldwork documentation.

Beyond the synchronous and asynchronous types of digital interactions explored above, you may have reason to create cultural documentation around more static digital environments such as web pages. Screen captures or exporting a website to a PDF document or image-based file format are methods for ensuring you document a site during a given visit. Projects such as the Wayback Machine—hosted by Internet Archive—propose to provide longitudinal tracking of specific URLs through periodic "crawling" of sites and storage of the HTML information. While the Wayback Machine may not exist in perpetuity, there are likely to be other services and similar efforts to archive websites. As you begin to plan documentation approaches for your own fieldwork project that involves digital spaces, spend time familiarizing yourself with the current options for scraping web data. While you do not necessarily need permission to make screen captures, be sure to seek both permission and consent if you intend to engage in more robust documentation. Additionally, you should examine an intellectual property or copyright issues that might arise in using screen captures or other means for reproducing content that belongs to someone else.

More dynamic digital spaces such as social network sites (SNSs) may present rich opportunity for your field project, as well as complex environments to navigate when it comes to cultural documentation (see boyd and Ellison 2007; Collins and Durington 2015). A social media space might provide a way for you to engage directly with members of a community linked to your fieldwork research, so it is worth exploring the means by which you can document. Take into considerations issues of privacy and other ethical questions, but also attend to the technical issues. Screen captures are fine for discrete moments in an exchange, but what about a thread of messages and images? Beyond visual (or audio) capture of information, be sure to think about the metadata as well. Time, date, and names (real or account handles) might be easily noted or even automatically captured. But what about IP addresses or even geocoded information: do you want this, or need it? While such data may easily be harvested for any given SNS, think through whether it is useful to your project and be prepared to discuss with participants why you are collecting it (or not) and how you plan to use it (or not).

When Recordings Fail

Every fieldworker using recording technology has had the dreadful experience of finding out at the last minute that they cannot record something they had intended to, their equipment failing, finding out after the fact that they had not recorded something after all, or losing a recording. Do not panic. This has happened to us all, and we have survived and successfully completed our goals. The first thing to remember is that for most projects, the use of technology is a means to an end and not the end itself. If you find out you cannot record or that you do not have a recording of an interview or the visual documentation of an event, write down everything you remember as soon after the event as you can. Our memories fade quickly, so the sooner you write things down and in as much detail as possible, the more complete your documentation will be.

In some cases, you may be able to document a subsequent activity to fill in gaps in your materials or you may be able to do an interview again. Note, however, that no two interviews are the same, and that sitting down with the same individual and asking the same questions just to get the answers on a recording may feel awkward since we are not in the habit of having the same conversations with the same people over and over. A better strategy might be to write down everything you remember from the interview. Then, if you need direct quotes or cannot remember something that was especially important, you could go back to the interviewee and ask them just for that information. Ask them to tell you a story again or elaborate on a certain topic so that you can get it on the recording. If you lose photographs or video footage, descriptive fieldnotes, sketches, and diagrams may be enough documentation for your needs, or you may want to return and take some photographs or video to fill in gaps. If the recordings were part of your goal and not just a means to an end, for example if you are making a documentary or taking photographs for a website or exhibit, then you may need to go back and replicate the fieldwork activity.

Conclusion

Learning how to document and determining which documentation strategies are most appropriate and productive for different fieldwork situations is something that develops with experience. In this chapter, we have shared with you some of the ways we think about documenting and given you multiple scenarios to think about and some exercises to help you develop skills. As with everything else we have discussed, an open mind and flexibility are integral to thinking about and doing documentation. And the most important thing, which we cannot emphasize enough, is keeping up with your fieldnotes. Audiovisual recording is a wonderful resource, but it can never replace the most important part of the fieldwork process: documenting your observations and what you learn through participating and noting down your thinking throughout the process.

11

ISSUES IN THE FIELD

CONDUCTING FIELDWORK IS AN ENJOYABLE and fulfilling experience most of the time. It also involves social relationships, money, health, and mobility. In as much as we have to contend with issues around these things in our everyday lives, challenges and conflicts inevitably arise during fieldwork. We cannot address everything that might come up or provide solutions to specific situations that might occur during fieldwork. However, we do think it is important to discuss some of the issues that more commonly arise. Our hope is that if you encounter these issues, you will not be surprised and that we will have provided some resources and information that will help you navigate them. If you face challenges other than the ones we cover, we hope that you will have already realized that everything may not go as you had hoped. It is okay for plans to change, and resources exist to help you. We will discuss health issues, social conflicts, identity politics, gender, sex, alcohol, and money and compensation.

First and foremost, fieldworkers and research participants are people whose basic needs should always be a priority. No folklore or ethnomusicology project is so important to justify anyone involved compromising their mental or physical well-being, putting themselves into danger, or not leaving a situation that is unsafe or is otherwise not productive for them. Our overarching message is that all sorts of issues may arise in the field; you should always prioritize your safety and well-being and that of the other project participants. Few if any projects should be continued if they are causing real problems for either the fieldworker or the participants.

Coupled with the well-being of the fieldworker is our emphasis on the respect owed to participants, even when there may be disagreements. For circumstances when respect is no longer possible, you should feel confident asserting your rights, terminating relationships, or leaving a project at any point.

Physical and Emotional Well-Being

Illness, mental or physical, can be a challenge during fieldwork. Some of you may have physical limitations that will restrict how much you can walk or how long you can stand. Some fieldworkers do research in foreign environments where there may be health risks. Some may live in situations where they do not have easy access to good hygiene, medicines, and health care. Even those doing research in locations where there is good access to health care may nevertheless get ill, injure themselves, or otherwise encounter physical challenges. Fieldworkers should not feel badly about stopping their research in order to obtain the care they need. In some cases, doing so might mean having to miss an important event or cancelling an interview. One might have to leave a field site for short times or even indefinitely, which can be discouraging. Usually new opportunities arise, and cancelled interviews can be rescheduled or new people identified to interview. In extreme situations, fieldworkers may have to stop a project completely, which may be disappointing, and could necessitate changing the direction of a research project, their studies, or their professional goals. Always remember that the project is less important than the fieldworker's well-being.

Attending to mental health is just as critical in fieldwork as it is in all aspects of life. Fieldwork can put pressure on one's psychological state. As Helen Myers (1992) explains, "By its very nature fieldwork provides a setting in which we feel awkward and disorientated, a disconcerting reality because fruitful work results from natural, honest, heartfelt and often spontaneous behavior" (22). Fieldworkers can feel anxious about meeting new people, entering foreign spaces, and engaging in intimate conversations about topics that make them uneasy. All of these feelings are normal, and most fieldworkers feel most or all of these things at some point. Pushing through these feelings is often satisfying, and the end results can be fulfilling. It is also important, however, to know yourself. Be cognizant of your strengths and weaknesses. Recognize what might be especially difficult or even impossible for you to do. We all have limitations. Knowing and being honest about what these are can help us either overcome them or make decisions most appropriate for our strengths or limitations. Someone who frequently suffers from social anxiety might find that when they go someplace new, bringing someone along or getting to know a participant in advance so that there is a friendly face may be enough to overcome the challenge. If this is not possible, you may need to establish other strategies. You could spend time with participants in one-on-one contexts before building up to participating in the more public social space. In some cases, though a fieldworker may have thought that they would be able to carry out a project, they might find that doing so is producing negative emotional outcomes. As with physical illness, your mental health should be the priority. Sometimes not completing a project or changing its focus or some of its methods to accommodate your emotional needs may be the best decision.

It is also common for fieldworkers to be anxious about whether they are doing enough, are getting the information needed, or whether they will meet timelines or other goals. From our experience, fieldworkers often gather far more than they realize at the time. Most can relax and appreciate the experience without worrying so much about whether the quantity is enough. However, some fieldworkers do not do enough to achieve the goals of their projects or they lose track of their focus and spend a great deal of time gathering information that may not be helpful for achieving their goals A well-designed research plan, along with a strategy for keeping track of progress in gathering the desired information and answering your research questions, should help alleviate these concerns, as described in chapter 3.

Interpersonal Relationships

Field sites are similar to other social situations in everyday life. As with the fieldworkers, Spradley (1980) reminds us that "informants are human beings with problems, concerns, and interests. The values held by any particular ethnographer do not always coincide with those held by informants" (20). People have different beliefs, there are social hierarchies, some people like some people more than others, people fight, and sometimes people do bad things (see Georges and Jones 1980; Jackson and Ives 1996; Stocking 1983). The onus is on the fieldworker to always treat others ethically and respectfully. The American Folklore Society published the AFS Statement on Ethics: Principles of Professional Responsibility in the *AFSNews*, New Series, Vol. 17, No. 1 (February 1988), which was approved by the AFS board in October 1987. This document provides explicit guidelines about fieldworkers' relationships with the people studied: "In research, folklorists' primary responsibility is to those they study. When there is a conflict of interest, these individuals must come first. Folklorists must do everything in their power to protect the physical, social, and psychological welfare of their informants and to honor the dignity and privacy of those studied." As indicated in this quote, a central premise of folklore (and ethnomusicology) research is that the priority for fieldworkers should be always to ensure the well-being of those studied.

Despite good intentions, it is not unusual to get into socially complicated situations that require thoughtfulness and sometimes a great deal of effort. You will inevitably have different types of relationships with different people, fit variously into social hierarchies, and have your own opinions. A fieldworker also can be involved as a participant (victim or perpetrator) of conflict, violence, or criminal activity. Participating in the social drama of the people involved in the folklore or musical practices you are researching can be some of the most productive experiences. Fieldworkers often learn a great deal about a community or individuals, people's values, what social dynamics prevail, and how the practice they are researching operates in life through their observations of and engagement in difficult situations.

As fieldworkers we often put aside some of our own principles when striving to gain a culturally relativistic perspective or in building rapport during fieldwork. In some cases, doing so may result in researchers compromising their integrity, as in when they don't comment upon or try to stop something happening that they find troubling. Fieldworkers can become allied with certain factions in a community, sometimes unwittingly, putting them into conflict with others regardless of what they say or do. It is also not uncommon for fieldworkers, whether they are already members of a community or not, to be committed to certain perspectives and to partake in community disagreements or discussions. Though this is not bad and can be productive, be aware that aligning yourself with a side will necessarily impact your relationships to members within that segment of a community and to those who may disagree. These associations will most likely impact what opportunities and perspectives emerge from the fieldwork experience. Some or all of the participants may decide that they do not want to help or participate in a project or even decide to try to sabotage it, for example, by giving false information, not telling you about important events, telling others not to participate, or spreading rumors. In these situations, we recommend that fieldworkers talk to members of the community whom they trust for guidance. Consider discussing the situation with your instructors, supervisors, or mentors. In some cases, the fieldworker may have to resort to local processes of conflict resolution, or in extreme cases, may find that they can no longer do the project successfully.

Identity in the Field

Fieldwork is often about building relationships with people who may be different from the fieldworker in a variety of ways: age, gender, ethnicity, race, nationality, politics, economics, religion, sexual orientation, or in their attitudes toward all these aspects of identity. Learning about others and cultural exchange can be transformative. Yet differences can also be uncomfortable or contribute to internal or social conflict.

A fieldworker might find that aspects of their own identity are not accepted in a social environment or that certain identity categories—for example, related to sexual orientation, gender, race, ethnicity, religion, educational level, occupation, or political affiliation—may be targets for derision or prejudice. For unmarked identity categories, those categories that may not be obvious to people without the fieldworker explicitly sharing information or otherwise being found out, a fieldworker might choose not to reveal certain aspects of themselves in order to do the research. There may be ethical issues involved, though. How honest should you be when you are asking and expecting fieldwork participants to divulge so much about themselves? And if you do choose to hide aspects of your identity, what happens if you are found out?

Let us explore some examples. The first considers the repercussions for someone doing research in an environment where people share a political perspective different from the fieldworker's. This difference could be relatively inconsequential if politics is not important to the project or in an environment where there is general respect for a plurality of political positions. On the other hand, if the fieldworker has been asking questions and attending events that would not be open to those from a different political persuasion or where there is animosity between the differing political factions, the revelation of the fieldworkers' political leaning and that they have been hiding it may be considered a real breach of trust.

The second example considers a fieldworker who identifies as gay, lesbian, or bisexual in an environment where same-sex relationships are not tolerated. If the fieldworker is used to being open and accepted about their sexuality and feels strongly that concealing their sexual identity is unacceptable, they might find that being open about their sexual orientation either precludes their developing rapport or being accepted in the research setting. If they think they would be rejected, they would have to decide whether to attempt to develop relationships while being open about their sexual orientation, hide their sexual orientation, or not do the project. If they chose not to reveal their sexual orientation, they may feel uncomfortable knowing that they might be unwelcome if the information were known. Furthermore, they might dislike not being honest about who they are, or they may be worried about being found out. The fieldworker would have to decide whether they were willing to experience these dynamics in order to pursue the project. In a case where the fieldworker decides to be honest about their sexuality, they might find that more attention is being spent on their sexuality than the project topic, which could be a distraction from the project's goals. On the other hand, the fieldworker could decide to change the focus to a topic related to sexuality, thus taking advantage of their interactions as important fieldwork data.

Other identity categories are marked or visible, and so fieldworkers do not have the choice of whether or not to reveal them. Some examples would be a woman doing fieldwork in a patriarchal male space, an African American doing fieldwork in a Euro American community (or vice versa), or a nongender conforming individual working on a project in a space where conforming to the gender binary is the norm. One should be thoughtful about these identity issues when selecting a project and developing a research plan, as discussed in chapter 3. In some cases, certain topics may not be accessible to persons because of their identity. In other cases, though the fieldworker may be concerned, the identity differences may not be much of an issue, or the process of building rapport could produce the necessary trusting and respectful relationships.

As discussed in the subsection "Positionality" in chapter 1, fieldworkers should be reflective about how their identity is interpreted during fieldwork and how it impacts the fieldwork experience. Think about how particular identity dynamics operate in different contexts. For example, a Euro American person doing fieldwork in a Native American community should be aware that ethnographic fieldwork is linked with the long history of exploitation of Native American groups by Euro Americans. An African American who identities strongly as "black" in the United States doing fieldwork in an African context might be disconcerted if they are classified as "white" in that context. We recommend that you be continually reflexive about your positionality in terms of how it might be impacting your experience in the field in addition to how it might be tangled with power differentials.

In addition to having to deal with aspects of one's own personhood and how it fits within the research context, fieldworkers also often confront attitudes or perspectives that they find troubling, regardless of their own identities. To return to a previous example, one might be doing research in the United States with a skilled musician who is an important leader in a community and who has been extremely welcoming of the fieldworker. The fieldworker might be troubled to hear the same talented musician utter prejudiced comments that conflict with the fieldworker's own values. These types of situations can be especially difficult for fieldworkers in their own communities. Through the process of doing research, one might learn a great deal about individuals or the community that they did not know previously. Some of the new information may reveal troubling historical happenings or something about people in the fieldworker's own family or community that the fieldworker finds disturbing. In these situations, as with others in their lives, the fieldworker has to decide whether to take a stance and confront the issue, which could be considered disrespectful and possibly jeopardize the research relationship. Or they might decide to ignore the comments and focus on the goals of the research project, which are about musicianship and not social issues. Each fieldworker will probably encounter moments like these at some point, and each will need to decide how to proceed depending on the situation, the goals of the project, their relationship with the individual, and how strongly they feel about the issues.

There are no right or wrong ways to deal with these situations. It is often important to recognize that you are a guest in the community and remember the objectives of why you are there. Some of you will engage in activist projects where the intent is to try to effect change around the issues that you find troubling. For others, your project might be about something other than the issues, in which case you might choose to mute some of your own values and continue with the project. Or, you might decide to incorporate the themes that trouble you into the final project. In some cases, fieldworkers might decide that they cannot comfortably or ethically continue the project. In making a decision, fieldworkers should review their objectives for the project. What are they trying to accomplish, and for whom? How would engaging these issues fit with the goals for the project as well as their personal ones?

The discussion thus far has been oriented toward those doing fieldwork in situations where they have a great deal of control over the topic and community being studied, such as those doing fieldwork in academic settings or for personal goals. These situations are always much more difficult when one is doing fieldwork for someone other than themselves, for example, as part of an internship or job in which case the fieldworker may have less freedom to confront issues or change the direction of a project because of social conflicts. In such instances, we recommend discussing your concerns with your supervisor to determine the best strategy to deal with specific situations.

Gender and Sex

Gender, sex, and sexuality in the field are topics often absent in general discussions of fieldwork methods. Yet, issues related to these categories occur with enough frequency that direct discussion is imperative. This is a complex topic about which we could easily write a full volume (see Babiracki 1997; Gluck and Patai 1991; Whitehead and Conaway 1986; "Folklore Fieldwork" 1990). We will address some of the more common issues that could emerge and provide thoughts about them. As we have discussed in previous chapters, the goal of participant observation is to immerse oneself in a cultural environment, become as linguistically and culturally competent as possible, and participate within that community from a culturally relativist perspective. Whether one is doing research in a community with which they are familiar or one that is foreign, a fieldworker might find that their way of being a gendered and sexual being diverges markedly from the expectations of the group. There may be gender divisions of labor and expectations about clothing and inter-action between people of different genders that is quite different from the norms typical in your life. These differences may be significant. If a fieldworker experiences such contrasts in the process of immersion, it could require them to go against how they identify or their own politics or ethical standards.

Issues around gender and sexuality can also have an impact on re-search access (see Golde 1986). A single woman, for example, may have access to certain spaces, but not others. A woman doing research on music in bar scenes may find that it is considered inappropriate for her to go to bars alone or that, in doing so, she receives sexual attention that makes her uncomfortable or unsafe. A man doing a project on high school girls about their joking practices may find that he is assumed to be lecherous, or conversely, that he becomes the object of the girls' crushes or unwanted sexual attention.

On the other hand, people sometimes use sexuality to gain access to field situations, raising a variety of ethical questions. A fieldworker may develop an intimate relationship with a member of a community. Though it might not be the motivation, doing so can be beneficial to the fieldwork goals: it can give entrée into a community, a companion who is an insider, or access to many events and activities that they might not otherwise have. Being introduced as both someone's significant other *and* a fieldworker can be much easier than introducing oneself as an outsider. In some cases, these relationships can be genuine and be fulfilling to both parties in the short or long term. At other times, these relationships can be problematic when there is lack of honesty or a power differential. Furthermore, devel-oping an intimate relationship with one person could inevitably impact one's social positioning in the fieldwork setting, how people think of the fieldworker, or to which people or events one is granted access. We cannot advise whether or not to have romantic or sexual relationships in the field, but we encourage fieldworkers to think carefully about their objectives and the implications. Developing relationships primarily for the fieldwork is disingenuous and unfair to the other party. It can also be deceptive to other participants in the project, who may think the fieldworker has a genuine connection to the community. If the relationship ends during the fieldwork or when the fieldworker is done with the project, this could cause animosity and distrust.

Part of developing cultural competency while preparing for fieldwork is understanding the sexual mores of the community where one is doing research. One might be doing research in a setting where there are a great deal of restrictions around sexuality, in which case what others know about the fieldworker's sexual activities could influence their reputation. On the other hand, some fieldwork situations might be characterized by a great deal of sexual openness and an expectation of sexual promiscuity, which could place expectations on a fieldworker to have sexual relationships in ways that may or may not resonate with their own level of comfort or morality (see Morad 2016). In these cases, it is important to be aware of these dimensions and to have agency and choice in how you approach the situation. You should have integrity and make decisions that align with what you want to do. You should not go along with the context merely for the sake of cultural immersion, unless doing so also fits with your own desires.

Sexual Harassment and Violence

This discussion leads us to the very important topic of sexual harassment and violence. As with all aspects of life, unfortunately, these issues occur in fieldwork situations. In some contexts, certain people will be more vulnerable than others. The power relationships in fieldwork are often inequitable in that the fieldworker might have more education, greater mobility (the power to come and go from the research site), money, and prestige than do participants or members of their communities. *It is imperative that fieldworkers be aware of their status and not use their greater power to manipulate or coerce someone into some type of intimate relationship.*

Part of doing fieldwork is often taking social risks: going to events alone that one knows little about, meeting someone one does not know for an interview in an unknown place or living in a new environment. It is important not to downplay the risks and to always be conscious of what is going on. One should also be aware of the risks for participants. Are participants vulnerable when doing certain fieldwork activities? Is the fieldworker expecting participants to be in spaces at times that might put them in physical danger or raise questions about their reputations?

Women of all sexual orientations are generally more likely to be victims of sexual violence as are gay men and transgender individuals, especially transgender women. In specific settings, particular categories of people may be more likely to be either victims or perpetrators. Without this knowledge, fieldworkers could be especially vulnerable if they were not familiar with the social landscape or did they know the reputations of particular individuals or the norms associated with certain social categories. If fieldworkers are attending an activity where they feel vulnerable, we recommend finding someone to accompany them. If they are planning an interview as already mentioned, we recommend selecting a public place where both parties will feel safest. We want to emphasize that taking these precautions in no way undercuts one's professionalism or one's skill as a fieldworker. Many years ago, Gilman had a graduate student who became entangled in a difficult relationship with an older man who was her main informant. Most of the fieldwork activities occurred in his home where only the two were present. When the student finally revealed that she did not feel safe at his home, Gilman immediately advised her not to see the person again and to discontinue the project. The student explained that she had continued for as long as she had and had not informed her professor earlier because she was developing herself as a professional. She felt that she should have been able to "deal" with the situation. We fully empathize with how this student felt. However, we want to underscore that professionalism does not require someone to "deal" with harassment, intimidation, unwanted sexual attention, or violence. Furthermore, there is often the misconception that only women or gender queer people experience sexual harassment or violence. This perception is damaging for men who may not recognize victimization or be reluctant to seek help because it conflicts with social expectations or normative ideas about masculinity.

If any type of harassment or violence happens to you regardless of how you identify, it is not your fault. It is always the fault of the perpetrator. It does not suggest anything about your abilities or professionalism. It is always imperative that the victim leave as soon as they can and seek help and support.

Alcohol (and Drugs)

Many fieldworkers enjoy alcoholic drinks as part of the fieldwork process, but what might be enjoyable or appropriate in one setting may lead to problems in others. Some might find themselves in settings where the consumption of alcohol (or certain drugs) is considered inappropriate for anybody or for certain categories of people. Though the fieldworker enjoys drinking, they might find that doing so during fieldwork is not acceptable or could lead to social stigma. In US contexts where alcohol consumption is acceptable, it is usually equally so for men and women, which is not the case in other parts of the world. Women accustomed to drinking publicly in the United States may find that it is deemed unacceptable where they are doing research. Different settings also have different laws. For foreigners doing fieldwork in the United States, for example, they should be aware that it is not legal to drink alcohol if one is under the age of 21, and there are strict laws about where and when drinking is permissible.

You might encounter situations characterized by a great deal of pressure to consume alcohol (or other substances) or to drink amounts greater than you can tolerate. Numerous toasts may be part of a ceremony, hosts might honor guests by frequently filling their glasses, or guests might be expected to take the first drink for every round. Some of you will enjoy taking part in the festivities. Others who typically enjoy alcohol may find the quantities or the speed of drinking to be too much. Still others may not drink at all, making these expectations challenging as you try to fit into the social situation.

We recommend learning about alcohol consumption as you develop cultural competency. If it is not appropriate for people in your social position to drink, we recommend not doing so publicly. If drinking is expected beyond your preference, you might select to sip small amounts rather than gulping a serving. For those who do not drink, be confident to say no. And even those who do typically drink might find that selecting not to may be a better option than being pressured to drink too much. One strategy is to establish from the outset that you are not a drinker by rejecting the very first offer and any that come after. Even if you do enjoy alcohol, defining yourself as a nondrinker can dissuade people from pressuring you to consume beyond what you can tolerate or enjoy. Note that men may be pressured to drink more than women in some settings and may be chastised for not living up to masculine ideals if they do not drink or consume enough. Remember that everyone's well-being is more important than succumbing to social pressures.

Drinking can also be tied to the quality of fieldwork. A drunk fieldworker may not pay as close attention to what is occurring, may make mistakes with recording technology, and may make social blunders. Safety is also a concern. Maintaining good health is necessary for successful research, and alcohol consumption can lead to poor choices and has been associated with increased risks of sexual violence. Being healthy and alert, especially in new environments, can promote the safety of all involved. One can often use fieldwork as the excuse not to drink by explaining that one is "working."

Money and Compensation

In most fieldwork situations, fieldworkers do not pay participants for time or labor, though paying research assistants and translators is common. The reasons for not paying are multiple and are context specific. Some common reasons include: (1) A fieldworker is typically participating in activities and engaging in conversations that would not normally be subject to payment in the contexts in which they occur. For example, we usually do not pay people to have a conversation or informally teach us how to cook something or how to sing a song. Following the culturally appropriate behavior in the context would thus suggest that payment would not be suitable. (2) Paying participants can shift the dynamic of the fieldwork relationship into more of an employer/employee relationship in which the person being paid feels compelled to provide what the payer wishes for. This could put undue pressure on the participant to feel that they do not have a choice but to do what is asked of them. It could also shape the participants' responses or activities. Rather than responding to questions honestly or doing an activity in the way they would otherwise, they might answer or do something based on what they think the fieldworker wants. (3) In as much as it can affect what and how information is shared, payment can also change relationships into more of a business relationship rather than the cultural immersive rapport that is the ideal for many fieldwork situations. (4) Many fieldworkers are working with small budgets and paying participants could make the research impossible. The funding for fieldwork projects is often far more limited than for social science or science research, such as large-scale psychology experiments, where compensation is sometimes offered as an incentive for participation. (5) Ideally, there is reciprocity in the relationship in that the research has some benefit to the community, and participation is motivated by people's own interest in having their cultural forms documented, made more visible, presented to public audiences, or other mutually beneficial goals.

Though formal payment for service is not usually the norm for fieldwork, many researchers find other means of compensating or expressing their gratitude for the time and effort of research participants. In chapter 14, we discuss the importance of providing copies of materials and sharing royalties or other proceeds after the fieldwork is completed. Here we will discuss ways of compensating while in the field. If one is working with someone who is selling artwork, recordings, or food items, purchasing some of their work and buying as generously as one can afford can be helpful to the participants and also be a way of expressing one's appreciation and support for what they do. Fieldworkers can find other ways of extending generosity throughout the fieldwork process. If one is doing an interview with someone at a coffee shop or restaurant, the fieldworker should ideally pick up the bill. If the fieldwork occurs at someone's house, bring food and beverages to share, or bring a small gift. As already mentioned, it is important to learn what is suitable in the cultural context. In some cultures, bringing food or drink to a meal is considered insulting; in other cultures, not doing so is disrespectful. Similarly, most cultures have specific ideas about gift giving, so be sure to use your ethnographic skills to learn about what is appropriate before deciding what to do.

Sometimes participants require certain materials or funds to pursue an activity, and the fieldworker can help make that happen. After spending several months doing fieldwork with a dance group in northern Malawi, Gilman bought fabric so that the group could make matching skirts, something that they would not have otherwise been able to afford. Fenn helped fund the recording of singles for several young musicians in Malawi who participated in his dissertation project. He also brought guitar strings and other supplies difficult for musicians to obtain in Malawi (see also Seeger 2008a, 2008b).

This type of giving can be important in the fieldwork process, but we also encourage you to always reflect on how it's affecting relationships and fieldwork dynamics. Are you doing enough? How do people perceive you? Are you overreaching what is appropriate? Are people depending on you in ways that feel uncomfortable? Are you taking advantage of the situation? Are others taking advantage of you? The issue of compensation and gift giving is especially complex in situations where there is significant disparity in economic status between the fieldworker and the participants. When the fieldworker has much less money or status than the people being studied, the issues are perhaps less. In these cases, fieldworkers might more easily accept the generosity of participants. Yet, fieldworkers might find themselves in situations where they are expected to spend more than they can afford, take their turn picking up the bill, or give gifts beyond their budget.

In situations where the fieldworker is in a much better economic situation than most or all of the participants, it can be far more complex because one or both parties may feel that the fieldworker *should* provide materially. You might feel badly about the poverty of individuals or communities. While it is important to provide and help out when one can, fieldworkers are rarely capable of radically altering the economic reality for individuals (unfortunately), communities, or the world for that matter. Finding ways of contributing that are appropriate to your financial ability and to the relationships you have are critical. In some cultural contexts it is common for people who have fewer resources to ask those with more for money or things. Receiving such requests may be uncomfortable for fieldworkers who come from a cultural environment, such as much of the United States, where asking for money outright is often deemed inappropriate. Learning when it is suitable to give and how to respectfully say no are vital to success in these situations. Here again we encourage fieldworkers to spend some time developing cultural competency. One strategy is to develop a friendship with someone who is well versed in local cultural practices and who is removed from the research situation who can help provide guidance and advice. Students working overseas may also benefit from a relationship with a local professor or professional who can provide guidance.

Conclusion

We have covered many topics and raised more issues and concerns than we have provided answers. Remember that fieldwork is an extension of living. In as much as we contend with the types of issues discussed in this chapter when engaging with our friends, families, coworkers, supervisors, neighbors, and strangers that surround us, we also have to deal with them in fieldwork. Frequently, some of the most challenging situations we face ultimately are those from which we learn the most about ourselves, our topics, and the participants. Being aware of physical, social, and economic issues and engaging with them in a thoughtful and respectful way should lead to opportunities for productive life-long learning and more informed, safe, nuanced, and in-depth research outcomes.

PART III

AFTER THE FIELD

AT SOME POINT, A FIELDWORKER determines that they are done with the active fieldwork phase, and it is time to start working with the data toward achieving the project goals. Because our research is built on human relationships, we typically continue to stay in touch with participants long after the active phase of research has finished, thus for some projects, fieldwork may never really end. Determining when the fieldwork is over can be confusing. Time, resources, or context-specific circumstances can be factors. This is especially true when the research is completed for an agency or when other limiting factors exist. For example, the fieldwork for a class paper is due at the end of the term, the duration of time that a fieldworker has to spend in the field comes to an end, money for a project runs out, or a grant deadline is reached. In other instances, the end is fuzzier, especially because most ethnographic projects could continue for a very long time. A well-thought-out research plan is helpful for determining whether the desired goals have been met. At some point, the fieldworker has to determine that they have completed enough to achieve their objectives, even if they also know that much more could be done.

In part III, we provide some guidance about the final phases of fieldwork projects. Note that the sequencing of fieldwork activities will vary between projects, so some of what we describe in this section may be completed during earlier phases. In chapter 12, we detail the processes for organizing and managing data, including logging, transcribing, and translating. These steps help assess what one has gathered, facilitate finding specific information within the data, and are critical for preparing materials for future use or to deposit in an archive. In chapter 13, we offer strategies for reviewing data and identifying themes for analysis or to highlight in fieldwork products. We also consider issues associated with using ethnographic data, such as power differentials, representation, subjectivity, and interpretative authority. Chapter 14, "Ethics and Final Products," addresses the human component of completing fieldwork and covers the value of continuing fieldwork relationships after a project is complete. It includes a discussion of intellectual property rights, reciprocity, and the importance of making fieldwork data and products available to communities of origin. The final chapter focuses on how to prepare your materials for preservation and future use by you, other folklorists or ethnomusicologists, and research communities.

12

MANAGING DATA

AFTER COMPLETING THE ACTIVE PHASE of fieldwork, most fieldworkers have a lot of data, ideas, and memories. It can be overwhelming and even paralyzing to contemplate what to do with all of it. In this chapter, we provide some strategies for taking a systematic approach to managing research materials and logging them so that you know what you have and can easily find it in the future. For some materials and projects, the additional time-consuming steps of transcribing or putting recording information into written representations will be valuable, and some materials might require translation.

Spreadsheets and Logs

In chapter 7 we recommended you develop a spreadsheet for overall management of your fieldwork materials and draft log sheets for individual items or series (such as photographs). Ideally you used these during fieldwork to capture metadata and organize your materials while it was fresh. However, we realize that depending on your fieldwork timeline and the nature of the activities, you may not have had time to do this work thoroughly. Now it is time to make sure your spreadsheet is complete and to refine metadata and expand logging by returning to each individual piece of documentation. Logging involves reviewing all interviews, photographs, videos, or other forms of documentation and creating detailed descriptions. How detailed your logs are and what information you include will vary depending on the nature of the materials and the goals of the project.

At the beginning of each log, provide the metadata. This is an important step even if you are logging multiple pieces of data associated with a single activity. You may have an audiorecording, a videorecording, photographs, and fieldnotes documenting a single concert. You should create individual logs for each piece of data. Though the metadata (other than information about media and format) would be the same for each log, be sure to include it at the beginning of each of the four. This attention to detail will greatly facilitate you accessing the metadata when you are working with the materials, and it will be invaluable for those who might engage with your data in the future.

In addition to providing the metadata, the log should provide more specific details, especially for longer recordings. You can use existing templates, such as those provided in *Folklife and Fieldwork*, or create your own based on your needs (Winick and Bartis 2016). Below is a sample template Gilman used to log video footage for her documentary:

Project name:
Project number:
Date:
Tape #:
Event:
Location:
Summary of contents:

Time in	Time out	People	Shot Description	Themes

The logging process involves reviewing your documentation and writing down brief summaries of its content. For photographs, create a numbering system so that you can easily note the content and themes of individual photographs. For websites, note names of sites, URL addresses, and details about content. For audio and visual recordings, note time codes for when specific topics, details, or stories appear. For fieldnotes, include topics and themes for different dates. Some logs briefly note a topic or theme for particular subsections of data, while others go into more detail providing summaries, descriptions or partial transcriptions of sections that are especially salient or that the fieldworker anticipates they will want to use in the future.

Following is a short segment of a log sheet from the American Folklife Center's *Folklore and Fieldwork*. Note that the metadata (as previously explained in chap. 7) is provided at the beginning of the time-coded interview log:

Identifier: afc2012034_00483

Title: Patrick interview, 2013-02-17

Names: Patrick (interviewee); Ellen E. McHale (interviewer) Place: Tampa Bay Downs Racetrack kitchen.

Date: 2013-02-17

Description: Patrick Bovenzi talked about his work in the horse business, and especially his current work as a horse identifier.

Language: English

Formats: 1 audio file, digital, WAV (55 min.); 1 video file, digital, sound, color, mpeg4 (55 min.)

Rights: No restrictions, permissions completed.

Tagging: Horses, Racetracks

00:10 Originally from Canandaigua, NY, not far from the Finger Lakes Racetrack. He started out walking hots at the Finger Lakes Racetrack when he was 14 years old. He has been in Florida 23 years. He has no other family members in the horse business. He was a kid who always had the Racing Form with him in high school, studying it in High School study hall. He started walking hots in 1968 when he was 14 (he had lied about his age, saying he was 16 years old). He worked at Finger Lakes Racetrack in the summers through high school and college.

1:38 In 1968 he started working for Marty O'Neill, a former jockey turned trainer.

2:10 He worked with the horses during college, worked the horses in the morning and evenings and went to RIT during the day. It took him a little bit longer to finish because of that – 5 years instead of 4. He majored in criminal justice, in the College of General Studies. He learned about law and when he's not a horse identifier, he is a steward so that is relevant to his degree.

4:10 Pat has done everything in the horse business – stable boy to steward: groom, hot walker, assistant trainer, jockey agent, paddock judge, placing judge, patrol judge, clerk of scales, horse identifier. He has been a horse identifier the longest. There are only 51 horse identifiers in the country. He works with four breeds and is very busy. (Winick and Bartis 2016, 26–27).

The log provides enough detail to allow the researcher to identity topics and themes in the interview, and the time code facilitates accessing the location on the audio file where particular topics came up. Note that this particular log contains extensive description for very short segments of time (two minutes or less). Other logs may be less detailed, for example, providing a brief description of the content every ten minutes. How much detail one provides depends on time constraints and how fieldworkers intend to use the log and the data.

Transcription

Transcription is the process of putting into writing something that was spoken or performed during fieldwork. Textual transcription includes such things as writing down verbatim an interview, song text, or story. Musical transcription involves using a written notation system to depict sound (notes, tonal quality, acoustics). There are also forms of transcription for movement and dance. We provide detailed discussion of textual transcription because it is the form most used across folklore and ethnomusicology. Fieldwork typically involves talking and listening to people, even if sound and movement are a focus, so interview transcripts can account for the bulk of one's field data.

Textual Transcription

Many fieldwork manuals highlight the value of verbatim textual transcription because of the importance of documenting data from the perspective of practitioners (Ives [1974] 1995; Spradley 1979). As folklorist Richard Dorson (1964) famously put it, the text "comes from the lips of a speaker or singer and is set down with word for word exactness by the collector" (1). In order to document and present participants' perspectives, explanations, or stories in their own words, some fieldworkers transcribe verbatim every interview and as much other fieldwork data as is possible. Logging systems, as an alternative, enables one to use data and to locate relevant portions as needed. Whether to transcribe verbatim and if so, how much to transcribe, will depend on your short and long-term goals. What are you planning to do with these materials? Do you plan for them to be accessible to other fieldworkers and scholars in the future? How much time do you have?

Textual transcription is a tedious and time-consuming process. It can take between six to fifteen hours to transcribe one hour of audiorecording. An experienced transcriptionist might take between three and four hours to fully transcribe one hour. We recommend using transcription software, which enables you to adjust the speed of the playback and to control the start and stop functions with either key strokes or a foot pedal. The software also keeps track of the time code and facilitates inserting it regularly into the written transcript. Using software greatly speeds up the process and improves accuracy. Available software is continually

Figure 12.1. Fieldworkers from a UNESCO team doing an Intangible Cultural Heritage survey log and transcribing field recordings after a long day of fieldwork. Karonga, Malawi, 2013. Photo by Lisa Gilman.

changing, so we recommend searching online or asking a supervisor or archivist for advice.

We all dream of the day that voice recognition software will accurately transcribe our fieldwork recordings. At the time of writing, no such software that works well has been identified. Most voice recognition software requires training the software to recognize users' voices, which is a time-consuming process. Since we tend to do fieldwork with a lot of different people who have their own speaking styles, accents, and linguistic codes, it is not feasible to train the software to recognize all of our research participants.

Folklorist Sandy Ives emphasized, and we agree, that the ideal person to transcribe an interview is the same person who conducted the interview: "You were there, you've had direct experience with the interviewee's speech patterns, and presumably you know what he or she was talking about. If, for instance, there are significant gestures or unexplained measures of distance—and in spite of your best efforts there will be some—you are the only one who will be able to make sense of them" ([1974] 1995), 75).For these reasons, it is best also to transcribe an interview or other fieldwork material yourself and to do so as soon after the event as possible.

Though writing down what someone said or sang might seem straightforward, in reality it is an inherently imprecise and messy process.

Communication happens through so much more than words, and the process of writing down involves interpretation. As Ives put it, "Even under ideal circumstances, a transcript is simply the best representation you can make of what is on the tape, but since it *is* a representation, it is unavoidably an interpretation" ([1974] 1995, 77). In *Oral Tradition and the Verbal Arts*, Ruth Finnegan (1992) explains some of the reasons why "the process of transcribing is a problematic one" (195). Some of the issues she raises are that language conventions are not neutral, but rather culturally defined and can be associated with status and the politics of language use in the local setting. Furthermore, it is difficult to represent multiple voices occurring simultaneously, at times interrupting or overlapping. And, there is often a discrepancy in tone between performance and writing. What might come across as eloquent and articulate in performance may appear incoherent or inarticulate in the written version because of the frequency of false starts, incomplete sentences, short utterances, and pauses that are typical of spoken language. Finnegan also emphasizes that though the aim might be for accuracy, the process of transcription is subjective; no two people will produce exactly the same transcription from the same oral text.

Nonverbals are also critical to in-person or mediated communication and performance. Facial expressions, tone of voice, posture, bodily orientation, pauses, silence, and intonation interact with words to produce an expressive act. The interpretations, perceptions, and meanings audience members take away from listening to people talk or perform is necessarily intertwined with nonverbal expressive channels. The process of transcription is thus also a process of translation in which oral communication is translated into written forms, and much of these nonverbals are missing in written transcriptions (see Fine 1984). Efforts to note them can be difficult or impossible for audiences to "read" and get a sense of the original performance. Aware of these issues, scholars have devised a variety of notation systems to account for nonverbals some of which are more detailed and complicated than others, and all of which fall short of "accurately" depicting all that happened communicatively when the original interaction took place.

We encourage you to transcribe interviews and other important textual recordings word for word, paying careful attention to accuracy in terms of taking the time to write down everything that was uttered, including false starts, repetitions, and exclamations. We also suggest you come up with a mechanism for noting nonverbals, such as laughter, pauses, sighs, chuckles, and so on. As Ives ([1974] 1995) recommends, in the process of transcribing, one writes down everything that is in the recording without omitting words or correcting grammar. After completing the transcription, review it closely while listening to the audio to improve accuracy.

You can develop your own format for transcription. We recommend starting with the metadata, such as the example of the log above, followed by one or two short paragraphs summarizing the interview. The transcribed text follows, formatted in dialog style, using conventional punctuation. Start a new paragraph each time there is a transition in speakers and provide the name of the person speaking with each transition. When doing a full transcription, one transcribes everything that was said by the interviewer, interviewee, and anyone else who was present. Even if you will not use the interviewer's words in final products, transcribing them provides important contextual information for interpreting the interview.

Pay attention to how much interpretation goes into the transcription process. Since most people do not speak with clearly delineated sentences or paragraphs, the transcriber decides where these breaks occur on the page. Transcribers decide how to punctuate and what descriptions of nonverbals to include. How one puts words down on a page will necessarily impact how the fieldworker and future audiences will interpret the material. Recognize that we are used to reading prose that has been carefully written and edited, which looks very different on the page than does a rendition of what somebody said. When deciding how to use the material, one might decide to "clean up" the passage to make it intelligible. Take into account the people you interviewed who may feel that including all the "uhms" and false starts makes them seem inarticulate.

The guidelines we have provided are intended for a general audience. For those of you who would like to learn more or whose research engages the intricacies of communication or ethnopoetics, we recommend that you review the literature on the strategies and challenges of transcribing a variety of texts (e.g., Briggs 1985; Fine 1984; Hymes 1981, 2003; Quick 1999; Seitel 1980; Sherzer 1990; Tedlock 1972).

Exercise

Assignment for students to complete individually outside of class. Each student transcribes word for word at least thirty minutes of a face-to-face interview they conducted.

DISCUSSION

- What is the relationship of the written transcript to the interview?
- Compare the comprehensibility of the written transcript to the original oral delivery.
- What choices were made while transcribing?
- What was omitted?

Musical Transcription

The emphasis on musical transcription in ethnomusicology has shifted in recent decades. Jeff Todd Titon explains that "not long ago, musical transcription was the distinguishing mark of our [ethnomusicology] discipline. . . . Music was objectified, collected, and recorded in order to be transcribed; and transcription enabled analysis and comparison. . . . Today it is not transcription but fieldwork that constitutes ethnomusicology" (2008, 25; see also Marin 2005). Despite this shift, sound transcription remains relevant to some projects. As with transcribing text, this is an imprecise process, and complicated symbolic systems have been developed to make it feasible. Notation systems were created with certain musical traditions as their base, making it difficult to note sounds that do not fall into the parameters of a particular system's symbolic codes. Those working in nonwestern musical traditions might find that they need to transcribe notes that do not fit the western musical scale or rhythmic patterns that cannot easily be depicted in western notation systems. Those working in nonwestern musical forms have developed notations specific to the traditions. We encourage those interested to explore what is available, develop their own notation systems, or work with their instructors and mentors to troubleshoot challenges. Guidance on the specifics of how to transcribe musical sounds is beyond the scope of this handbook, but much scholarship exists on the topic (Allgayer-Kaufmann 2010; Ellingson 1992; Hood 1971; Kaufman 1990; Nettl 1964).

How Much to Transcribe?

For the purposes of archiving and future use, the general rule is the more you transcribe the better because it can facilitate you working with the materials and others accessing them in the future. Some fieldworkers advocate partial transcriptions, while others insist that full transcription is necessary. With partial transcription, you review recordings and select those parts that are most significant to a project or that you will likely use in final products. Partial transcriptions entail logging the full recording, but only transcribing the selected segments. For full transcription you would produce logs in addition to the word-for-word text document of an interview.

Be realistic with regard to your particular project. How are you using the materials? How might transcriptions assist you with your interpretive process or your strategies for producing something out of your data? There may be certain materials that are especially important or valuable for you to transcribe, whereas for others, listening or watching recordings could be adequate. Consider whether there are materials that you need to transcribe because of an agreement with participants or because they will be valuable and accessible to members of your research community. In making decisions about what and how much to transcribe, consider your time constraints, resources, and what you need to produce the best outcomes. Also consider the value material might have for future practitioners, community members, or cultural workers.

Linguistic Translation

For those fieldworkers researching in an environment where one or more languages different from the one that will be used for the research product are spoken, part of the management of texts will be translating all or certain parts of the data from the original language into another language for the purposes of presentation, analysis, and preservation. This is a tricky process that deserves a great deal of thought and linguistic expertise.

Finnegan (1992) outlines some of the issues in linguistic translations. She explains that literal or word-for-word translation is often considered to be the ideal, but that there is "no such thing as a neutral 'literal' or 'exact' rendering. Any translation involves "multiple decisions about models of meaning, delimitation of units, purposes, audiences, and so on" (188). Finnegan elaborates that translation can have different aims. While word-for-word translation has its value, much translation "implies trying to somehow convey the original to foreign listeners/readers" (188). Word-for-word translations often do not acknowledge ambiguity, the subjectivity of interpretation, or the possibility that the translator did not understand what was intended in the original language. Some translations attempt to provide information about what the translator thought was the intended meaning in the utterance or integrate elements of aesthetics, tone, or other communicative dimensions. Take, for example, the use of symbols or metaphors, common in songs and verbal performances that are meaningful in the original language but that bear little significance in the language of translation. The translator could choose to provide the literal translation alone, provide the literal translation with a footnote with some explanation of its possible meanings, provide alternate symbols or metaphors that make sense in the language of translation, or select some other choice. Another problem in translation is that direct translation may be interpreted as simplistic, unintelligible, or erudite in the language of translation. As a result, readers might add levels of meaning to the text that are derived from the translation rather than from the initial performance.

Much has been written about translation that extends far beyond the scope of our expertise or this handbook's objectives (see Feleppa 1988; Okpewho 1990). Here, we emphasize the need to recognize and take into consideration the problems and shortfalls and to be cognizant of the choices one makes and why one is making them. As with so much we have discussed, some problems can be mitigated by honesty. Being up front in final products about the issues of translation in written texts, documentary videos, exhibits, or events does not take away the problems. Yet, it can help audience members interpret and understand that translation has occurred and is contributing to their experiences and interpretations of the material.

Conclusion

The processes of logging, transcribing, and translating data are time-consuming and complex. Nevertheless, the time spent is productive beyond the goals of organizing the data and making it usable. In as much as they are a necessary step for managing one's data, all the steps described in this chapter also provide valuable opportunities for review and reflection and contribute to ongoing skill building. Ives makes the excellent point that the transcription process forces you "to listen carefully to what went on," which "will help you plan for future interviews. And finally, I know of no better way than self-transcription to teach what good interviewing is and is not, what succeeds and what does not" ([1974] 1995, 75–76). The review process, another valuable step in the process of interpretation and analysis, is the topic of the next chapter.

13

CODING, ANALYSIS, AND REPRESENTATION

ONCE YOU HAVE LOGGED, TRANSCRIBED, and translated your data it is time to decide what to produce and what to include in the final product. This chapter begins by suggesting that fieldworkers (with their collaborators if appropriate) revisit their original goals at this point and determine whether what they set out to do is still the best choice. We then suggest a system for reviewing and coding data to identify themes and patterns for the purposes of determining what one wants to "say" with the materials. We end by discussing issues of representation and the power dynamics associated with interpretation.

Deciding What to Produce

What should you do with the material? You probably started with a specific goal in mind: a thesis, documentary video, musical recording, an exhibit, festival, or blog. Or, you may have planned to use the information for some type of activism intended to produce social change. Some of you will not have the choice about whether or not to pursue the original plan. The outcome of your projects may be predetermined in that it was stipulated by an instructor, supervisor, or granting agency. Others might have been working collaboratively with a community to produce a preagreed upon outcome. For those of you who have more flexibility, it can be fruitful at this point to take stock of your fieldwork materials and reflect on what would be the best product. If you planned to make a video, is it still the best choice given the topic, materials you gathered, and the priorities of the participants? It can be valuable to share materials with participants to find out what their preferred outcome would be now that the fieldwork is complete. Be sure to keep in mind availability and your limitations (Spitzer [1992] 2007). Consider what time, skills, and material resources would be needed for what they hope to accomplish. Sometimes communities have resources that they can put toward a project. Other times they have great hopes for what a fieldworker can accomplish, which could be within or outside of the fieldworkers' capacity. Fieldworkers should avoid making promises unless they can reasonably expect to fill them. As an example, a community could decide that they would like a documentary video, website, and book produced out of the fieldwork that was carried out by a single person. It would be important for the fieldworker to determine whether these ambitious goals were feasible, and the fieldworker should be honest about their own limitations. Collaborative decision-making is an ideal, but it does not obligate the fieldworker to do more than what they can reasonably do. If a request is beyond the fieldworker's capacity, they could offer to do what they could, help find resources to complete the other parts, and respectfully explain their own limitations. Note that it is common to underestimate the time it will take to bring a project to completion, especially when it involves multiple players and collaborators. Be sure to budget a much longer timeline than you hope for to ensure your success and not to mislead the collaborating community members.

Aside from the hopes of participants, in reviewing the fieldwork materials, one might find that the materials are useful for a variety of products beyond the original plan. Somebody might have planned to write a thesis. In the process of doing the fieldwork, they might realize that they have audiorecorded performances and interviews that could be produced into a podcast. Or, they might have photographs of artists and their creations that would work well as an online exhibit. If they originally planned to make a video or create an exhibit, they may want to write an essay for a local publication or write an article for a scholarly journal in addition to the original plan.

Sometimes, what was originally intended is not the best option given the data collected or how the fieldwork transpired. Someone planning to do a documentary video might have found that they were able to get plenty of access to events and opportunities to learn about the topic. However, they were not able to get permission to record enough to produce an effective documentary. While they do not have adequate footage for a video, they might be able effectively to switch gears and write about the topic. Or, they might be able to create a multimedia presentation that relies primarily on text but integrates bits and pieces of video footage and photographs.

Once again, we emphasize ongoing reflection and flexibility. Thinking beyond the original goal can be fulfilling for the fieldworkers, as well as for the participants, because it often extends the audience for the project and sometimes the value for all involved. Researchers who produce a book, public presentation, video, exhibit, and event about a topic will invite a much broader audience to engage with the material than they would if they only did one of these.

Reviewing Data, Coding, and Identifying Themes

The process for reviewing data and deciding how to use it will vary depending on the context for the fieldwork, objectives, and the nature of the data. An instructor, advisor, or supervisor may direct you to use a specific mechanism for working through your data. For those seeking some direction, we offer a process intended primarily for those producing written scholarly texts. It is based in the social sciences and may or may not align with the approach of you or your instructors. In the authors' experience as students, we received little guidance about moving from data to analysis, so we hope this outline will prove to be useful to some of our readers.

Fieldwork data is at the center of ethnographic products. Whether one is producing an exhibit or a scholarly dissertation, the thick descriptions and audiovisual documentation should be front and center. Central to how ethnographers approach presenting and analyzing data is the recognition that the process of description and selecting what and how to present fieldwork data is an inherently subjective and interpretive process. Furthermore, fieldwork participants make decisions and interpret their lives using analytical frameworks, which are often not those of the theorists who are popular at any given time in the academy. Many contemporary folklorists and ethnomusicologists use a process called grounded theory to develop analyses (Glaser and Strauss 1967). For this approach, the focus, themes, and selectivity of the end-product are rooted in the ethnographic data.

Organizing and analyzing data using a grounded theory approach requires an ongoing and systematic process of moving back and forth between a close review of data, one's emerging thoughts on a topic, and engagement with the relevant scholarly literature (especially for those working in academic settings). One builds an analytical framework based on what one interprets from the data and uses the scholarly literature to contextualize, elaborate, or deepen the description or analysis. For those whose products will not engage the scholarly literature, the process involves moving back and forth between the close examination of the data and one's emerging plans for what to present and how, always making sure the decisions are informed first and foremost by the fieldwork materials.

In going through this process, the foci of your final project may or may not align with the lines of inquiry that drove your project. The first step is to examine your data to determine what are the most salient, significant, or even just most interesting themes that came out of the research process, a process called "open coding" (see Emerson, Fretz, and Shaw 1995, 142–60). To accomplish this step, review all the fieldwork materials (fieldnotes, photographs, video and audiorecordings, interview recordings and transcripts, archival materials, and ephemera) so that you are familiar with your data and can start to make sense of the scope of your material and some directions that you might want to take. During this process we recommend not taking extensive notes or attempting to determine a plan or focus; rather become familiar with what you have. Those who take copious notes at this phase often find that the notes add to the pile of data that may already be overwhelming. After you review the data, jot down ideas or themes that come up frequently or seem especially significant.

Step two is to identify themes. Go through your data a second time, focusing line by line, image by image, or minute by minute. As you do so, be attentive to the themes you have already noted while adding new ones that emerge. Identify themes that seem to be especially important both in the data but also for your project. In truly open-ended grounded theory, you would focus primarily on those topics that emerged from the data. However, your positioning and goals will probably also determine what themes might be most important.

Below are some hypothetical examples:

- In an activist collaborative project with a community where the goals are to determine how to utilize storytelling in conflict resolution, the themes that emerge could be those related to storytelling and conflict resolution, such as crossgenerational conflict, performer audience interaction, and storytelling and trust-building
- In a documentary project about the relationship between a popular contemporary musical form and the musical traditions of a community, themes of instrumentation, conflicting values, cultural appropriation, and intellectual property might arise as important themes
- In a more open-ended project for a PhD dissertation about a ceramic tradition in a community, the themes might be less related to any questions preconceived before the fieldwork was carried out, and instead might include such things as aesthetics, shifting values between generations, changing materials, or transmission of techniques

Once you have noted down themes in your second review of the data, examine the list, which might be quite long, and begin to organize it.

Are there terms that basically refer to the same thing? Are there clusters of interrelated ideas? Are there themes that seem to emerge more than others? Are there ones that are the most salient for participants? Are there themes that would be most possible for you to address with the data that you have, your background, or time limits? Are there ones that would be ethically or otherwise problematic for you to tackle? Are there ones for which you already have a strong background? Are there themes that you could best engage using the formats you intend to use for your final project? Create an organizing system. If there are interrelated themes in a cluster, use an umbrella term for the group. Label themes that are more prevalent versus those that are less so. Note down themes that may be interesting but for which you do not have much data.

After creating a long list of themes and having organized them into categories, step three involves selecting a cluster that will work together well for the project. The idea is to identify multiple themes that integrate into a larger focus. How many themes to select and how the themes interrelate will vary depending on the project. The important thing is that you select ones with which you can produce something coherent. Make sure that you narrow the scope appropriate to your goals. At this time, you may want to refer to existing scholarship or materials on the topic and select themes of focus that do not replicate existing work or that complement and add to discussions taking place.

Focused Coding

Once you have a short list of interrelated themes that you have decided to use as the focus for your project, go through the data again, marking where in your data these themes emerge. Look for quotes, images, or performance segments related to each theme. This process is often referred to as "focused coding," which involves "building up and elaborating analytically interesting themes, both by connecting data that initially may not have appeared to go together and by delineating subthemes and subtopics that distinguish differences and variations within the broader topic" (Emerson, Fretz, and Shaw 1995, 160). Software programs for facilitating the coding of qualitative data exist, though not all folklorists and ethnomusicologists use them. These programs enable you to work across multiple formats, including text, audio, and visual materials. Such programs can be useful but will likely involve dedicated effort to become proficient. You can also code using your metadata spreadsheet or logs, a notebook and colored pens, or a wall full of sticky notes (Fenn's method with his dissertation).

Ultimately, the objective of coding your data is to mark where in the data the themes arise. In its simplest form this can mean writing in the margins of hard copy documents, color coding text and images with highlighters, or organizing images/recordings/texts into outlines or folders. It can involve using software to tag materials, making it possible to easily aggregate all the data that is coded to a particular theme. No matter which way you decide to code, you should end up with a robust and navigable system for tracking the themes and content of your materials.

Analysis

Once you have coded your data, you can begin to review the data that has been coded under a specific theme and start to draw out what you want to present or say about the material. Depending on your project, your goals and processes will be different. A fieldworker making a film can use the focal themes and coded data to conceptualize the narrative arc for the documentary, selecting the audio and visual segments to include. Someone creating a visual exhibit could use the coding to identify and group images and contextual information around thematic foci to create a coherent product.

For those doing academic writing, this is the phase where most of the analysis happens. Bear in mind that the process of identifying themes and coding also involves interpretation. In this grounded approach, your analysis grows from the themes and apparent patterns. You create an overarching argument, or thesis statement, from the patterns that emerge from your coding of the themes of focus. The subsections of your argument come from the data that you have aggregated within the thematic foci.

Many beginner fieldworkers become frustrated when they find that their data does not fall into neat clear-cut arguments. There typically are diverse perspectives and conflicting information in fieldwork materials, making it difficult to provide clear descriptions, explanations, or interpretations. In quantitative research, these differences are accounted for through analytical tools that allow for the organization of patterns in the data as numbers—for example 22 percent of the saxophone players enjoy faster songs, while 62 percent prefer slower melodic ones. Or, if a certain percentage of the study group concurs or fits into a similar category, conclusions about the whole population can be made. In ethnographic research, by contrast, the goal is *not* to produce broad conclusions that claim to be authoritative for everyone in the study group, nor is the purpose to produce information associated with different percentages of the population. Rather, the objective is to produce nuanced presentations and analyses of how real people and groups think about and do what they do, which will necessarily be varied and multifaceted. Some of the best ethnographic research teases out this messiness to offer insights into the complexities of social and artistic life. Rather than providing percentages about the aesthetics of the hypothetical saxophone players, the theme "musical taste" might reveal that different people prefer differently paced music. Noting this difference, an exhibit or film could highlight this diversity of perspectives. A scholarly analysis could focus on themes related to aesthetic differences, such as relationships between age and aesthetics in the community or how music pacing is associated with emotion.

It is difficult to offer a set way to draw on scholarly literature in analysis, but instead we explain the principle. As you developed the research plan, you should have examined the literature relevant for understanding the topic and developing lines of inquiry. Now that you are in the phase of analyzing the data, we recommend engaging the literature *after* having done the initial identification of themes and coding. This ensures that you are grounding your analysis in *your* data and not what others have said. Engaging the scholarly literature as you begin the process of identifying patterns in your data can help you identify and articulate arguments. Again, we suggest a back-and-forth approach. Review the data and begin to figure out what you want to say. Start putting together arguments grounded in the data. Go to the relevant scholarship and use it to assist you in making arguments and to identify ways of putting your project in conversation with existing scholarship. Once you start writing, keep going back and forth between the data and the literature—but remember (for most of you) that the bulk of your thinking and writing will be about the ethnographic data rather than what others have written. We offer this process very generally, understanding that each fieldworker will engage the scholarship differently depending on their goals and idiosyncratic process.

Issues in Using Data

Throughout the handbook we have touched on the power dynamics that can occur in the preparation for and doing of fieldwork. Here we discuss the power issues involved with producing products out of fieldwork data. Though we have placed this discussion in section III of the handbook, the issues we discuss should be taken into consideration in all phases of the fieldwork process. Regardless of the power relations during the research process, the people *producing* the products hold the decision-making power about what data to use and how to use, interpret, and present the material. We will discuss several types of issues that relate to these power inequities, including subjectivity, selectivity, and the politics of representation.

Group Exercise

1. Group does a shared activity. The activity can be anything that the group can do together relatively quickly—for example, take a walk to buy beverages at a nearby store or visit someone located nearby.
2. Everyone in the group spends seven minutes writing a description of what took place.
3. Some or all members of the group read their descriptions to the group.
4. Hold a group discussion about similarities and differences between each description. Reflect on the following questions related to subjectivity, selectivity, and representation.
   - What contributed to these differences?
   - What does each reveal about the event or activity?
   - What is left out?
   - What do the descriptions reveal about the people writing them?
   - How do the descriptions relate to what happened?
   - What details about individuals were included?
   - What details were omitted?
   - Were intentions attributed to individuals? If so, were they accurate?
   - Were thoughts, values, or perspectives attributed to individuals? If so, were they accurate?
   - Did students present participants differently depending on their interpersonal relationships?

Subjectivity

There are many ways to think about and interpret any material involving human beings. In as much as the people you may have interviewed, observed, or otherwise engaged with while doing your research had different opinions and perspectives, so do different authors, filmmakers, exhibit designers, or event planners. This variety of perspective can come from individuals' personalities, political perspectives, cultural identities, relationships to the group being studied, aesthetics, or goals. Two different people taking exactly the same material to create something with the same stated objective will always produce two different products, as should be evident after completing the exercise above.

Knowing this could be paralyzing—realizing that research cannot be objective could convince someone that there is no point in doing it. After all, whatever one presents will necessarily be subjectively based on the priorities and through the lens of the producer. In contemporary social science and humanities research, many fieldworkers, including the authors, feel strongly that our research is important and contributes to knowledge even though we acknowledge its subjectivity. Rather than trying to pretend that it is not biased by presenting our findings as objective fact, what we do instead is honestly address our subjectivity (see Clifford and Marcus 1986). Michelle Kisliuk (1977) articulates this position especially well when she writes, "I can only presume to speak from my own experience, hoping that I have been a rigorous and sensitive enough researcher to have gained insight into a mutual dialogue." She recommends that the fieldworker provide relevant information about their experience within the ethnographies they produce, allowing the reader to "decide whether to trust my [their] insight and how best to use it" (33). Integrating reflexivity into final products contributes to honesty and provides information as audiences interpret fieldwork products (see Barz and Cooley 1997, 2007). Producers can be explicit about their biases, explaining their goals and information about their identities to help inform their audiences about how they might approach and interpret the product. An author can provide information about their fieldwork process and integrate themselves into their descriptions and analyses. A filmmaker can include footage of themselves in the field and make audible questions that they asked to provide evidence of the filmmaker's presence and relationship to the participants.

As we discussed in earlier chapters, these issues of subjectivity exist whether or not the fieldworker is a member of the group in which they did research. A musician studying her own community of musicians might have greater access and comprehension of certain aspects of the study than would someone from outside. However, that one already is passionate and feels a strong sense of value for a community and its music may bias the fieldworker's perspective so that she is not able to see conflict within the group or the ways that the community implicitly excludes nonmembers. Someone who is not a member of a group needs to be especially attentive to what they do not know as they present what they do know. And, if there are significant differentials in the social status of the researcher and researched, they need to be attentive to how these disparities impact how and what they present through the material. It might seem that being a member of the group takes care of this problem because a group member will necessarily have accurate information. However, being a member does not mean that the individual can speak for the whole group. Fieldworkers with an insider perspective can sometimes be less aware of how their own position impacts their relationships, whom or what they had access to, and how they are presenting information. Furthermore, it can be difficult for a member to present material or interpretations that are critical because they may be concerned about how doing so could impact people's feelings or even their relationships within the group.

Collaborative projects at their best have the benefit of integrating multiple subjectivities. Because multiple people are involved there can be a built-in system for recognizing differences in perspective, since rarely would everyone on a team agree. Disagreements can make bias visible and evoke discussions: ideally decisions about representation and interpretation come from a negotiation of a diversity of perspectives. Yet, even when a group decision-making process occurs, the result is still subjective. Minority positions might be excluded, or the people involved might not represent everyone involved in the practice being studied.

Selectivity

Another set of issues illustrated in the exercise above has to do with selectivity, a process that always occurs in the production of fieldwork outcomes. Certain themes, ideas, quotes, footage, songs, art objects, individuals will be selected to be included while others will not. The selection process can be frustrating because fieldworkers often end up with a great deal of really interesting and wonderful data, much more than they could possibly integrate into their final product. Fieldworkers should make decisions about what to include or exclude deliberately. Be aware that you are making choices and think about the implications they have for what is presented and from whose perspective. In addition to considering how selectivity factors into what a product communicates, reflect upon interpersonal issues. Someone who contributed greatly to a project might be unhappy about being left out, or it might be necessary to include the perspective of a community leader for political reasons. Alternately, including perspectives of those in less dominant positions might be important, but could be controversial for the community.

It is difficult to discuss these issues in the abstract because each project will necessarily be unique and the possibilities for issues that arise out of selectivity are endless. We recommend each fieldworker take a moment to consider the following:

- What are the goals of the project?
- What do you want to include from your data?
- How have you made those decisions?
- What have you left out?
- Why?
- Think about or ask (if possible) what would participants or other members of your team (if the project is collaborative) want to include or exclude? Why?
- Do their answers (anticipated or real) change your thoughts?
- What biases are expressed by what you have selected and omitted?
- Do you have other materials to put into conversation with these that could be used to present a more nuanced perspective?

Also tied to the selectivity of material is being aware that your data may include sensitive materials. You may learn about and possibly document illegal activities, infidelities, conflicts, or some other type of information for which there might be negative consequences to an individual or group if revealed. Institutional IRBs attempt to minimize the possible risk of research, which is important. As the people doing the fieldwork, we have an added responsibility to think beyond the IRB as there may be consequences that are not considered "risk" by an IRB board but that nevertheless have social consequences. It is each fieldworker's responsibility to think carefully and to make decisions that they feel are ethically appropriate. Sometimes omitting identifying information is enough to mitigate a situation. Other times, excluding certain information or individuals may be the right choice. These decisions can be difficult when it means not using a piece of data that is especially vital for telling a story or in analysis. Remember that relationships and the well-being of everyone involved should always be the priority.

Representation

At the heart of this discussion is the inherently complex nature of representing people and cultural practices to audiences. This is a big and complicated issue that we cannot address in full, though we provide thoughts and questions based on our own experiences. Why are issues of representation so crucial to consider? The straightforward answer is that people are always changing, and the social world is a fluid ever-shifting reality, making it impossible to provide definitive declarations about social life or people. In the process of fieldwork, we are only ever accessing information from specific moments and times and through the messiness of the social relationships in which the fieldwork occurred. Thus, at best, fieldwork materials always represent "partial truths" (Clifford 1986). We only know as much as we were able to glean from the limited interaction with the participants or activities at particular times and places. Any statement we present is necessarily anchored in the context of interaction. Thus, intricately tied to the information are the dynamics in which the information was shared: How did we obtain it? Who was involved? What else was going on? What was on the minds of the people involved? What happened before and after? How did participants understand the nature of the interaction? What did the people providing the information think the fieldworker was trying to accomplish? What was the power relationship between the information gatherers and the ones providing it?

When Gilman was doing fieldwork for the documentary *Grounds for Resistance*, the participants in the project were combat veterans of the US military who had deployed to one or both of the US conflicts in Iraq and Afghanistan. Each was struggling with mental and physical challenges while they collaborated to run a proveteran antiwar coffee house. Over the course of filming, individuals' political identities and perspectives on the war and on the antiwar movement shifted multiple times. Gilman had the challenge of selecting clips for the final product, knowing that anything veterans said during a given interview was reflective of their thinking at that moment and had most likely changed by the time of editing. She collaborated with the participants to try to ensure that they agreed with the representations in the final product. Nevertheless, the mindset of some changed after completion. In the end, the documentary provides only partial truths composed of bits and pieces of individuals' fleeting perspectives and only that which they were willing to share on camera at various moments over the course of the fieldwork.

Furthermore, in many research situations in folklore and ethnomusicology, the fieldworker is identified with or comes from a social category that is dominant to the ones being studied. The fieldworker might be more educated or have higher economic status. In social situations where there are hierarchies associated with gender, race, or ethnicity, many fieldworkers fall into the dominant group. In these cases, there is a built-in power relationship within the fieldwork situation that the production phase amplifies, in that the fieldworker has the power to make decisions about what to do with the materials, how to analyze, and how to represent the group.

To add to the power dynamics, even if a fieldworker does not come from a socially dominant position and is researching "up," as some have put it, they usually wield the most power in determining what comes out of the research. As an example, in the case of a college student interviewing a prominent local musician who is older and has much higher status in a community than the student, the musician may wield the most power during the fieldwork in determining when and where the interview will take place, who can be present, and what questions they are willing to answer. At the time of producing something from the interview, however, the power shifts to the student. The student decides how to represent the musician, what to include and exclude, and in the case of certain types of products, how to interpret or analyze something about the musician.

Group Exercise

Pick a topic that everyone in the group is willing to discuss (foodways and musical listening habits are usually good topics that are not too sensitive and with which all participants probably have some experience).

1. Divide into pairs.
2. Each person jots down three questions to ask the other one about the topic
3. Each person interviews the other by asking the three questions and jotting down notes.
4. Each questioner writes up the interview and reads it to the other
5. Pairs discuss how they felt about the relationship between the write-up and their own perspectives.
6. Bring everyone to debrief as a group.

A variation on this exercise is for one student to interview the professor or other "higher status" person present. The discussion can explore how the power/status differential impacted what was asked, what was answered, and how people represented the interview.

This exercise is useful because the person asking the questions and writing up the "interview" is usually especially aware of how they are representing the person they interviewed, knowing that the person will read or hear their representation shortly after. Remember that you should be just as concerned about how someone or a group will respond to what you say or show about them even if they are not sitting in front of you while you are writing. It is also a valuable exercise because everyone has the experience of being represented. More likely than not, participants found that they did not feel completely comfortable with the tone or accuracy of how they were represented. Remember that feeling as you represent those in your project.

Some strategies for addressing issues are to be sensitive to audiences' interpretations of how you represent a group or individuals. Are you respectful? Are you attributing feelings or perspectives to individuals that might be inaccurate, biased, or temporary? As has already been discussed, every fieldwork interaction happens within complex social relationships that are often tied to power differentials associated with factors such as economics, class, education, ethnicity, gender, sexuality, and religion. How are you presenting people in relationship to these dynamics, and how do you think audiences will interpret what you are presenting? For example, you may be doing research with a group that is often the target of prejudice or that is generally misunderstood by the types of people who would most likely be the audience for your work. Consider how your project interacts with what you think audience members' preconceived ideas might be. Would your product feed or counter such prejudices?

In situations where there are clear distinctions between the fieldworker and the research participants, the fieldworker can work collaboratively with participants in the phases of data management and analysis. Fieldworkers and participants can review data together, identify themes, code, and decide on the final product together. This can help to diffuse the power differential and give opportunities for participants to contribute to decisions about how they are represented.

This type of collaborative process is one that many of us hope for, and while it is possible for some projects, it proves to be challenging for many. Time and physical constraints are often an issue. Participants may not be as motivated or interested in the goals or deadlines of the project as is the fieldworker, so they may not be willing. Or, it may not be appropriate to ask participants to expend time and energy on a project that may not be as high of a priority for them as it is for the fieldworker. Also note that the participants may not have the knowledge base or interest in the academic goals of the project, for those who are producing more conventional scholarship. Furthermore, many projects emerge because of a fieldworker's or institution's interests and priorities rather than those of the participants, making it difficult to involve participants in the interpretive process. Being aware of these challenges can inspire creative ways of engaging participants rather than quickly giving up if they are not as responsive as you would hope. Consider the value of feedback interviews as discussed in chapter 9.

Interpretive Authority?

A fieldworker may be focused on certain types of practices or research questions and/or come to conclusions that do not resonate with those of participants and may even be offensive to them (e.g., Borland 1991; Feld 1987). This raises the question of interpretive authority. Who gets to interpret whom? And, who gets to decide how to interpret? For example, someone doing research in a musical community who is interested in Judith Butler's theory of performativity may find that participants cannot read, are not interested in trying to read or understand Butler's thick philosophical prose, or that gender performativity conflicts with how they think about their musical engagement. An illustrative example is the documentary *The Order of Myths* about Mardi Gras celebrations in Mobile, Alabama, by Margaret Brown (2008). Brown's Euro-American family features prominently in the documentary that ultimately reveals and critiques the racist structures underlying the celebrations and by extension the racism inherent in her family's role. Brown faced the difficult conflict of wanting to address the community's racism while also wanting to maintain relationships with her family members and the larger community.

Some folklorists and ethnomusicologists would argue that our job is to work with participants to document and represent folklore and musical practices in ways that resonate with the community, and that therefore, our interpretations should not deviate from or be critical of the people with whom we did research. Producing something that might be deemed judgmental of the very people who so generously participated in our fieldwork can seem inconsistent with the importance of rapport in the fieldwork process and after. Yet, even among those who participate in a particular type of folklore or music, there will necessarily be differences in perspectives or interpretation. Some of these differences may be based in social inequities or outright conflicts between members, making it impossible to be equally attentive to or respectful of everyone's perspectives all the time. Imagine a cultural practice that is exclusive to men and is used to bolster their power within a community. If a fieldworker provided only the perspective of the men, they would neglect the important perspectives of half the community. If they decided to provide the perspectives of men and women in order to provide a more inclusive analysis, the men may not appreciate the criticism. It would be difficult to provide an analysis of this situation without either implicitly or explicitly leaving out an important perspective or being critical.

Strategies exist for presenting critical perspectives or differences in interpretation that emphasize respect despite the conflicting views. The grounded interpretive model described earlier provides a structure that can make it possible to provide a nuanced and complicated analysis that includes the perspectives of participants in a respectful manner while simultaneously providing social critique. Giving opportunities for participants to read and provide feedback can also be one way of integrating a variety of perspectives and providing information. The fieldworker could present their critical perspective and then include responses from participants about their interpretation, so that audiences can read both and come to their own conclusions.

Folklorist Elaine Lawless uses the term "reciprocal ethnography" to refer to a process for integrating the interpretations of participants into the research and analysis process. After publication of her book, *Handmaidens of the Lord: Women Preachers and Traditional Religion* (1988), one of the women ministers read it and took issue with Lawless's feminist interpretation, raising the question of who had the authority to provide an analysis. In her article, "'I Was Afraid Someone like

You. . . an Outsider. . . Would Misunderstand': Negotiating Interpretive Differences between Ethnographers and Subjects," Lawless explains that while she had shared many aspects of the book with the women prior to its publication, including sharing her rendition of the life story with each of the ministers, she had not shared her interpretations, which ultimately differed significantly from how the women perceived themselves (see Lawless 1992). This experience ultimately motivated Lawless to develop a process for analysis based in dialog that allowed for multiple voices and points of view rather than fore fronting that of the scholar. In developing this process, Lawless drew on many scholars, including ethnomusicologists Jeff Todd Titon (1988) who advocates for "reinterpretations that are based on our informant's interpretations of our interpretations" (13).

Conclusion

Given the diverse types of projects, contexts for fieldwork, and objectives that we anticipate for our readers, we have not provided guidance for all the types of situations and materials that our readers are most likely working with. The goal of this chapter was to provide you with some ideas about how to use your data to create something, whether that something is a scholarly text, a musical performance, a documentary, or an exhibit. Regardless of your specific project and goals, paying careful attention to power dynamics and to your role in representing others, whether the others are members of a community of which you are a part or not, is critically important both for the quality of your work and in terms of the ethics and relationships that are so central to the ethnographic enterprise.

14

ETHICS AND FINAL PRODUCTS

WE HAVE EMPHASIZED THE IMPORTANCE of rapport and the inter-personal relationships between fieldworkers and research participants that are necessary for the success of most ethnographic projects. In this chapter we consider what happens to these relationships when the field-work phase is complete and all too often the fieldworker moves on to other activities and priorities. We emphasize the important of maintaining relationships beyond the time of fieldwork. We also consider the importance of making fieldwork materials, the raw data and final products available to participants, and to think carefully about issues of intellectual property. We end by discussing who benefits from fieldwork and the importance of maximizing the benefits to participants.

Relationships

As we have discussed throughout, relationships with participants are at the core of ethnographic fieldwork. They are critical for carrying out successful research, and these relationships should be genuine and reciprocal. Yet as sincere as fieldworkers might be during the course of the fieldwork, the power over whether, how, and when the relationship will persist after the fieldwork ends frequently lies with the fieldworker. In cases where a fieldworker is a member of the community, the relationships often persist separate from the research endeavor. Yet the onus is still on the fieldworker to communicate with participants about the progress and outcomes of the research and to provide them with any copies or access to materials, as will be discussed shortly. In cases in which they are not members of the community, fieldworkers often make the decisions while doing the fieldwork about when and how to participate in the community and the extent to which they will continue the association. Frequently, fieldworkers feel strongly about the relationships while doing the fieldwork, but as time passes after the project is finished everyone drifts back into their own lives. It may also become more difficult to maintain the relationships due to time constraints, physical distance, or changes in the fieldworker's priorities or life situations (see Patai 1991).

While we emphasize the importance of honoring relationships that develop during fieldwork, we also recognize that lots of different types of affiliations develop and not all will be productive to continue. Our intention is not to romanticize fieldwork relationships because we realize that some will be contentious and difficult, some will be friendly but not terribly deep, and others may become more intimate and meaningful over time. As with other people in our lives, it makes sense to nurture and continue some relationships over others. But it is also important for fieldworkers to balance the relationships with people with whom they feel some friendship versus those whom they might not feel close to, but who nevertheless were critical to a project's success. In other words, our social relationships in our everyday lives ebb and flow for all sorts of reasons. In fieldwork relationships we need to be especially attentive to the reality that fieldworkers often initiate and nurture relationships *because* we hope to gain something from them, access and information for *our* projects. Once the project is done, participants may continue to be invested in the relationship and feel disappointed, hurt, or exploited if the fieldworker disappears. Letting the relationship die when it is no longer valuable to the fieldworker can feel like a real betrayal to the people who were generous and helpful, sometimes because of a shared commitment to the project, but at other times because of a feeling of genuine friendship.

Sustaining fieldwork-related relationships can involve similar efforts that one might make in other contexts, such things as finding time to spend together, sending greetings for special occasions, commemorating deaths or other significant events, remaining informed about things happening in the community, or engaging with people through phone calls, email, and social media networks. Often during this research phase, the fieldworker spends a great deal of time with participants. Participants may invite them to their homes and special events; yet, the fieldworker may not be in a position to reciprocate during the active phase of research. If the relationships expand, it can be important to invite participants into the fieldworker's home or social activities. This can be especially significant when the fieldworker comes from a different social or cultural group than the participants. In as much as the fieldworker enjoyed the opportunity to learn about a community other than their own, participants may also enjoy learning about and gaining access to the fieldworker's.

Giving Copies of What Is Produced

Aside from maintaining interpersonal relationships it is important to make fieldwork materials available to participants (see Seeger 2008a, 2008b). Fieldworkers should always provide copies, and sometimes originals, of everything that comes out of fieldwork to the participants and to the communities, organizations, institutions, or countries that are relevant to the materials. At a basic level this includes giving copies of books, videos, articles, and documentation of exhibits or live events to participants as is feasible. For those working in digital formats, we recommend providing digital files, links to websites, and so on. Giving participants access to all that was produced is important for maintaining honesty and integrity. Participants, members of the community, and future generations have a right to be aware of and have access to what was produced about them.

In some cases, participants will not be able to access the materials. For example, plenty of books are written about the artistic practices of people who may not read and write, or who may not do so in the language of publication. It is still necessary to provide written copies because they may appreciate seeing and having the final product; their family members or other members of the community may read it in the present or in the future. The fieldworker also can spend time explaining orally the content of the material in addition to presenting the written version. In some cases, fieldworkers can produce informal translated versions for fieldwork communities or produce official versions (such as published texts, videos, exhibits) in local languages. Remember that the value of fieldwork products typically extends far into the future. A participant in the moment may not be interested or may be unable to read something. Five, ten, twenty, or thirty years in the future the work may prove to be significant, and participants deserve to have access.

For projects whose format are inaccessible to participants, such as documentary videos or websites requiring equipment for access unavailable in a community, the onus is on the fieldworker to make the effort to make the material accessible. For example, in the case of video footage, the fieldworker can invite participants to a place where viewing is possible or bring equipment to a community—much easier today because of the portability of laptops and speakers, which can be brought to participants. The fieldworker can share the work with participants in person while also providing copies or links to them for possible future access. As an example, Gilman did fieldwork on dance practices in rural Malawi where

Figure 14.1. Fenn produced an installation of boutique guitar pedals made by Devi Ever for an exhibit called "Designing Sound" in Eugene, Oregon. Devi and members of her band at the time attended the exhibit at Fenn's invitation. Eugene, Oregon, 2011. Photo by John Fenn.

most participants did not have access to regular electricity or a device for playing the video. She made the effort to visit communities and show them footage she had taken. Later she burned footage to DVDRs, which she left with members of the community. Though they did not themselves have DVD players, they knew someone in town with a laptop who was able to show the film to a broader audience.

For physical exhibits, shows, and other ephemeral events, the field-worker should make sure to notify and if possible invite participants to attend. If necessary, they should go to some extra effort to help people do so by providing transportation, free tickets, and for some types of events, making sure they have a comfortable way to participate. If this is not possible, documenting the exhibit with photographs and videos and either sending these to participants or bringing the images to the participants as described above for videos can be effective. As a collaboration between the Oregon Folklife Network and University of Oregon's Center for Intercultural Dialogue, a team of students, staff, and faculty from the University of Oregon, including Gilman, did fieldwork at the Oregon State Correctional Institute on a men's crochet group, resulting in the 2011 exhibit, "Hooks, Yarn, and Bars." The men whose lives and work were the focus of the exhibit could not attend because of prison restrictions. The team photographed and videotaped the event, which one of the members edited into a documentary. The team then planned a follow-up visit to the prison during which they showed the video and discussed their experience at the exhibit. This was one of the most powerful interactions during the fieldwork process because the men were able to see people outside of the prison walls interact with their art and learn about the personal and social work they were doing. It was also powerful for the fieldworkers because they heard how important their efforts had been to the men, increasing the meaningfulness of the project to all involved.

This example also highlights that nurturing relationships after the fieldwork is over can be valuable if there are opportunities for continuing to do the fieldwork. In the case above, that the team made the effort to make the video and return to show it greatly enhanced the men's trust. Their concerns that the team might portray them in ways that fed negative perceptions of them as criminals were largely assuaged. They welcomed the team to continue to do research with them, enabling one team member to eventually write a thesis based on his research and produce subsequent physical and online exhibits.

Sometimes a fieldworker may be reluctant to provide copies of final products because they think that participants will not be pleased with how they are represented or that they may disagree with conclusions or analyses. It would be easy for a fieldworker to attempt to avoid conflict by not sharing in the hopes that participants never had the opportunity to see the interpretation or representation. Even in these cases, however, fieldworkers should be up front about what they produced in as much as they hoped for and often relied on participants being honest throughout the fieldwork process. Not providing copies does not preclude the participants gaining access, and it can cause even more conflict if the

Figure 14.2. A team of fieldworkers associated with the Oregon Folklife Network produced an exhibit about the Crochet 4 Community group at the Oregon State Correctional Institution as part of the University of Oregon's Center for Intercultural Dialogue's "Prisons, Peace, and Compassion" conference. Because the participants could not attend, the team documented the exhibit and produced a short documentary to show to the men at a later date. Mount Vernon, Washington, 2011. Photo by Shelise Zumwalt.

participants find the materials on their own and feel that the fieldworker was being disingenuous.

Intellectual Property

It is especially important for fieldworkers to consider intellectual property issues. To what extent is their data their own "property," and to what extent does it belong to the participants or communities of origin? Fieldworkers should consider legal as well as ethical dimensions of intellectual property issues during and after the fieldwork process. Much of the work of folklorists and ethnomusicologists falls into grey areas in which there may not be legal obligations about what to do with materials, but there may be significant issues around ownership or ethics. Consider such questions as who owns the materials you collected and who *should* own them? Or how is ownership determined? And what are the relationships between ownership and custody of materials? Consider the power structures within which your research took place. It may be that the institution you work for or study within habitually takes ownership of research data, though it should rightly belong to the communities that were documented. In such cases decisions need to be made about how best to deal with the materials. Questions of ownership and custody can be especially important when there is esoteric information, when a community has a long history of having physical objects or documentation of their cultural practices taken or removed from them, and when there is a financial component to how materials might be used—for example, in the case of musical recordings that might be compiled and distributed or sold. Even if it makes sense for a fieldworker to retain control over materials, consider whether there are people who would benefit from having access to the materials—for example, to promote themselves or their folklore or musical practices, or for personal reasons.

Deciding what to do with field materials can be especially difficult if there are concerns about the implications of granting access. The consent procedure we outlined creates some protection for participants because they have input into how the materials will be used and whether they should be archived. However, the fieldworker should also think about the potential implications of making materials accessible even when consent was granted. In some fieldwork scenarios, participants may not have the perspective to understand the possible risks, for example someone not familiar with archives or the internet might have a limited standpoint for deciding whether they want materials in these spaces. The fieldworker should explore whether making them publicly accessible would pose any "risks" to any one or to a community. Is there esoteric information that is culturally or religiously inappropriate to make public (see Toelken 1998)? Are there issues of expatriation or taking materials outside of a community? Would these materials be better retained in their own communities?

The issues and questions surrounding intellectual property are rarely clear or simple. While a fieldworker may hold copyright on any recordings she made during research using audio and visual technologies, there may be other rights attached to the content (or even context) attached to those recordings. Having consent from participants to conduct interviews, take photographs, or record musical performance is one thing. Getting permission to use these recordings (often granted through release forms) is another thing, intertwined with consent but not the same. No matter the end product, become familiar with approaches to intellectual property, both general and specific to the cultural settings of your research (see Seeger 1992, 1996; Perullo 2008). In addition to scholarly research and analysis of these issues, initiatives from the World Intellectual Property Organization (WIPO) provide guidance for navigating work with traditional cultural expressions.

Benefits from Research

Some fieldworkers emphasize that the motivation for research should be some benefit to the community being studied, as we have mentioned before (see Ancelet 2003). The process and outcomes of a project should be driven by the goals and needs of the people being studied. Many public folklorists and ethnomusicologists develop projects and goals in collaboration with the communities they study. In these types of projects, participants usually clearly benefit.

For many academic and some nonacademic fieldwork, however, the benefits to participants are less evident. Many fieldworkers do research for their own academic or professional goals rather than those of the communities they study. Much cultural work does not produce tangible benefits, such as much revenue for those doing the fieldwork. Cultural work in general tends to be underappreciated and underpaid, and many of us who do this work expend a great deal of our own resources, including time, energy, and passion in addition to financial and material resources. It therefore can seem that it is not relevant to think about financial benefits of doing research and who should gain from it. After all, if one is a student or even a relatively underpaid public sector employee or university faculty member, none are getting rich from doing folklore or ethnomusicological fieldwork.

While this is true, we should be honest about the benefits that many fieldworkers do enjoy. The products of fieldwork have led to many students getting a degree and ultimately employment. Publications and videos have led professional academics to get jobs and promotions. Speaking tours, exhibits, and shows have helped public sector workers build their careers, which have led to jobs, promotion, recognition, and so on. Unfortunately, we live in an inequitable world. We are all operating in some way or other within the hierarchical systems that surround us, and we cannot hope to change these structures through our own personal practices. Yet small decisions and actions that acknowledge and seek to mitigate the inequities even in small ways are possible.

Though royalties from academic books are often quite small, some fieldworkers who produce books choose to give some or all of the royalties to the individuals or communities who enabled them to write the book or to donate to an organization that resonates with the topic or communities. Many individuals find small ways of contributing to communities or individuals they work with, for example, when appropriate they buy or help sell recordings and art products, contribute to fundraising campaigns, and give materially to individuals and family members in culturally appropriate ways. Others who have the means choose to do more substantial things, such as contributing to organizations or institutions

Figure 14.3. Gilman and Fenn developed a lasting friendship with Gresham Mzomera, whom they first met when he was a teenager while they were doing fieldwork in Nkhata Bay District in 1998–99. They enjoyed introducing their children to one another in 2013. Nkhata Bay, Malawi. Photo by Lisa Gilman.

that are important to the people or topic—for example, performance venues, research centers, galleries, archives, activist organizations, or recording studios.

Not all benefits are immediate or apparent at the time of research. As Anthony Seeger (2008b) explains, "Sometimes the results of field research have a profound impact on the lives of the communities or individuals we study for reasons unimaginable at the time we undertake the research" (283). For example, the detailed descriptive data of many communities have proved to be valuable sometimes decades later in efforts at linguistic or cultural revivals, highlighting the value of preservation efforts for ethnographic materials.

Conclusion

We have emphasized the responsibilities of fieldworkers to be respectful and consistent in the relationships they develop while doing research, and we have suggested some ways that the relationships can be reciprocal. To conclude this discussion, we share with you that while some relationships developed through fieldwork will be focused primarily on the fieldwork experience, many of us find that some of the relationships extend far into the future. There are numerous examples of long-term friendships, marriages, family alliances, artistic collaborations, and business endeavors that have grown out of relationships that began through fieldwork. Some of the most valuable, profound, and loving relationships that the authors have are with people we first met over the course of our research.

15

PRESERVATION AND FUTURE USE

THE MATERIALS FOLKLORISTS AND ETHNOMUSICOLOGISTS produce through fieldwork—their collections of audio and visual recordings, notes, photographs, permission or consent forms, and various other items—have value for their own projects, but also hold potential future significance for communities of origin, other researchers, and the public in general. Preserving these materials and enabling future access are important postfieldwork actions. These are far from neutral actions, however, and almost always pose a range of ethical, moral, technical, and practical issues. Fieldworkers do not have to navigate these issues on their own, as scholars, practitioners, and professional archivists have discussed process and practice for some time, generating a range of recommendations and options (Brady 1999; International Association of Sound and Audiovisual Archives 2011; Seeger 1986; Topp Fargion 2009). We recommend communicating directly with staff at an archive about your fieldwork—especially if it is an institution you have identified as one to which you hope to donate your collection in the future. They can give the most up-to-date information about technical and procedural aspects of cultural documentation, including recommendations on file formats, descriptive information to gather, and preparing your materials for donation. This chapter will walk you through several steps, highlighting key issues along the way. We provide only general guidelines, though, as changing digital technologies and related archival practices preclude specific recommendations.

Sources for information on archival practices and standards:

- Society of American Archivists (SAA) online glossary: http://www2.archivists.org/glossary
- Society of American Archivists' Describing Archives: A Content Standard: http://www2.archivists.org/groups/technical-subcommittee-on-describing-archives-a-content-standard-dacs/dacs
- American Folklore Society (AFS) Ethnographic Thesaurus: http://id.loc.gov/vocabulary/ethnographicTerms.html
- International Association of Sound and Audiovisual Archives: https://www.iasa-web.org/iasa-special-and-technical-publications

Ethnomusicologist Anthony Seeger, a prominent thinker on the roles of archives, wrote:

> When the field researcher recognizes the importance of depositing his or her collection in an archive, the archiving process begins in the field, not in the archives. Important issues of documentation, recording technique, and ethics can only be addressed by the field researcher. . . . All ethnomusicological methodology demands that sound (or video) recordings be clearly identified. Traditionally this includes the answers to the questions "who, what, where, when, by whom" for each item. We call this identification "documentation." The best person to do it is the collector. Documentation is most easily done when the recordings are made, preferably on the tape as well as on paper. It is still not too difficult to do when the field trip is over. It is exceedingly difficult to document a collection after many years, and infernal to document one after the death of the collector. If we are to look toward an age when we can quickly and easily copy sound recordings, it is first essential to know which recordings are which, where they were made, in which language, when and by whom.
>
> Information about the recording process itself is also important to future users. It includes "how" (the recording technique), "for what" (the research intent of the recording strategy), and "ethical status" (implied or contractual consent to and restrictions on the recording). These are crucial issues for the posterior use and evaluation of any recording. Only if the field researchers assume the responsibility of providing proper documentation will archives have the information necessary to do their jobs well. (1986, 269)

The extended quote from Seeger highlights several central considerations for a fieldworker. First, the processing of archiving starts in the field—not after you have returned with an unorganized body of recordings, photos, and notes. Earlier in this book, we discussed this body of materials as the cultural documentation produced during fieldwork, but Seeger extends this notion. "Documentation" as he refers to it comprises both the recordings and the information *about* the recordings. Second, his observations underscore the responsibility of the fieldworker in acquiring and organizing all the necessary metadata about a collection: technical descriptions, dates, locations, names, permissions, and restrictions. Third, he implies that archives have "jobs," or multiple activities they are responsible for—an important consideration in the age of born-digital materials that offer many complexities when it comes to preserving, storing, and providing stewardship through access. Archives are more than the places fieldworkers dump their collections when their hard drives are full. These institutions are dynamic centers of knowledge and, increasingly, means for repatriation and sources of cultural vitality (Kolovos 2010, 25).

Metadata and Preservation

As noted earlier in this handbook, metadata is most simply described as "data about data." For example, a single digital photograph from your fieldwork is a piece of data that records a moment of cultural practice, such as a traditional pottery process. When you look at the photograph, you might see the individual potter you worked with and can identify her by name. You recall the exact location in the photo, from the room in the house to the name of the village or town. Maybe you have only recently finished fieldwork, so you even remember the date—or know where to find it in your fieldnotes. But others looking at your photograph without you there—either the next day, or thirty years on—will not have access to all that information. They will only see a photograph of a woman with pottery. All the information you "see" or know is the kind of documentation needed to most fully ensure fieldwork materials are meaningful for future users.

Metadata frames the ways in which fieldwork materials can be discovered, accessed, and used. Metadata also gives future users the ability to assess if collections or individual items such as a photograph or an audio recording meet their needs, whether those be connected to academic research, repatriation, or general interest. Taking seriously the responsibility outlined by Seeger, fieldworkers need to do more than create robust and honest documentation of cultural practices through textual, audio, and visual means (the data). We also need to create accurate and clear documentation of our fieldwork materials (the metadata), if only so that the cultural experiences, practices, and meanings that communities agreed to share with us during fieldwork remains useful and accessible in the future.

> Metadata makes possible several key functions–the identification, management, access, use, and preservation of a digital resource–and is therefore directly associated with most of the steps in a digital imaging project workflow: file naming, capture, processing, quality control, production tracking, search and retrieval design, storage, and long-term management (Puglia, Reed, and Rhodes 2004, 6).

Access can be a fraught concept, as can use. The broad concept of metadata breaks down into narrower categories that can help determine the different kinds of access and uses for a collection or specific items. There are four categories of metadata about which it is useful for a fieldworker to know: administrative, descriptive, preservation, and structural. Here are brief definitions for each category from the Society of American Archivists online glossary (accessed December 12, 2016):

- Administrative metadata: Data that is necessary to manage and use information resources and that is typically external to informational content of resources. Administrative metadata often captures the context necessary to understand information resources, such as creation or acquisition of the data, rights management, and disposition
- Descriptive metadata: Information that refers to the intellectual content of material and aids discovery of such materials. Descriptive metadata allows users to locate, distinguish, and select materials on the basis of the material's subjects or "aboutness." It is distinguished from information about the form of the material, or its administration
- Preservation metadata: Information about an object used to protect the object from harm, injury, deterioration, or destruction
- Structural metadata: Information about the relationship between the parts that make up a compound object

As a fieldworker preparing materials for preservation, descriptive and administrative metadata are the more important categories to consider; the two others relate mainly to archival practices and procedures. The "descriptive" and "administrative" categories contain the kind of information that impact access and use from an end-user's perspective. Accurate and complete descriptive metadata enables fieldwork materials to be discoverable after they are cataloged by an institution, while administrative metadata outlines any restrictions on use that the fieldworker has listed. Restrictions may be in place for any number of reasons but should align with cultural rules or expectations held by the community of origin and/or the individuals with whom the fieldworker interacted. Ideally you will have captured any restrictions in the field during the consent or permission process, either in writing or verbally. Administrative metadata also accounts for the embedded information captured by many digital devices, such as date-time stamp, file format and settings information, or geolocation codes.

The spreadsheet described in chapter 7 will help you gather descriptive and administrative metadata and start to form a documentation "map" of your materials. This spreadsheet will be invaluable to an archivist or cataloger should you donate your collection to an institution but will also be of great use to you as you work with the materials in finishing your project. But, the spreadsheet only has the metadata—not the data itself. Remember that your field data exists as a body of digital files (images, videos, audio files, and text documents), and possibly analog or physical items such as field notebooks, flyers for events, maps, or other ephemera. All these materials need to be organized.

Born-digital files afford a range of ways you can organize them in directories or folders on a hard drive, and we will focus on those to the exclusion of any physical items for the purposes of this handbook. A simple organization scheme with "human-readable" folder or directory names is most efficient, as it enables someone other than yourself to make sense of the organization. "Human readable" refers to the ability a person has to determine the content of a file (or folder) from its name alone. For example, "IMG_0001.jpg" indicates that the file is in the JPEG format via the extension, but the name does not tell much else. From the file extension, some people might be able to discern that this is likely a digital photograph, but that is about it. However, a name such as "2016-12-5_Malawi_basket-maker0007.jpg" indicates a bit more about the content of the file. By listing a specific date, a geographic location, and a cultural practice, the file name tells a user just enough about it to help them decide what they might learn by opening or examining it further.

In addition to naming your individual files, you will want to organize them in an easily navigable manner. Here is a recommendation of a folder organization scheme:

- Top level folder = YEAR_PROJECT-CODE
- Second level folders = YEAR_PROJECT-CODE_LOCATION or EVENT_DATE (YYYY-MM-DD) [this is National Information Standards Organization 8601 date formatting]
- Third level folders = IMAGE/VIDEO/AUDIO/FIELDNOTES/ EPHEMERA

Your fieldwork data or content would live in the third level folders. It is good practice to make at least three copies of all digital fieldwork materials, including metadata or spreadsheets, and store them in separate locations (i.e., on three different hard drives and physical places). This is especially true if you do not plan to deposit your collection in an archive or have not gotten that far in your thinking.

A question surrounding born-digital materials when it comes to issues of access is availability via the web or other electronic means. With analog materials, "access" commonly entailed physical travel to archives and/or "access copies" produced by the archive upon request—and often at some cost to the patron. Digital files present the opportunity for remote access through streaming or download. Whether fieldwork materials appear on servers hosted by an institutional archive, a private service, or a commercial entity (such as YouTube or SoundCloud), many ethical considerations present themselves. First, a fieldworker should have permission from individuals or communities of origin to share any type of cultural documentation beyond the scope of the project, including permission to deposit in an archive and/or make things available. Second, the fieldworker needs to consider what type of "control" they might lose upon making files electronically accessible. Once someone downloads or copies a digital file, they can do anything with it—despite restrictions attached to the file (barring any Digital Rights Management software embedded). Finally, a fieldworker needs to address copyright and intellectual property issues. In general, a fieldworker holds copyright over the recordings or files they create but does not necessarily retain rights over the cultural content of those recordings. Intellectual property law—especially in transnational settings—can be incredibly complex (and well beyond the scope of this handbook). When considering whether to make your field materials available via the web or other digital distribution system, consult with an archivist or other professional on these issues.

In addition to legal questions surrounding digital access or distribution of your field materials, there will also likely be ethical considerations. Keeping in mind that ethics statements crafted by professional organizations such as the American Folklore Society or the Society for Ethnomusicology identify the responsibility of fieldworkers to the people they engage with in the field. Any interest you have in making your recordings widely available via online means should be vetted by the communities or individuals who have shared their creative practices or heritage with you.

Conclusion

The preceding discussion of steps and issues related to preserving your fieldwork materials comprises basic guidelines for describing and organizing the data and metadata of your project. Such description and organization will be important whether you plan on keeping your materials in your immediate possession or intend to donate them to an archive. If you decide to hold onto the body of data you have gathered in the field, work to fully engage the responsibility articulated by Seeger at the start of this chapter. If you move toward donating your collection to an archive, remember that each institutional repository has its own standards and procedures. In deciding whether or not to deposit—or in deciding which archive to go with—it is best to contact staff members and discuss your collection with them. Professional advice and guidance will be invaluable at this stage.

CONCLUSION: JUST SAY YES!

WE HAVE COVERED A GREAT deal in this handbook by providing a combination of general and specific strategies. Our goal has been to provide guidance and reflection useful to diverse audiences. We anticipate that our readers will be involved in fieldwork that produces outcomes spanning numerous types of folklore and musical practices in many different geocultural, face-to-face, and online spaces. Some will do fieldwork to try to effect change, others will publish theoretically driven scholarship, and many will produce public presentations in multiple platforms and media. We hope that bits and pieces or all that we have covered will be useful to each of our readers.

We recommend using this volume strategically. Read through it all from beginning to end or read chapters that are most relevant to your project. But also refer to it throughout your project. We are always developing and honing our fieldwork skills, and with each new project comes a different setting, set of questions, and objectives. Fieldworkers continually add to their toolboxes and adapt to new situations, not to mention having to contend with the never-ending changes in technology. As you approach new projects or encounter new challenges, we hope that you will return to this handbook to revisit sections that might be helpful.

For those teaching classes or leading workshops, our intention is for this handbook to be used as a sole resource or in combination with the many excellent resources that complement, provide more detail, or diverge from our orientation. It can be used in the sequence we have created. Or, we have divided the book into short topic-specific chapters to facilitate individuals using parts in the sequence of their choice to best meet their needs.

While we have provided plenty of suggestions, thoughts, and technical detail, the most important aspects of fieldwork are the interpersonal relationships that are at the center of this research approach. Take the time to meet people, get to know them, and develop trusting relationships, all while paying attention to everything you observed and experienced. Be genuine in these relationships and nurture them long after a project is complete. Be methodical, deliberate, and reflective as you systematically document every fieldwork activity—always make time to record your experiences in your fieldnotes! Many fieldworkers will encounter issues associated with inequitable power relationships, representation, and intellectual property. Remember the importance of attending to these issues thoughtfully and deliberately while always maintaining high ethical standards. The well-being of all involved should be your priority!

Most important, fieldwork is about experience: enthusiasm and flexibility are the keys to success. Fieldwork is about people and social interactions, and these can rarely be anticipated or controlled. Recall that people do not always think or behave the way we expect them to. Sometimes activities are cancelled, organizations are dissolved, people who are central to our projects leave, or resources run out. These are only a few examples of what can happen to disrupt a fieldworker's well-meaning goals. Go with the flow! Change plans, adapt, try new methods, talk to different people, and spend time in new spaces. The authors have each had amazing experiences as a result of the "just say yes" philosophy. Attending unexpected events, sharing meals with strangers, joining in an unfamiliar activity, doing something that was not part of the original plan—even when it might mean extra-long days, missing meals, feeling socially awkward, or otherwise extending oneself—often leads to the most productive, inspiring, and fun fieldwork!

Works Cited

Allgayer-Kaufmann, Regine. 2010. "From the Innocent to the Exploring Eye: Transcription on the Defensive." *World of Music* (51): 416–31.

American Folklore Society. 1988. "AFS Statement on Ethics: Principles of Professional Responsibility." *AFSNews* 17:1.

Ancelet, Barry Jean. 2003. "The Theory and Practice of Activist Folklore: From Fieldwork to Programming." In *Working the Field: Accounts from French Louisiana*, edited by Jacques Henry and Sara Le Menestrel, 81–100. Westport, CT: Praeger.

Anderson, Kathryn, and Dana C. Jack. 1991. "Learning to Listen: Interview Techniques and Analyses." In *Women's Words: The Feminist Practice of Oral History*, edited by Sherna Berger Gluck and Daphne Patai, 11–26. New York: Routledge.

Babiracki, Carol M. 1997. "What's the Difference? Reflections on Gender and Research in Village India." In *Shadows in the Field: New Perspectives for Fieldwork in Ethnomusicology*, edited by Gregory Barz and Timothy J. Cooley, 121–36. Oxford: Oxford University Press.

Barz, Gregory F. 1997. "Confronting the Field(Note) In and Out of the Field: Music, Voices, Texts, and Experiences in Dialogue." In *Shadows in the Field: New Perspectives for Fieldwork in Ethnomusicology*, edited by Gregory F. Barz and Timothy J. Cooley, 45–62. Oxford: Oxford University Press.

Barz, Gregory F., and Timothy J. Cooley, eds. 1997. *Shadows in the Field: New Perspectives for Fieldwork in Ethnomusicology*. Oxford: Oxford University Press.

———. 2007. *Shadows in the Field: New Perspectives for Fieldwork in Ethnomusicology*, 2nd ed. Oxford: Oxford University Press.

Bendix, Regina. 2000. "The Pleasures of the Ear: Toward an Ethnography of Listening." *Cultural Analysis: An Interdisciplinary Forum on Folklore and Popular Culture* 1: 33–50.

Benmayor, Rina. 1991. "Testimony, Action Research, and Empowerment: Puerto Rican Women and Popular Education." In *Women's Words: The Feminist Practice of Oral History*, edited by Sherna Berger Gluck and Daphne Patai, 159–87. New York: Routledge.

Borland, Katherine. 1991. "'That's Not What I Said': Interpretive Conflict in Oral Narrative Research." In *Women's Words: The Feminist Practice of Oral History*, edited by Sherna Berger Gluck and Daphne Patai, 63–75. New York: Routledge.

boyd, danah, and Nicole Ellison. 2007. "Social Network Sites: Definition, History, and Scholarship." *Journal of Computer-Mediated Communication* 13 (1): 210–30.

Brady, Erika. 1999. *A Spiral Way: How the Phonograph Changed Ethnography*. Jackson: University of Mississippi Press.

Briggs, Charles L. 1985. "Treasure Tales and Pedagogical Discourse in Mexicano New Mexico." *Journal of American Folklore* 98: 287–314.

———. 1986. *Learning How to Ask: A Sociolinguistic Appraisal of the Role of the Interview in Social Science Research*. Cambridge: Cambridge University Press

Brown, Margaret. 2008. "The Order of Myths." Documentary Film. Distributed by the Cinema Guild.

Clifford, James. 1986. "Introduction: Partial Truths." In *Writing Culture: The Poetics and Politics of Ethnography*, edited by James Clifford and George E. Marcus, 1–26. Berkeley: University of California Press.

Clifford, James, and George E. Marcus, eds. 1986. *Writing Culture: The Poetics and Politics of Ethnography*. Berkeley: University of California Press.

Collier, John Jr., and Malcolm Collier. 1986. *Visual Anthropology: Photography as a Research Method*. Albuquerque: University of New Mexico Press.

Collins, Samuel G., and Matthew S. Durington. 2015. *Networked Anthropology: A Primer for Ethnographers*. New York: Routledge.

Cooley, Timothy J. 1997. "Casting Shadows in the Field: An Introduction." In *Shadows in the Field: New Perspectives for Fieldwork in Ethnomusicology*, edited by Gregory F. Barz and Timothy J. Cooley, 1–19. Oxford: Oxford University Press.

Cooley, Timothy J., Katherine Meizel, and Nasir Syed. 2008. "Virtual Fieldwork: Three Case Studies." In *Shadows in the Field: New Perspectives for Fieldwork in Ethnomusicology*. 2nd ed., edited by Gregory F. Barz and Timothy J. Cooley, 90–107. Oxford: Oxford University Press.

Coyne, Richard. 2010. *The Tuning of Place: Sociable Spaces and Pervasive Digital Media*. Cambridge, MA: MIT Press.

Dewalt, Kathleen M., Billie R. Dewalt, and Coral B. Wayland. 1998. "Participant Observation." In *Handbook of Methods in Cultural Anthropology*, edited by H. Russell Bernard, 259–99. Walnut Creek, CA: AltaMira Press.

Dorson, Richard. 1964. *Buying the Wind: Regional Folklore in the United States*. Chicago: University of Chicago Press.

Ellingson, Ter. 1992. "Transcription." In *Ethnomusicology: An Introduction*, edited by Helen Myers, 110–52. New York: Norton.

Emerson, Robert M., Rachel I. Fretz, and Linda L. Shaw. 1995. *Writing Ethnographic Fieldnotes*. Chicago: University of Chicago Press.

Etter-Lewis, Gwendolyn. 1991. "Black Women's Life Stories: Reclaiming Self in Narrative Texts." In *Women's Words: The Feminist Practice of Oral History*, edited by Sherna Berger Gluck and Daphne Patai, 43–58. New York: Routledge.

Feld, Steven. 1987. "Dialogic Editing: Interpreting How Kaluli Read Sound and Sentiment." *Cultural Anthropology* 2 (2): 190–210.

Feleppa, Robert. 1988. *Convention, Translation, and Understanding: Philosophical Problems in the Comparative Study of Culture*. Albany: State University of New York Press.

Fenn, John. 2004. "Rap and Ragga Musical Cultures, Lifestyles, and Performances in Malawi." PhD diss., Indiana University.

———. 2010. "The Building of Boutique Effects Pedals—the 'Where' of Improvisation." *Leonardo Music Journal* 20: 67–72.

Fine, Elizabeth C. 1984. *The Folklore Text: From Performance to Print*. Bloomington: Indiana University Press.

Finnegan, Ruth. 1992. *Oral Traditions and the Verbal Arts: A Guide to Research Practices*. New York: Routledge.

"Folklore Fieldwork: Sex, Sexuality, and Gender." Special Issue. *Southern Folklore* 47 (1).

Garcia, Angela Cora, Alecea I. Standlee, Jennifer Bechkoff, and Yan Cui. 2009. "Ethnographic Approaches to the Internet and Computer-Mediated Communication." *Journal of Contemporary Ethnography* 38 (1): 52–84.

Georges, Robert A., and Michael O. Jones. 1980. *People Studying People: The Human Element in Fieldwork*. Berkeley: University of California Press.

Gilman, Lisa. 2016. *My Music, My War: The Listening Habits of U.S. Troops in Iraq and Afghanistan*. Middleton, CT: Wesleyan University Press.

Glaser, Barney G., and Anselm L. Strauss. 1967. *The Discovery of Grounded Theory: Strategies for Qualitative Research*. Chicago: Aldine.

Gluck, Sherna Berger, and Daphne Patai, eds. 1991. *Women's Words: The Feminist Practice of Oral History*. New York: Routledge.

Goggin, Gerard, ed. 2006. *Cell Phone Culture: Mobile Technology in Everyday Life*. New York: Routledge.

———. 2008. *Mobile Phone Cultures*. New York: Routledge.

Golde, Peggy, ed. 1986. *Women in the Field: Anthropological Experiences*. Berkeley: University of California Press.

Goldstein, Kenneth S. 1964. *A Guide for Fieldworkers in Folklore*. Hatsboro, PA: Folklore Associates.

Herndon, Marcia, and Norma McLeod. 1983. *Field Manual for Ethnomusicology*. Norwood, PA: Norwood Editions.

Hood, Mantel. 1971. *The Ethnomusicologist*. New York: McGraw Hill.

Howard, Robert G. 2011. *Digital Jesus: The Making of a New Christian Fundamentalist Community on the Internet*. New York: New York University Press.

Hughes, Everett C. 1960. "Introduction: The Place of Field Work in Social Science." In *Field Work: An Introduction to the Social Sciences*, edited by Buford H. Junker, x–xv. Chicago: University of Chicago Press.

Hunt, Marjorie. 2016. *The Smithsonian Folklife and Oral History Interviewing Guide*. Washington, DC: The Smithsonian Center for Folklife and Cultural Heritage. Accessed February 13, 2018. https://folklife-media.si.edu/docs/folklife/interviewing_guide/InterviewingGuide.pdf.

Hymes, Dell H. 1981. *"In Vain I Tried toTell You": Essays in Native American Ethnopoetics*. Studies in Native American Literature 1. Philadelphia: University of Pennsylvania Press.

———. 2003. *Now I Know Only So Far: Essays in Ethnopoetics*. Lincoln: University of Nebraska Press.

International Association of Sound and Audiovisual Archives. 2011. *Ethical Principles for Sound and Audiovisual Archives*. IASA Special Publication No. 6.

Ives, Edward D., 1995 [1974]. *The Tape-Recorded Interview: A Manual for Fieldworkers in Folklore and Oral History*. 2nd ed. Knoxville: University of Tennessee Press.

Jackson, Bruce. 1987. *Fieldwork*. Urbana: University of Chicago Press.

Jackson, Bruce, and Edward D. Ives. 1996. *The World Observed: Reflections on the Fieldwork Process*. Urbana: University of Illinois Press.

Kaufman, Kay. 1990. *Musical Transcription*. New York: Garland.

Kippen, James. 2008. "Working with the Masters." In *Shadows in the Field: New Perspectives for Fieldwork in Ethnomusicology*. 2nd ed., edited by Gregory F. Barz and Timothy J. Cooley, 125–40. Oxford: Oxford University Press.

Kisliuk, Michelle. 1997. "(Un)Doing Fieldwork: Sharing Songs, Sharing Lives." In *Shadows in the Field: New Perspectives for Fieldwork in Ethnomusicology*, edited by Gregory F. Barz and Timothy J. Cooley, 23–44. Oxford: Oxford University Press.

Kolovos, Andrew. 2010. "Archiving Culture: American Folklore Archives in Theory and Practice." PhD diss., Indiana University.

Lassiter, Luke Erik. 2005. *The Chicago Guide to Collaborative Ethnography*. Chicago: University of Chicago Press.

Lawless, Elaine J. 1988. *Handmaidens of the Lord: Pentecostal Women Preachers and Traditional Religion*. Philadelphia: University of Pennsylvania Press.

———. 1991. Women's Life Stories and Reciprocal Ethnography as Feminist and Emergent Author(s). *Journal of Folklore Research* 28 (1): 35–60.

———. 1992. "'I Was Afraid Someone like You. . . an Outsider. . . Would Misunderstand': Negotiating Interpretive Differences between Ethnographers and Subjects." *The Journal of American Folklore* 105 (417): 302–14.

Ling, Rich, and Jonathan Donner. 2009. *Mobile Phones and Mobile Communication*. Cambridge, UK: Polity.

Lomax Hawes, Bess. 1992 Practice Makes Perfect: Lessons in Active Ethnomusicology. *Ethnomusicology* 36 (3): 337–43.

———. 2007 (1992). "Happy Birthday, Dear American Folklore Society: Reflections on the Work and Mission of Folklorists." In *Public Folklore*, edited by Robert Baron and Nicholas Spitzer, 65–67. Jackson: University of Mississippi Press.

Marin, Marian-Bălașa. 2005. "Who Actually Needs Transcription? Notes on the Modern Rise of a Method and the Postmodern Fall of an Ideology." *The World of Music* 47 (2): 5–29.

Modan, Gabriella, and Amy Shuman. 2011. "Narratives in Interviews, Interviews in Narrative Studies." *Language in Society* 40 (1): 13–25.

Morad, Moshe. 2016. *Fiesta de Diez Pesos: Music and Gay Identity in Special Period Cuba*. New York: Routledge.

Myers, Helen. 1992. "Fieldwork." In *Ethnomusicology: An Introduction*, edited by Helen Myers, 21–49. New York: Norton.

Nettl, Bruno. 1964. *Theory and Method in Ethnomusicology*. New York: The Free Press of Glencoe.

Okpewho, Isidore. 1990. *The Oral Performance in Africa*. Ibadan, Nigeria: Spectrum Books.

Paredes, Américo, and Richard Bauman. 1972. *Toward New Perspectives in Folklore*. Austin: University of Texas Press.

Patai, Daphne. 1991. "U.S. Academics and Third World Women: Is Ethical Research Possible." In *Women's Words: The Feminist Practice of Oral History*, edited by Sherna Berger Gluck and Daphne Patai, 137–53. New York: Routledge.

Perullo, Alex. 2008. "Conceptions of Song: Ownership, Rights, and African Copyright Law." *English and Cultural Studies Book Publications*. Paper 7. Accessed February 2, 2018. http://digitalcommons.bryant.edu/eng_book/7.

Phillips, Whitney. 2016. *This Is Why We Can't Have Nice Things: Mapping the Relationship between Online Trolling and Mainstream Culture*. Cambridge, MA: MIT Press.

Post, Jennifer C. 2011. *Ethnomusicology: A Research and Information Guide*. New York: Routledge.

Puglia, Steven, Jeffrey Reed, and Erin Rhodes. 2004. *Technical Guidelines for Digitizing Archival Materials for Electronic Access: Creation of Production Master Files—Raster Images*. National Archives and Records Administration.

Quick, Catherine. 1999. "Ethnopoetics." *Folklore Forum* 30 (1/2): 95–105.

Rice, Timothy. 1987. "Toward the Remodeling of Ethnomusicology." *Ethnomusicology* 31 (3): 469–88.

Sanjek, Roger, ed. 1990. *Fieldnotes: The Makings of Anthropology*. Ithaca, NY: Cornell University Press.

Schensul, Jean J. and Margaret D. Lecompte, eds. 2016. *Ethnographer's Toolkit*. 2nd ed. Lanham, MD: AltaMira Press.

Seeger, Anthony. 1986. "The Role of Sound Archives in Ethnomusicology Today." *Ethnomusicology* 30 (2): 261–76.

———. 1992. "Ethnomusicology and Music Law." *Ethnomusicology* 36 (3): 345–59.

———. 1996. "Ethnomusicologists, Archives, Professional Organizations, and the Shifting Ethics of Intellectual Property." *Yearbook for Traditional Music* 28: 87–105.

———. 2008a. "Long-term Field Research in Ethnomusicology in the 21st-century." *Em Pauta* 19 (32/33): 3–20.

———. 2008b. "Theories Forged in the Crucible of Action: The Joys, Dangers, and Potentials of Advocacy Fieldwork." In *Shadows in the Field: New Perspectives for Fieldwork in Ethnomusicology*. 2nd ed. edited by Gregory F. Barz and Timothy J. Cooley, 271–88. Oxford: Oxford University Press.

Seitel, Peter, and Sheila Dauer. 1980. *See So that We May See: Performances and Interpretations of Traditional Tales from Tanzania*. Bloomington: Indiana University Press.

Sherman, Sharon. 1998. *Documenting Ourselves: Film, Video, and Culture*. Lexington: The University Press of Kentucky.

Sherzer, Joel. 1990. *Verbal Art in San Blas*. Cambridge: Cambridge University Press.

Shuman, Amy. 1986. *Storytelling Rights: The Uses of Oral and Written Texts among Urban Adolescents*. Cambridge: Cambridge University Press.

Slawek, Stephen M. 1994. "The Study of Performance Practice as a Research Method: A South Asian Example." *International Journal of Musicology* 3: 9–22.

Society for Ethnomusicology. 2001. *A Manual for Documentation, Fieldwork & Preservation for Ethnomusicologists*. Bloomington, IN: Society for Ethnomusicology.

Spitzer, Nicholas R. 2007 [1992]. "Cultural Conversation: Metaphors and Methods in Public Folklore." In *Public Folklore*, edited by Robert Baron and Nicholas Spitzer, 77–104. Washington, DC: Smithsonian Institution Press.

Spradley, James P. 1979. *The Ethnographic Interview*. New York: Holt, Rinehart and Winston.

———. 1980. *Participant Observation*. New York: Holt, Rinehart and Winston.

Stocking, George Jr., ed. 1983. *Observers Observed: Essays on Ethnographic Fieldwork*. Madison: University of Wisconsin Press.

Stoeltje, Beverly. 1993. "Power and the Ritual Genres: American Rodeo." *Western Folklore* 52 (2–4): 135–56.

Stoller, Paul. 1989. *The Taste of Ethnographic Things: The Senses in Anthropology*. Philadelphia: University of Pennsylvania Press.

Stone, Ruth M., and Angela Stone-MacDonald. 2013. "The Feedback Interview and Video Recording in African Research Settings." *Africa Today* 59 (4): 3–22.

Stone, Ruth M., and Verlon L. Stone. 1981. "Event, Feedback, and Analysis: Research Media in the Study of Music Events." *Ethnomusicology* 25 (2): 215–25.

Sunstein, Bonnie Stone, and Elizabeth Chiseri-Strater. 2007. *Fieldworking: Reading and Writing Research*. Boston: Bedford/St. Martin's.

Taussig, Michael. 2011. *I Swear I Saw This: Drawings in Fieldwork Notebooks, Namely My Own*. Chicago: University of Chicago Press.

Tedlock, Dennis. 1972. *Finding the Center: Narrative Poetry of the Zuñi Indians*. New York: Dial Press.

Titon, Jeff Todd. 1988. *Powerhouse for God: Speech, Chant, and Song in an Appalachian Baptist Church*. Austin: University of Texas Press.

———. 2008. "Knowing Fieldwork." In *Shadows in the Field: New Perspectives for Fieldwork in Ethnomusicology*. 2nd ed., edited by Gregory F. Barz and Timothy J. Cooley, 25–41. Oxford: Oxford University Press.

Toelken, Barre. 1998. "The Yellowman Tapes 1966–1997." *Journal of American Folklore* 111 (442): 381–91.

Topp Fargion, Janet. 2009. "'For My Own Research Purposes'?: Examining Ethnomusicology Field Methods for a Sustainable Music." *The World of Music* 51 (1): 75–93.

Underberg, Natalie M. 2006. "Virtual and Reciprocal Ethnography on the Internet: The East Mims Oral History Project Website." *Journal of American Folklore* 119 (473): 301–11.

Underberg, Natalie M., and Elayne Zorn. 2013. *Digital Ethnography: Anthropology, Narrative, and New Media*. Austin: University of Texas Press.

Weller, Susan C., 1998. "Structured Interviewing and Questionnaire Construction." In *Handbook of Methods in Cultural Anthropology*, edited by H. Russell Bernard, 365–409. Walnut Creek, CA: AltaMira Press.

Whitehead, Tony Larry, and Mary Ellen Conaway. 1986. *Self, Sex, and Gender in Cross-Cultural Fieldwork*. Urbana: University of Illinois Press.

Winick, Stephen, and Peter Bartis. 2016. *Folklife and Fieldwork: An Introduction to Cultural Documentation*. 4th ed. Washington, DC: American Folklife Center, Library of Congress.

Wong, Deborah. 2008. "Moving: From Performance to Performative Ethnography and Back Again." In *Shadows in the Field: New Perspectives for Fieldwork in Ethnomusicology*. 2d ed., edited by Gregory F. Barz and Timothy J. Cooley, 76–89. Oxford: Oxford University Press.

Index

access
  to archives, 31
  to "born-digital" materials, 240
  to field materials, 231
  gender and, 26, 189
  linguistic competency and, 32
  metadata and, 237, 238
  outsiders and, 20
  in participant observation, 136
  preservation for future, 235
  in project development, 26–27
  research location requires, 41
  research plan for obtaining, 46
  sexuality and, 26, 189
  to spaces, 109, 111
  topic selection affected by, 25
  to virtual fieldwork sites, 59, 60, 61
accessories, 71–73
accommodations, 57
  budgeting for, 80–82
activism, 188, 209
administrative metadata, 238–39
after the field, 197–241
  analyzing data, 214–15
  benefits from research, 232–34
  deciding what to produce, 209–11
  focused coding, 213–14
  giving copies of what is produced, 227–30
  intellectual property issues, 230–31
  issues in using data, 215–24
  maintaining interpersonal relationships, 225–27
  managing data, 199–208

preservation and future use, 235–41
reviewing data, 211–13
alcohol consumption, 191–92
American Folklife Center (Library of Congress), 31, 94
American Folklore Society (AFS)
  ethics statement of, 49, 50, 60, 184, 240
  Ethnographic Thesaurus, 236
  Position Statement on Research with Human Subjects, 126
  research funding information from, 89
analog-digital conversion, 70
Anderson, Kathryn, 156–57
annotated bibliographies, 30
anthropology, networked, 41
anxiety, 183–84
archives, 30–31
  archiving text-based electronic interviews, 178–79
  consent and permissions for use of materials, 53, 231
  managing data from, 93
  as means for repatriation, 237
  for preservation, 235–37, 239, 240, 241
  for questions of method, 44
  release forms required by, 124
  requirements for accepting materials, 45
  research questions for identifying, 40
  of websites, 179

253

artwork, purchasing, 86, 193
asynchronous communication, 60–61
    documenting, 179
    for interviews, 144, 145, 154
    See also email
ATMs, 56, 78
audiences
    at induced events, 101
    interpretation of ethnographic projects by, 217, 221
    at musical performances, 110–11
    observing, 105–6
    in participant observation, 136
audio recording
    born-digital materials for, 64, 83
    budgeting for equipment, 83
    date and time settings in recorders, 95
    digital versus analog equipment, 66–67
    documentation for archiving, 236–37
    in documentation strategies, 168, 171–72
    equipment choices for, 68–70
    external microphone for, 71
    of feedback interviews, 161–62
    of informal conversations, 141
    of interviews, 65, 143, 149–50, 171–72, 178
    learn to use the equipment, 177
    legal issues in international fieldwork, 52
    log sheets for, 200
    managing data from, 93
    for online interviews, 144
    power adapters for, 73
    quality metrics for cameras, 66
    recording strategy in research plans, 45
    sample list of equipment for, 82
    transcribing, 202–5
    when recordings fail, 180–81
    See also microphones

banking, 78
Bartis, Peter, 7, 67–68, 82, 94, 95, 151–52, 200, 201
Barz, Gregory F., 96, 97, 99
batteries, 71, 76, 82, 83, 98

Benmayor, Rina, 12
biases, 217–18
bibliographies, 28, 29–30, 40
blogs
    for acquiring cultural competency, 33
    bloggers as participant type, 11
    fieldnotes, 96
    interview materials on, 158
    of research participants, 31
    as research product, 209
"born-digital" materials, 64, 83, 237, 239–40
Botkin, Benjamin, 103
Briggs, Charles, 162
Brown, Margaret, 222–23
budgeting
    for accommodations, 80–82
    compensation for participants, 193
    creating a budget, 79
    for equipment, 82–86
    for food, 80–82, 86
    for incidentals, 86–87, 146
    for reciprocation, 87–88
    for research assistants, 86
    time duration and, 78
    for travel, 79
bureaucracy
    in domestic fieldwork, 52–53
    in international fieldwork, 51–52
Butler, Judith, 222

cables, 72, 82, 83
cameras. *See* photography
capture technologies, 64
    budgeting for, 83
    digital versus analog, 66–67
    See also recording
cash, 56, 78
"Casting Shadows in the Field" (Cooley), 7
cell phones
    for fieldnotes, 98
    in fieldwork, 85–86
    See also smartphones
cellular networks, 76, 85
Center for Folklife and Cultural Heritage (Smithsonian Institute), 31, 142
charts, 173

LISA GILMAN serves on the faculty in Folklore and English at George Mason University. Her research interests include performance, music, dance, oral literature, intangible cultural heritage, war, trauma, gender, and sexuality in southern Africa and the United States. She is author of *My Music, My War: The Listening Habits of U.S. Troops in Iraq and Afghanistan* and *The Dance of Politics: Performance, Gender, and Democratization in Malawi*. She is also editor with Michael Dylan Foster of *UNESCO on the Ground: Local Perspectives on Intangible Cultural Heritage* and producer of the documentary *Grounds for Resistance: Stories of War, Sacrifice, and Good Coffee*.

JOHN FENN is Head of Research and Programs at the American Folklife Center at the Library of Congress. Throughout his career he has brought an ethnographic perspective to field research, focused on the roles of creative and artistic practice in communities. Conducting fieldwork on arts and culture in Malawi (SE Africa), China, Indiana, and Oregon, he has documented a range of dynamic cultural practices, traditions, and groups—working individually as well as in collaboration with teams of other researchers and cultural practitioners. Interpretive output based on his fieldwork experiences include academic and popular publications, exhibitions, and public programming.